THE THREE POISONS

A Buddhist Guide To Resolving Conflict

Ross McLauran Madden

authorHOUSE®

AuthorHouse™
1663 Liberty Drive
Bloomington, IN 47403
www.authorhouse.com
Phone: 1-800-839-8640

Illustrations by ALISSA MADDEN

Author photo by Frank Pryor

First published by AuthorHouse 7/23/2010

ISBN: 978-1-4389-8813-9 (e)
ISBN: 978-1-4389-8811-5 (sc)
ISBN: 978-1-4389-8812-2 (hc)

Library of Congress Control Number: 2009905168

Printed in the United States of America
Bloomington, Indiana

This book is printed on acid-free paper.

Harih Sri Ganapataya namaha

ACKNOWLEDGMENTS

There are many people who helped me with this project – whether they knew it or not.

First, Maia Madden and my children Evan, Alissa, Luke, Paul, and Malia, and my brother Erik, for showing me in the first place that the little "self" I tried to shore up for so long was much smaller than the love we all feel for one another, and ultimately had no substance whatsoever. I also owe the deepest gratitude to my lovely and talented daughter Alissa for her beautiful pen and ink drawings that grace these pages.

Second, my Aikido teacher of thirty years, Robert Nadeau, who taught me Mindfulness and Compassion in a different, more physical format, and who has been a great inspiration to me always. Also, my fellow teachers and students at City Aikido, for their support and companionship over the years.

Third, the faculty and staff at Pepperdine University's Straus Institute for Dispute Resolution, for showing me that it is indeed possible to have the values we hold dearest be the basis for the work we do in the world. In particular, Kenneth Cloke, who not only acted as the faculty thesis advisor for this book, but also gave me in his class the first inkling that conflict resolution is actually about Loving Kindness and Compassion.

Fourth, Sasha Georgeson for being such a good friend throughout the writing of this book, and for helping me make the personal transformations necessary to write it.

Fifth, my co-workers Pamela Lanza and Cris McDermott, for listening so patiently to my innumerable ruminations about Buddhism over the past few years.

Sixth, the teachers and staff at Spirit Rock Meditation Center in Woodacre, California, for providing such a wonderful place to·learn the practice of Mindfulness.

Seventh, Alise Halbert for her prodigious efforts getting this book into its final form, but even more for showing me how to make Loving Kindness and Compassion a real part of everyday life.

Eighth, though certainly not last, the Buddha, because it is his remarkable wisdom that provides the basis for whatever is helpful in what follows.

Ross McLauran Madden
San Francisco, California
November 2009

CONTENTS

FOREWORD

Mediation and Meditation: The Deeper Middle Way

By Kenneth Cloke

"Now, there are many, many people in the world, but relatively few with whom we interact, and even fewer who cause us problems. So, when you come across such a chance for practicing patience and tolerance, you should treat it with gratitude. It is rare. Just as having unexpectedly found a treasure in your own house, you should be happy and grateful to your enemy for providing that precious opportunity."

The Dalai Lama

Conflict is everywhere, not only between human beings, but throughout nature, from quantum mechanical particles to dark energy and the soap bubble structure of galactic superclusters. Nonetheless, we each take our conflicts personally, and far from being happy or grateful to our enemies, we often allow ourselves to be thrown off balance and drawn into unpleasant ideas, negative emotions, and destructive behaviors.

So what is the solution? How do we return to balance and equanimity, and perhaps even to happiness and gratitude? We can start by reframing conflict through the lens of the "four noble truths," as originally taught by the Buddha. For example, we can recognize that our lives are filled with conflict; that conflict is a form of suffering that is caused by attachment; that we can stop, settle, resolve, transform, and transcend our conflicts by reducing our attachment; and that the way of doing so is by following the middle path – in other words, not merely by medi*t*ation, but medi*a*tion as well.

However, as we quickly learn, while the middle path may *seem* simple, it conceals a number of profound truths, one of which is that there is simplicity both this and the other side of complexity. As the famous Zen saying puts it,

> "Before I started meditating, blue mountains were blue mountains and white clouds were white clouds. After meditating a while, blue mountains were no longer blue mountains and white clouds were no longer white clouds. But after meditating further, blue mountains are blue mountains and white clouds are white clouds"

In conflict, we often delude ourselves into thinking we are following the middle path, but are actually, in a simple way, only withdrawing from our opponents, remaining silent, and avoiding engagement or controversy. But if we want to become "Bodhisattvas of conflict," we need to follow a different path, one that leads us through, and to the other side of complexity and conflict.

This "middle" path consists of engaging with the conflicted parts of ourselves and our opponents, and discovering through awareness and the experience of authentic relationship, a deeper source of compassion than the abstract, purely meditative one that is often devoid of genuine experience, and as a result, does not *require* us to grapple with or overcome our attachments at their source.

There are actually two different middle paths, leading to entirely different outcomes. The first consists of adding two things together and finding their average. We do this when we add two sums and divide by two, or when we combine something hot with something cold to produce something that is lukewarm.

The second middle way consists of combining entirely different things in a creative way, as when we combine water with flour and heat to create bread, which is not an average, but an outcome that is completely new and different. The same transformation takes place when we ask questions that reveal the underlying reasons for a dispute, which often have nothing in common with the issues people are vigorously fighting over

This deeper, *transformational* middle way can be accessed through "skillful means," which include not only meditation techniques that assist us in becoming more centered, compassionate, and aware of ourselves and others; but mediation techniques that enable us to engage in authentic and committed listening, openhearted communication, empathetic dialogue, creative problem solving, collaborative negotiation, genuine forgiveness, and reconciliation. These quintessential conflict resolution skills allow us to escape the ruts our conflicts draw us into, and reveal to us that it is the *mind*, and not just the flag or the wind that is waving. How do we reach this awareness?

Within Buddhism, there are not only mindfulness or awareness practices, but concentration and insight practices. These ultimately merge into a single practice that encompasses every part of us. As the great Rinzai teacher Hakuin wrote:

> "What is the true meditation? It is to make everything – coughing, swallowing, waving the arms, motion, stillness, words, action, the evil and the good, prosperity and shame, gain and loss, right and wrong – into one single *koan*."

A *koan*, of course, is a brief story, question, or dialogue that conceals a paradox, or to paraphrase, a conflict containing two truths, and does so in such a way as to illuminate their essential unity. The most commonly referenced *koan* is "what is the sound of one hand clapping." To rephrase this paradox in relation to conflict, we might ask: "what is the disagreement between one party?"

In doing so, we see that if we act in such a way that there are no longer two parties, but only one, the conflict between us must disappear, simply because there cannot be a conflict without two or more sides. Yet there is an even deeper truth about conflict. The brilliant physicist Neils Bohr, in describing the paradoxes of quantum theory, coined the useful expression "complimentarity," which he defined as "a great truth whose opposite is also a great truth."

When we apply this idea to conflict, we discover that a more profound outcome than the simple disappearance of conflict is the unification of what we formerly regarded as opposites. But if all the individuals and ideas that are locked in conflict, at a deeper level, simply represent partial expressions of a deeper underlying truth, what is the point or purpose of their conflict? Doesn't it all seem a bit silly and pointless? Perhaps it was this realization that led Hakuin to also write:

> "As for sitting in meditation, that is something which *must* include fits of ecstatic blissful laughter – brayings that will make you slump to the ground clutching your belly, and even after that passes and you struggle to your feet, will make you fall anew in further contortions of side-splitting mirth."

What is the source of this laughter and mirth, as applied to conflict? I believe it is the profound recognition that all our fuss and bother amounts to precisely nothing; that it is all simply an opportunity for transformation and transcendence; that it is a chance to be grateful to our enemies and learn from them, and happy that they finally brought us back to sanity and equilibrium.

Using this *koan*, we can now understand that there is a deeper "middle" path than the one mentioned above, one that opens for each of us when we transform and transcend our conflicts by finding a middle path that includes *both* of our opposing truths, that integrates mediation and meditation into a single *koan*, and that practices both as a single, undifferentiated whole. Zen writer Bernard Phillips suggests:

> "In Zen, the effort and the result are not two different things, the means and the goal are not separated, the finding occurs in the very seeking itself. For ultimately, what is sought is the wholeness of the seeker, and this emerges only in the wholeheartedness of the seeking."

In other words, the "simple" middle path that lies on the far side of complexity appears only when we "walk the talk," and *become* not just the resolution, and the integrated expression of both sides legitimate concerns, but the conflict as well, as revealed in the way that we approach and engage in it. As the 12th century Chinese Zen monk Ta Hui (Dahui) wrote, "When a person is confused, he sees east as west. When he is enlightened, west itself *is* east." In practical terms, what does this realization mean for conflict resolution?

As mediators, we routinely enter the conflicts of others, but do not always understand that, as a consequence, their conflicts also enter us. As Friedrich Nietzsche wrote, "When you look into the abyss, the abyss looks into you." Meditation is a way of looking into the abyss of conflict and allowing it to enter us without overwhelming our equilibrium, but instead, pointing us in the direction we need to go -- not only to assist others in stopping, settling, resolving, and transforming their conflicts, but to finally and completely transcend them within themselves. How can meditation assist mediators in achieving these outcomes?

There is a natural affinity between mediation and meditation, inasmuch as both recognize the simultaneity of unity and opposition; both acknowledge the presence of diverse and multiple truths; both seek a middle way; and both encourage us to have a *complete experience* of our conflicts, allowing us to evolve and leave them behind.

While there are dozens of personal benefits that flow from meditation, experienced mediators may find, as I have, that Buddhist awareness, contemplation, and insight practices can enhance our professional skills as well. It is not uncommon, for example, for mediators who meditate regularly to experience the following benefits:

• Improved ability to remain calm and balanced in the presence of conflict and intense emotions

• Greater willingness to move beyond superficiality in conversation and move into the heart of whatever is not working effectively

- Expanded sensitivity to the subtle clues given off by the parties, indicating a shift in their thoughts, feelings, and attitudes

- Deeper insight into the nature of suffering and what might be done to release it

- Greater awareness of what apparent opponents have in common, though they emphatically disagree and even dislike each other

- Improved creative problem solving skills, and ability to invent or discover imaginative solutions

- Expanded capacity to calibrate and fine-tune insights and intuition

- Greater sensitivity to the natural timing of the conflict

- Increased willingness to engage in "dangerous" or risky conversations and raise sensitive issues without losing empathy

- Decreased investment in judgments, attachments, expectations, and outcomes

- Increased ability to be completely present, open, and focused

- Reduced stress and burnout

Of course, this does not mean that meditators always make superior mediators. Buddhists have not always been the best role models in conflict, and Buddhism has, in my experience, fallen short in developing the *social* practice of what I call "inter-mindfulness," or what meditation teacher Shinzen Young calls "the monastery of relationships," which is an essential part of many conflict resolution practices.

Nonetheless, it is clear that within Buddhism, as within mediation, lie a clear set of instructions on how each of us can improve our skills in handling conflict and untangling the knots they create inside us. What are these instructions, and how exactly do we develop these skills?

While meditation is traditionally oriented to internal sensations, awareness is a generic source of skillful techniques and insights – not only into ourselves, but into others and our relationship with them, and as a result, into the nature and sources of conflict. Buddhism and conflict resolution can therefore both be said to operate by improving awareness, which can easily be applied to a wide range of difficult conversations, interactions, and relationships.

Whereas Buddhist meditation focuses attention primarily internally, for example on the breath, noticing thoughts, emotions, and internal bodily sensations, then letting them go; mediation focuses attention primarily externally, for example on communications and interactions between conflicted parties, noticing and discussing what is not working in their relationship, then asking what might be done to improve or let go of it. By combining these approaches creatively, we are able to produce new combinations.

We can say, for example, that *"mediative meditation"* consists of using awareness to expose the false expectations, self-judgments, and suffering that lie hidden beneath the surface of our conflicts. These keep us attached to our opponents and issues, and create the sensation of a solid, separate "Self" that congeals quickly around unresolved antagonism. They encourage us not simply to imagine or verbalize loving-kindness, but to act and make it real.

"Meditative mediation," on the other hand, can be said to consist of being keenly aware of what is taking place inside us in the midst of conflict, using empathy and compassion to increase our awareness of what is happening internally within ourselves and the parties, and helping to bridge the gap between them so they can discover a way out of their antagonism, attachment, and suffering. These combined practices enable us to move beyond merely settling, or even resolving disputes to discover insightful ways of transforming and transcending them.

We can do so, for example, using mediation techniques such as empathetic storytelling and private reflection; by creatively reframing differences to reflect underlying unities; by asking conflicted parties to empathetically imagine what it might have been like to have experienced what the other person experienced; by ask them to speak directly to each other from their hearts; and by drawing their awareness to what they are experiencing right now, or the way they are talking to each other, and asking each what the other could do that would help them listen or speak more openly, then doing that, and using feedback to reinforce awareness and on-going practice.

It is one thing, of course, to use these techniques in mediation with complete strangers, and quite another to avoid losing our balance when *we* are the ones in conflict. How do we use these skills in such a way as to remain authentically ourselves, and become *unconditionally* openhearted and aware in the presence of our opponents? Even a strong intention to practice compassion and loving-kindness may not suffice to achieve this goal, so it is useful to ask ourselves some difficult questions that will help us draw our attention to what really matters. Here are a few to start with:

- What do I really know about my opponent?
- What would make me decide to act or speak like that?
- What is true for him/her?
- What questions could I ask to find out?
- What am I doing that is helping to fuel the conflict?
- What am I *not* doing that is helping to fuel the conflict?
- What is the crossroads I am standing at right now in this conflict?
- What is the deeper "third path" or "middle way" in this conflict?
- How might changing my attitude, behavior, or response help me resolve, transform, or transcend it?
- What would it take for me to do so?
- What is preventing me from moving forward or letting go?

·   Can I maintain awareness of my breath and what is happening in my body, mind and emotions while I am in the midst of conflict?

·   What price have I paid for this conflict? What has it cost me?

·   How much longer am I prepared to continue paying that price?

·   What is the most difficult aspect of this conflict for me? What makes that difficult?

·   What would it take for me to let it go completely and open my heart to the person I am fighting with?

·   What is one thing the other person could do that would change my entire attitude toward the conflict? What is one thing I could do?

·   Is there anything I would be willing to apologize for, or offer without any expectation of return?

·   On a scale of 1 to ten, how sincere and deep was the apology I gave or the gesture I made?

·   What would it take to make it a 10?

·   What does my heart tell me to do?

The opportunities for integrating Buddhist awareness, insight, and contemplation practices into dispute resolution, both personally and professionally, are limitless. Yet the modern world makes it much more difficult to sustain these attitudes and practices. The highly respected Zen scholar and practitioner D. T. Suzuki, who was invited to speak in London in 1936, noticed the contrast between traditional contemplative practices and the demands of modern life:

> "How can I construct my humble hut right here in the midst of Oxford Circus? How can I do that in the confusion of cars and buses? How can I listen to the singing of birds and also to the leaping of fish? How can one turn all the showings of the

shop window displays into the freshness of green leaves swayed by the morning breeze? How am I to find the naturalness, artlessness, utter self-abandonment of nature in the utmost artificiality of human works? This is the great problem set before us these days."

The problem today is even greater, as it includes an additional difficulty: How we do so not just in the midst of our own internal conflicts, or even the deeply upsetting interpersonal conflicts that transpire in our families, workplaces, and neighborhoods; but in response to wars, bombings, genocides, ethnic prejudices, religious intolerances, mistreatment of women and children, and seemingly endless international conflicts over environmental choices, economic policies, and political beliefs that affect us all deeply, no matter how far we may imagine we are from the turmoil and terror.

These larger conflicts reinforce the Zen saying that:"The believing mind believes in itself," thereby turning belief in a circle so that it becomes a source of conflict. Sometimes, as May Sarton wrote, "One must think like a hero to behave like a merely decent human being." But sometimes one must also think like an ordinary human being, merely chopping wood and carrying water, in order to be heroic enough to find ways of transcending the conflicts that separate us.

In order to escape the downward gravitational tug of antagonisms on any level, and resolve, transform, or transcend them, we require a combination of inner and outer skills. If we do not transform ourselves, we will find it much more difficult to transform the world; and if we do not transform the world, we will find it far more arduous to transform ourselves. In meditation as in mediation, inner and outer increasingly merge and reveal themselves as one.

These are just a few of the important lessons we are able to learn by seeking the places where Buddhism and conflict resolution intersect. What is fascinating to me as a practitioner of both over the course of many years are the ways they call out to each other, invite each other in, and increasingly *require* the skillful practice of the other. Trying to meditate without addressing underlying conflicts makes our practice superficial, frustrating, and incomplete. Trying to mediate without cultivating awareness traps us at the surface of our conflicts and ignores what is taking place in their depths. When we combine these practices, we are led to the deeper middle way, and to profound insights, both for ourselves and others.

These are difficult tasks and a lifetime's work, but this book will help you make a start. It reveals the richness and relevance of Buddhism as an approach to understanding what lies beneath the surface of our conflicts, and guides us in discovering their sources deep within ourselves. It is full of insightful stories and examples, and of clarity and insight, and I encourage you to consider how you might use it as a source of techniques for resolving your own and other people's conflicts.

I want to go further, however, and encourage those of you who decided to read this book because of its focus on Buddhism to learn more about conflict resolution as a practice; and for those who chose to read it because of its orientation to conflict resolution to start or continue a regular practice of sitting meditation, as an integral part of your work in dispute resolution. As the great Buddhist sage Dogen wrote, "Practice and enlightenment are not two." Neither are mediation and meditation.

May you find yourself in these pages, and delight in what you find.

Kenneth Cloke
Center for Dispute Resolution
Santa Monica, California

THE THREE POISONS:

A BUDDHIST GUIDE
TO CONFLICT RESOLUTION

1. INTRODUCTION

"Every cell in our body contains all the talent, wisdom, goodness, and happiness
of the Buddha, and also of all our spiritual and blood ancestors…Of course,
every cell also contains within it the seeds of hell, of violence: jealousy, anger,
and other negative emotions. But we can practice so that hell does not overpower
the energies of Mindfulness, understanding, and loving-kindness in us."[1]

We live in a world of conflict. Within us and without, locally and globally, in every person, couple, situation, family, company, business, religion, state, country and continent, conflict arises and passes, leaving in its wake both the resulting synthesis of the clash of opposing forces – which is often good or necessary for all concerned – as well as its victims and detritus.

Conflict is not therefore the exception but, rather, the rule. You may not like it, and might prefer a conflict-free world, but really that's just the way it is. Look around – individuals living in maelstroms of confusion and pain, families in denial and dispute, countries insulting and attacking each other, groups in turmoil – it's really quite

---

1   Creating True Peace, Thich Nhat Hanh (2003), Free Press, Page 29.

1

remarkable. It appears that conflict is somehow hardwired into the way the human mind works and as a result encoded as well into how we treat each other at all levels of human intercourse.

Our hardwired conflict is not the same as the aggressiveness of animals. I have a lovely male Staffordshire terrier named Aiko, who is kind to me and my children, but who goes psycho when he's around cats or other small furry animals and wants to attack them. Since he's a pit-bull mix, the species-aggression he exhibits is natural to him. The conflict that's hardwired into his genes operates by rote and instinctually, without compunction or remorse about any of his behavior, no matter how incomprehensible or reprehensible it appears to me. I've trained it out of him not by appealing to any sense of right or goodness or possibility, but simply by superimposing over it a fear of displeasing me.

Human conflict is different because unlike Aiko's, our human brains consist not only of reptilian and mammalian components, but have also a greatly enlarged neo-cortex, which allows us to conceptualize, develop morality and wisdom, and actually transform ourselves and the world around us in an intentional and compassionate way.

So whereas Aiko stops chasing a cat when I tell him to, yank on his collar, and say "heel", you and I can stop a conflict and turn it into something else through self-knowledge and the desire to do so. We have free-will, which means we can choose the ethics and morals we wish to abide by. We have the ability to be mindful – the ability to watch our own minds and feelings, and learn what their patterns are and what triggers them. And whereas Aiko "loves" me and is loyal by instinct, you and I are able to love ourselves and others, learn to see and feel the suffering of others, and choose a path of compassionate transformation for ourselves and the conflicts that embroil us and them.

Ultimately, if conflict is imminently present in each of us and all of our situations, we have perhaps mis-designated its role in our collective life. It has an inherently negative image for us, somewhat better than "death" but worse even than "doing the laundry", and is rarely recognized as the catalyst for personal and situational growth that at its best it surely is.

Because of this failure to recognize the transformational aspect of conflict, we have failed by and large to develop the art of dealing with conflict as it arises, concentrating instead on developing the art of war. War is the response to the confrontational part of conflict which fails to recognize the human possibilities for growth and cooperation in each opposing event. Because we have been unclear about the difference between what conflict is and what its true function is, and unclear about the nature of the emotions and psychological processes that are unleashed during conflict situations, we often have failed to derive the benefits of conflict, coming instead out of the process with bitterness and a feeling of alienation.

While that may be unavoidable in certain conflict situations, it is entirely avoidable in a majority of others. We don't have to be the puppets of our passions in conflict, nor do we have to come away from them with a feeling of defeat or anger. What we need is an understanding of and language for the conflict process, and some basic principles and procedures to help navigate through the perilous passages in the journey through that process. Since there is never an absence of conflicts, but rather only unresolved and resolved ones, we need an understanding of how the one molts into the other, and what we can do to aid in that process. Resolved conflicts aren't conflicts anymore, because the energies that caused the difference in wants to become active struggles have been transformed from negative to positive, from poison to elixir. To do "conflict resolution", whether for ourselves or others, we need to be at home with conflict, kneading and playing with it with acceptance and a feeling of possibility, and not just with a closed feeling of dread. Instead of seeing it as an anomaly or as "something wrong", we need to see it as perhaps painful yet necessary, and then work it lovingly with tools that transform it intelligently into a new set of possibilities for growth.

In what follows I try to fashion just such a language for the resolution of conflict out of the teachings of the Buddha, and the practices and theories that have grown out of those teachings. As in so many other areas of our lives, there is a wealth of wisdom for the resolution of conflict in the teachings of the great spirits in human history, people like the Buddha and Jesus, Mohandas Ghandhi, Henry David Thoreau, and Martin Luther King. Indeed, their many messages seem to converge, all of them boiling down to Christ's Golden Rule or the Buddha's teachings on Loving Kindness and Compassion. If you do unto others as you would have them do unto you, then you probably won't let greed and hatred control your dealings with them when you find yourselves in conflict. If you've developed Loving Kindness for all sentient creatures and empathize with their inherent suffering, you'll try to reduce suffering for everyone in a contentious situation.

But while these basic credos provide a measuring stick for the success of our efforts to live as compassionate beings, in actual conflict situations we also need techniques that acknowledge and work with the dynamic structure of conflict itself. Most social groups have some form of conflict resolution structure in place to deal with disputes between members of the group. For example, in Islamic society, *shura* (groups of people chosen by the parties to mediate or decide a controversy) and consultation between the parties are preferred methods to quell conflict[2]. Similarly, as you will see from the story of "the Dirty Basin" later in this book, during the life of the Buddha he and the members of the sangha (his followers who lived together to follow his Way) had to develop methodologies to deal with conflicts as they arose between the monks living in the community.

While these existing methodologies are of interest, it is a primarily historical or sociological one. Historical or sociological study is not the real purpose of this book, however, since the modern world (a world bursting at the seams with strife) is much different than a sangha in Northern India 2500 years ago, and might benefit from a fresh look at how Buddhism applies to the resolution of new-world conflicts not set within the confines of a religious commune. So we'll look

---

2   *Informal Dispute Resolution and the Formal Legal System in Contemporary Northern Afghanistan*, (2006), Page 2, Draft Report to the Rule of Law Program, The United States Institute of Peace, http://www.usip.org/ruleoflaw/projects/barfield_report.pdf

instead primarily at the basic concepts of conflict and its alleviation in Buddhism.

In Buddhism, techniques and precepts develop out of two intertwined major pathways, commensurate in strength and depth with each other, each fostering the other through the expression of itself. First, there is a pathway of self-understanding, of Mindfulness. On this pathway one expands awareness of and comfort with one's own consciousness, so that the world becomes clearer and less filled with *maya* (which is Pali and Sanskrit for illusion) and *moha* (which is Pali for ignorance or delusion, and which in Sanskrit is *avidyā*).

Second, there is the path of Loving Kindness (*metta*) for one self and thereby for others, from which grows Compassion (*karuna*) for who they are and the suffering they must by dint of their human life endure. This path develops often through learning to positively practice Compassion for others, but also develops quite naturally to the extent that self-understanding or Mindfulness has been developed.

These two pathways are relevant to the resolution of conflict in each of the three contexts dealt with in the pages that follow: the individual level (i.e. internal conflict within the individual), inter-personal (such as between husband and wife, lovers, or co-workers, neighbors, and so on), and in situations where you are acting as a mediator to help two or more opposing sides resolve their conflict.

The twin pathways of Mindfulness and Compassion are relevant to each of these three contexts. If it's your own internal conflict, then through Mindfulness and honesty with yourself, and through the development of Loving Kindness and Compassion towards yourself, you can learn to see yourself and those conflicts in new ways that allow them to transform you into a more centered and harmonious person. In inter-personal situations, Buddhist principals and practices can help you to not only be mindful of your emotions, but also to communicate them in such a way that they can be actually heard, and alert to what the other party is actually communicating, so that they can be heard as well. If you've signed on to help resolve someone else's conflict, in addition to being mindful and compassionate yourself, you can use Buddhist psychology and precepts to help the disputants become aware of what is actually going on in the situation, and to let go of their attachments to their own delusions so as to develop Compassion for the other side.

In this book, we shall first look at conflict itself, and how it is viewed from a Buddhist perspective. In that perspective, conflict arises where there is a) some factual or situational nexus that creates a perceived divergence of interest within an individual or between the opposing sides to a conflict, and b) the arising of any or all of what the Buddhists call "the Three Poisons" of i) anger or hatred, ii) greed or grasping, and iii) ignorance or delusion. As we shall see in the next chapter, if you have (a) without (b), you have a debate, disagreement, or a theoretical difference but there is no *conflict* because there is no emotional or physiological attachment or aversion to the prospective result of the divergence.

The resolution of conflict in its truest and fullest sense is the conversion of the Three Poisons of anger, greed and ignorance into the Four Sublime States of Loving Kindness, Compassion, Appreciative Joy, and Equanimity. In fact, in deference to the Four Noble Truths expounded by the Buddha upon his enlightenment, and the Buddha's Noble Eightfold Path which is laid out in the Fourth Noble Truth, and by which he declared suffering to be resolved, we might fashion the schema for the arising and full resolution of any conflict as follows:

The Four Truths of Conflict

1) Life is Conflict

2) Conflict is caused by Attachment

3) Conflict can be resolved and reconciled through transformation of Attachment

4) The way to resolve and reconcile conflict is the Eightfold Path To Resolve Conflict.

These truths acknowledge that conflict is unavoidable in human life, and that (as we shall discuss in the next chapter) attachment in one form or another is the root cause of all conflict. This attachment can be released and transformed, through using Mindfulness to convert and transform destructive emotions into Loving Kindness and Compassion. This conversion process is the one referred to in the Fourth Truth of Conflict, to wit:

Eightfold Path To Resolve Conflict:

1) a **Situation** causes *Attachment* and thereby Conflict

2) which is the arousal of one or more of the **Three Poisons**

3) which persist through a **Refractory Period** (a period where they are highly resistant to change) leading to stasis

4) after which the parties can **Acknowledge** to themselves and each other – through the development of *personal or interpersonal Mindfulness* –the nature of the Three Poisons present in the situation, making possible

5) a **Settlement** of the (external) Situation, during which process

6) the parties can develop **Loving Kindness** and **Compassion** for themselves and the others, which allows for

7) **Appreciative Joy** in the benefits that each side has gained through the Situation, which allows each person to achieve

8) **Equanimity** and peace with themselves, the others, and the outcome of the process.

Certainly, not every conflict resolves in this order and not every conflict resolves completely through all these phases before the actual situation giving cause to it terminates, but then neither is every baseball hit a home-run, nor does every game go a full nine innings before being called. Indeed, it's only from a short-term perspective that one might say that not every conflict resolves, since I'm quite sure that all will have been resolved before the next Big Bang.

With this Eightfold resolution schema in mind, after discussing the nature of conflict itself, we will look at the life of Siddhartha

Gautama[3], and see what role divergence and conflict played in that life. The Buddha is a very unusual person to view in a conflict context, because he was always Mindful (having in fact invented Mindfulness), and seemingly always expressed Loving Kindness and Compassion. And by the way that the characteristics of Mindfulness, Loving Kindness and Compassion manifested in the various conflicts swirling around him, they are instructive to our own attempts to foster those qualities in our own conflicts. They are also instructive in that even the Buddha could not prevent the development of conflicts in his own life or those of the people around him, nor could he always successfully quell them once they started. Which means that any failures to resolve our own conflicts are both understandable and unavoidable. It also points out that an important part of the art of healing inter-personal conflict is often the ability to foster Mindfulness, Loving Kindness and Compassion in others as well as in oneself.

Certainly, one could say that in the history of Buddhism there are many examples of Buddhists (whether singly or in organizations) not expressing Loving Kindness and Compassion towards each other, and of them failing to be mindful of their true motivations or attachments in their own conflicts. Indeed, in any faith or system for the improvement of the human condition there are examples of shortcomings and cruelties. When I told a friend I was writing this book, he opined that Buddhist monks and temples are often sources of social or personal oppression in Southern Asia, somewhat akin to the coercive and restrictive aspects of Christianity in the West.

While that may be true, it is also true that Buddhism offers a very profound and real framework for the resolution of suffering and conflict, along with instructions on how to achieve those goals. Any acknowledged shortcomings in their previous application – whether by ourselves or others – should merely warn and catalyze us to have integrity and diligence in our ongoing use of the proffered framework and instructions.

---

3   Essential Buddhism, Jack Maguire (2001), Pocket Books, Page 242. Siddhartha is Buddha's birth surname, "All is fulfilled". Gautama is the family name.

Because Buddhism is largely a system for the refinement of human consciousness based upon a schematic conception of how our minds and perceptions function and go astray and become conflicted, we shall outline herein some of the salient characteristics of that conceptual schema, both to understand its portrayal of conflict and how it applies to its resolution. We'll then discuss Mindfulness, Loving Kindness and Compassion, because of their pivotal role in the resolution of conflict, and then discuss ways in which they can be utilized in the process of resolving the various types of conflicts we encounter in our lives. Finally, we'll look at how the Buddhist concept of "Wheel of Becoming" – the progression of steps through which ignorance and mistakes arise and continue in our lives – is relevant to the resolution of conflict, and how the introduction of Mindfulness and Compassion into the progression leads to resolution and freedom.

Finally, I want to note something about the "Buddhism" to which I refer in the following pages. Since we live in a world fraught with conflict, it is not surprising to learn that conflicts have arisen within Buddhism itself, leading to different interpretations of what the Buddha's teachings mean, and how they are to be applied. In fact, it would have been incomprehensible if a 2,500 year-old teaching currently practiced in one form or another by some 400 million people didn't have doctrinal or practical differences. Despite these perceived differences between the various schools of Buddhism (in the Theravada, Mahayana, and Vajrayana vehicles), the reader should know that this book is based on the "synoptic" view[4] that all Buddhist teachings are part of a unified field of knowledge (with some schools emphasizing certain aspects and other schools emphasizing others), and that all are linked in one form or another to the original teachings of the Buddha himself. In the parts of the book where I offer ideas for meditation or Compassion practices, they are the ones I have learned or studied, which isn't meant in any way to suggest that they are better than other forms of such practice that the reader may

---

4   A Survey of Buddhism, Sangharakshita (4th Ed. 1976), Shambhala Books, Page xxi.

have tried or be interested to learn. Similarly, when I refer to texts, treatises, or theories of one school or another, it's because it's helpful and illuminating, not because I think the material is better than that of any other tradition.

2. THE NATURE OF CONFLICT

The Rising of the Three Poisons

"Greed, hatred, and delusion of every kind are unwholesome. Whatever action a greedy, hating, and deluded person heaps up - by deeds, words, or thoughts - that too is unwholesome. Whatever suffering such a person, overpowered by greed, hatred, and delusion, his thoughts controlled by them, inflicts under false pretexts upon another - by killing, imprisonment, confiscation of property, false accusations, or expulsion -being prompted in this by the thought, 'I have power and I want power,' all this is unwholesome too."[5]

Conflict is a term "so broadly applied that it is in danger of losing its status as a singular concept"[6]. This is particularly true since conflict is a concept that refers to us internally as well as in our social aspects. While many of the treatises on mediation and conflict resolution do not define it, a working definition is an essential aid to our purposes here.

On a simple level, conflict is the state where the parts of the equation do not agree with each other. In other words, a perceived

---

5   In the Buddha's Words, Bhikkhu Bodhi (2005), Wisdom Publications, Pages 36-7, from the *Ariguttara Nikaya* 3:69; 1201-2.

6   *Social Conflict: Escalation, Stalemate, and Settlement*, Pruitt and Kim, 2004, McGraw Hill, Page 7.

divergence of interest or opposition of interests. Conflict can also arise on getting up in the morning on the wrong side of the bed, out of sorts, or off-center. Interpersonally, it can and usually does show up whenever two or more of anybodies other than best friends congregate for very long. And the draw towards conflict is very powerful. There is always a shortage and competition for limited resources, and differing needs for respect or love or whatever, so there are innumerable chances for "conflict" to arise.

Although we are going to give our own special definition to conflict, we should see what other sources have to say about it, since there must be some nexus between ordinary understanding of the word and a Buddhist definition of it. The American Heritage Dictionary of the English Language (4th Ed.) defines it thusly:

"**Conflict** ... **1.** A state of open, often prolonged fighting; a battle or war. **2.** A state of disharmony between incompatible or antithetical persons, ideas, or interests; a clash. **3.** *Psychology* A psychic struggle, often unconscious, resulting from the opposition or simultaneous functioning of mutually exclusive impulses, desires, or tendencies. **4.** Opposition between characters or forces in a work of drama or fiction, especially opposition that motivates or shapes the action of the plot..."[7]

The first of these – essentially *war* – is listed first because it is perhaps the most common understanding of what conflict is, but in a Buddhist framework is actually more definitional of the *result* of what the Buddha said underlies conflict. In other words, the open, prolonged fighting and warfare comes about as a result of a conflict that already exists, and is merely the fruit of the tree.

The second definition – a state of disharmony – is the often internal view of conflict as a state of disharmony between incompatibles. This is closer to what our Buddhist definition will be, since a disharmonious state is the seed-bed of conflict, though in our definition there will

---

7   The American Heritage Dictionary of the English Language (4th Ed.),
      Houghton Mifflin, New York 2000, page 386.

be slightly more emphasis on the venomous internal states that occur within the conflicted party or parties.

The third definition – a psychological one – is again closer than the first definition to the Buddhist definition because it also refers to the cause of the conflict, rather than the result as does the first definition.

The fourth definition – opposition between forces or characters in a drama – might at first blush seem to be irrelevant to our discussion here, since it deals with drama and fiction, rather than the meat and potatoes of "real world" drama. Yet that would be a mistaken assumption. For in the Buddhist model attachment and delusion lie at the base of every conflict, so to some extent all conflicts are fictional works of drama, hatched in the minds of the participants as they "motivate or shape the action of the plot."

In Buddhist "psychology", as we shall explore more fully in Chapter 4, there are certain unmistakable aspects to human consciousness. First, the mind attaches to phenomena immediately, and changes them through the act of perception just as quickly. In fact, only about twenty percent of any perception of a sensory event is the actual sensory impression itself – the other eighty percent is created or manufactured within our own minds. In the process of changing the perceived phenomena, the mind creates "mental formations" (ideas and opinions as well as what we usually call "feelings") about the changed phenomena, and also becomes attached to the mental formations as well. The mental formations lead primarily to the arising of the Three Poisons – greed or craving, anger or hatred, and delusion or ignorance.

In a Buddhist definition, then, the root cause of conflict is attachment (to both our mental activities as well as to the "outcome" of the conflict), and its driving force is one or more of the Three Poisons. Because of the importance of these two aspects of conflict in a Buddhist analysis, they deserve to be looked at more carefully.

Attachment

"Attachment" is a very loaded term, much more complicated than ordinarily presumed. It tends to be interchangeable for Buddhist writers and teachers with the words "desire" (which should not be confused solely with the idea of sexual or romantic desire for another) or "craving", no doubt because all these words are attempts to translate the Sanskrit word "*trishna*", which encompasses them all but is not itself exactly encompassed by any of them. Common types of response from those learning that the Buddha in his Second Noble Truth said "All suffering comes from desire (attachment)" tend to be things like, "Gee, maybe I shouldn't want that new car so much!" or "Maybe I am too attached to my vices!" Both of these are in fact examples of attachment, but at a fairly superficial level. At a more basic level, the Buddha was talking about attachment to perceptions and emotions occurring at a much, much deeper and more immediate level, attachments which infuse our consciousness generally before we even know they've arisen.

We are in the habit of assuming that we control our minds, and that what we experience is a "true" perception of "reality". Therefore, when something goes wrong, or we get in a conflict with someone (or with ourselves), we assume that we are "right" since according to our perception of reality things aren't working out the way they should. If it's an internal conflict, the dominant voice will criticize the self or lesser voice for having failed to do what it views as "right". If the conflict is inter-personal, we will objectify the other side and demonize them, holding more and more strongly to our view of what has occurred.

In fact, we haven't necessarily seen anything "real", nor are we "right" – we have attached on various levels to our perceptions and feelings about events surrounding us, based upon what we want and fear, and assumed that the mental construction we have thereby fabricated is correct.

So…what things might we get attached to? The list is endless, but certainly includes:

a) *attachment to the moment's perception.* For instance, right now you're attached to what your eyes see on this page, as well as to the changes to those perceptions that your brain is making. You're also likely starting to attach to other things arising in your mind, like "is it lunch time yet? or "what is this guy getting at?" So your brain has attached to the sensory input of the visual stimuli, and your mind has started to change that input based both upon what it wants (or doesn't want) and your historical experiences;

b) *attachment to our sense of who we are.* We each have a history, things we want, things we don't like and things we do. We each have a "story" about who we are, and about the things that have occurred to us. This attachment will act as one of the modifiers of the sensory input in (a), above.

c) *attachment to our analysis of the situations we're in.* Within each situation, and within each conflict, we will develop a "story" that is contoured to fit our perceptions and wants. Because we've already attached to our perceptions, we will generally believe this story to be "true".

d) *attachment to false expectations of ourselves and others.* In conflict situations especially, we attach to our story about our own role in the situation or what it "should" be, and/or to expectations of how the others involved "should" be acting or what is "really" motivating them. Of course, as often as not this is based upon a false concept of who you are and why you're doing what you're doing, and also on a biased perception of the other and the situation which is colored by your own desires.

The list goes on and on, because the things that present to each of us change from minute to minute. In each moment, our attachments shift to accommodate this ever-changing phenomenal world we float through everyday. And though the identity of the attachments differ, they all are similar in that each involves in some way desire or aversion. In other words, each one has to do with getting more of what you want and less of what you don't.

In fact, attachment on all levels is deemed by the Buddha to be the basic cause of suffering – his Second Noble Truth (after the First, which is that life is suffering) is that suffering is caused by attachment or desire:

> "The Buddha's Second Noble Truth is that human beings suffer because we live in an almost constant state of desire. According to the Buddha, we are born into this condition as well: it is part of our evolutionary inheritance, the karma of taking form. He explains in detail how simply having a body and senses and coming into contact with the world will create pleasant or unpleasant sensations that will automatically lead to reactions of desire or aversion. This process is instinctual, a function of our nervous system, which operates according to the biological law of stimulus-response. The Buddha saw that this organic condition keeps us continually dissatisfied and off-balance"[8]

According to the Buddha, we are basically desire machines – we are driven on a creature level by our likes and dislikes. And because of this, we are always somewhat dissatisfied with the way things are, since we're already attached to the next thing which will make it better (or less worse).

A corollary of this desire-aversion aspect to attachment is that attachment tends to make us *ignorant* of what's actually going on around us. When we want something, our perception of it changes to reinforce its desirability, and the things and situations around the desirable object/person appear as either favorable or unfavorable towards us getting the desired thing. This, of course, is the basis of much of modern advertising. But since we no longer are seeing the situation for itself, but rather as it serves our needs, we have become ignorant of the true nature of the world around us.

---

8   Buddha's Nature: A Practical Guide to Discovering Your Place in the Cosmos, Wes Nisker (1998), Bantam Books, Page 22.

Of course, then you might ask, what does this have to do with conflict? Since we attach or grasp for everything throughout our phenomenal existence, and since that means we regularly are ignorant of the true nature of the reality in which we live, but are only in conflict for some of those issues, what's the relevance?

The relevance of the basic concept of grasping or attachment to that of conflict is a matter of degree. The more basic, deep-rooted and/or universal the issue or need, the stronger the attachment, and the more likely a conflict situation will arise through the unleashing of the Three Poisons. I may want a mocha this morning, but my attachment to heading to a coffee shop is low to moderate. My desire (through the form of aversion) to not be run over by the car that doesn't stop properly for me on the way to the coffee shop is much, much stronger. And I'll probably get angry at the driver and frightened by that car, which will increase the likelihood of a conflict. In other words, there are levels of attachment each with differing likelihoods of creating conflict.

Levels of Attachment

As a general rule, the deeper the attachment, the more likely the conflict, and the more difficult it is to achieve a true and complete resolution. That's because the deeper levels of attachment relate to more and more critical areas of human life, with each being more essential to the well-being of the organism than the former.

In the Kudatanta Sutra, the Buddha recited a tale to the Brahmin Kudatanta, who had asked him how to properly prepare for a sacrifice he wished to hold for all the notables in his region of Northern India (the Buddha would through the Sutra convince him to release all the animals instead of sacrificing them, but that is beside our point). The tale he told the Brahmin was that of a long-ago King named Wide-Realm, who himself sought to have a large sacrifice because he believed it would help him maintain the wealth and power he had accumulated during his life but which he feared to lose. Wide-Realm had in turn asked his Brahmin chaplain (a previous incarnation of the Buddha) how to successfully organize such a sacrifice.

Instead of giving Wide-Realm a recipe for a successful barbecue, the chaplain told him that his kingdom was plagued with thieves and social unrest because the factors needed to provide meaningful work for the people were lacking. He stated further that were the king to impose additional taxes, or try to capture and punish all the miscreants, he would be misspending his resources and efforts. Instead, he should provide seed for the farmers, capital for the tradespeople, and decent wages for the government workers. The chaplain goes on:

> *"Then those men, following each in his own business, will no longer harass the realm, the king's revenue will go up; the country will be quiet and at peace; and the populace, pleased with one another and happy, dancing their children in their arms, will dwell with open doors."* [9]

Wide-Realm took his chaplain's advice, and his kingdom was in fact thereafter a model of peace and harmony. The Brahmin Kudatanta was so impressed by the Buddha's story that he cancelled the sacrifice, set free the "seven hundred bulls, and the seven hundred steers, and the seven hundred heifers, and the seven hundred goats, and the seven hundred rams" who were to have been slaughtered, and asked to be and was accepted instead as a lay disciple of the Buddha.

This sutra is often cited as an example of the Buddha's social and economic theories because it demonstrates implicitly his understanding that a person's basic needs must be met in order to allow harmony to prevail.

Abraham Maslow presented a modern, psychologically-based parallel concept in what he called the "hierarchy of needs", which we mention here insofar as it relates to the idea of attachment and the power of different types of attachment. Maslow presents the following hierarchy as being the order (reading from bottom to top) in which needs present (generally), and each of which levels needs to be substantially satisfied to permit the individual to start trying in earnest to fulfill the next[10]:

---

9   Kutadanta Sutta, http://tipitaka.wikia.com/wiki/Kutadanta_Sutta
10   Motivation and Personality, Abraham F. Maslow (1970, 2d Edition) Harper & Row, Pages 35-58.

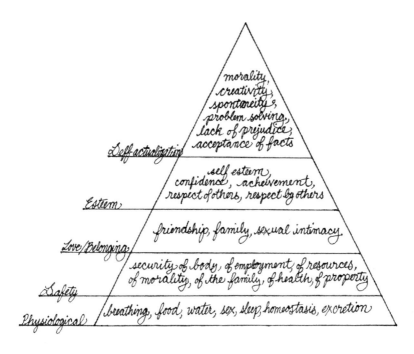

The physiological needs are the most basic – they are the needs for water, food, air etc. that must be met in order for the human being to survive, the lack of any of which will pre-empt any other thoughts or activities on the part of the individual. In other words, if I'm starving all my thoughts will be of food, and the world will be seen as a food-providing and/or food-hiding set of possibilities and obstacles. Until I get enough food to survive, I will not really be able to focus on satisfying any other levels of need I might otherwise have (unless the lack of food is not based upon a physiological need but, rather, a subverted safety or love need). As Maslow says:

> "For the man who is extremely and dangerously hungry, no other interests exist but food. He dreams food, he remembers food, he thinks about food, he emotes only about food, he perceives only food, and he wants only food. The more subtle determinants that ordinarily fuse with the physiological drives in organizing even feeding, drinking, or sexual behavior, may

---

11   Adapted from Wikipedia, http://en.wikipedia.org/wiki/Maslow

now be so completely overwhelmed as to allow us to speak at this time (but only at this time) of pure hunger drive and behavior, with the one unqualified aim of relief."[12]

This effect is readily apparent in nations where famine has led to mass starvation – all activities and thoughts become focused on food and its acquisition, and no ethical strictures on behavior appear relevant to the starving people until it has been acquired. The Buddha stated much the same in the Sixth Realization of the *Sutra on the Eight Realizations of the Great Beings*, in which he recognized not only the power of the physiological needs, but their generative effect for destructive emotions:

"THE SIXTH REALIZATION is the awareness that poverty creates hatred and anger, which creates a vicious cycle of negative thoughts and activity. When practicing generosity, Bodhisattvas consider everyone, friends and enemies alike, as equal. They do not condemn anyone's past wrongdoing, nor do they hate those who are presently causing harm."[13]

The next ascending level is the safety needs, which Maslow defines as "security; stability; dependency; protection; freedom from fear, from anxiety and chaos; need for structure, order, law, limits; strength in the protector; and so on."[14] Maslow claims that these needs, while less strong than the physiological ones, can likewise dominate the entire personality and become its sole organizing principle in cases where these needs are sufficiently threatened. Many of the endless crises in the Middle East focus heavily on these issues, with each side being firmly attached to its position because of fears for its security and safety.

---

12 Motivation and Personality, Abraham F. Maslow (1970, 2d Edition) Harper & Row, Page 37.

13 Sutra on the Eight Realizations of the Great Beings, (trans Thich Nhat Hanh), http://www.buddhanet.net/pdf_file/beingssutra.pdf

14 Motivation and Personality, Abraham F. Maslow (1970, 2d Edition) Harper & Row, Page 39.

Unlike physiological needs, which are driven by the need to achieve an acceptable homeostatic state, safety needs are often distorted or exaggerated by the psychological make-up of the individual. The clearest example of this is the obsessive-compulsive, for whom a simple need like making sure the bathtub is turned off or that the door is locked becomes of life-and-death concern, and takes over the entire personality. Since attitudes, fears and desires regarding safety needs tend to be formed during childhood, if there has been a trauma with regards to safety needs in childhood the adult will carry forward that trauma unhealed into his or her present situations. This doesn't necessarily mean that these attachments can't be transformed, just that their resistance to lessening or shifting can be surprisingly strong, and that the importance of seemingly inconsequential matters may take on an unreasonably great importance for an individual involved in a conflict. Everyone who as ever acted as a mediator is familiar with situations where one party will have an overly-strong attachment to a seemingly inconsequential need – usually, some historical safety need trauma has gotten mixed into a current situation and exaggerated the party's perceived need for a certain result. The overly strong attachment to a seemingly inconsequential need can also be symbolic, as in a divorce where who gets a piece of furniture suddenly becomes all-important.

Once the safety needs are met, the belongingness and love needs become prevalent. These are the mammalian needs for comfort, protection, physical contact, and a place within a group or family. Maslow notes that the thwarting of these needs is "the most commonly found core in cases of maladjustment and more severe pathology".[15]

Next, Maslow posits the esteem needs, which are in two subgroups, although he acknowledges that these may operate in our society but not be universal. The first subgroup is the need for achievement and mastery within one's life, leading to self-confidence and a feeling of usefulness – in other words, internal feelings or sense of accomplishment and worth. The second grouping is that of recognition of this achievement by others – the external part of

---

15   <u>Motivation and Personality</u>, Abraham F. Maslow (1970, 2d Edition)
      Harper & Row, Page 44.

the equation, the esteem and respect that inure to someone because of his or her internal/life mastery. So one feels good about his or her accomplishments, and enjoys the status they have accorded him within his social milieu.

These four lower tiers are the basic needs – in other words, failure to substantially achieve a working comfort level with each of these will leave one less able or possibly even unwilling to approach the pinnacle of the hierarchical pyramid, the need for self-actualization. For Maslow, the need for self-actualization is the set of needs to become what one should or must become based upon his or her predispositions and gifts. This tier reminds me of how Morihei Ueshiba, the founder of Aikido, defined *winning*: "Winning means winning over the mind of discord in yourself. It is to accomplish your bestowed mission."[16] At this level, the need for personal, idiosyncratic fulfillment – whether it be in the arts, business, family, religious or spiritual pursuits, or any possible amalgam of any or all of these – as part of a life-long unfolding process is the key to psychological motivation.

Maslow's thesis was that until one has substantially satisfied the needs at each of the "basic" lower four tiers of the hierarchy (physiological, safety, belongingness and love/esteem), he or she will not have the psychological or biological "space" to develop or act fully upon needs at the highest tier:

"In actual fact, most members of our society who are normal are partially satisfied in all their basic needs and partially unsatisfied in all their basic needs at the same time. A more realistic description of the hierarchy would be in terms of decreasing percentages of satisfaction as we go up the hierarchy of prepotency. For instance, if I may assign arbitrary figures for the sake of illustration, it is as if the average citizen is satisfied

---

16   Aikido, Kisshomaru Uyeshiba (1978) Hozansha Publishing Co. Ltd, Page 178.

perhaps 85 percent in his physiological needs, 70 percent in his safety needs, 50 percent in his love needs, 40 percent in his self-esteem needs, and 10 percent in his self-actualization needs."[17]

Maslow also acknowledges certain exceptions to the order of the tiers. For example, some people prefer esteem or self-esteem to love. Artists tend to value their artistic endeavors at the risk of basic needs (for that matter, wandering Buddhist monks valued their path more than their physical needs). Religious or political martyrs will try to accomplish their goals despite failure to satisfy their basic needs. Psychopaths tend to have a permanent loss of love needs, or get them drastically twisted into something else. Some people permanently lose their ambitions within higher tiers and accept their lot in life as long as the physiological and safety needs are substantially met.

Ultimately for our purpose here, the hierarchy of needs is useful because it illustrates in a schematic way certain principles which relate to the Buddhist concept of attachment:

a) underlying all of the tiers on the hierarchy is the concept of motivation or grasping for fulfillment. In other words, the Buddhist concept of *trishna* as reflected in a more modern "psychological" garb;

b) in the absence of overriding religious, political, artistic, or psychopathological motivations, the lower on the hierarchy we are, the stronger the attachment. Needs and desires tend to arise at various levels of importance – the closer the attachment is to a "basic need", the stronger it is likely to be as well;

c) there are certain needs or prerequisites that are not the immediate need, but without which the basic need cannot be met. For instance, if Israel prevents a worker from crossing the border to get to work, the worker might perceive this as

---

17   Motivation and Personality, Abraham F. Maslow (1970, 2d Edition) Harper & Row, Pages 53-4.

a threat to both physiological and safety needs, even though strictly speaking it is neither. The worker will react to a deprivation of this right to cross the border with the same intensity as he would to a direct danger to any of his basic needs; and

d) because every factor in each person's world is viewed in terms of whether it fosters or harms satisfaction of needs at the various tiers in the hierarchy, no one is actually viewing reality in its true light – Maslow's theory supports well the Buddhist idea that our attachments make us ignorant of the true nature of our life.

Every mediator knows that the parties to the mediation get "stuck" in their positions, and that one of his or her primary jobs in resolving the dispute is to get them "unstuck" – in other words, to get them to let go of their attachments. Similarly, most couples that have had an argument knows that each person has held firm to their "story" throughout the tumultuous parts of the conflict, only letting it go (hopefully) once the heat of argument has started to subside. These are both examples of the Buddha's Second Noble Truth that suffering is caused by desire or attachment. As we'll see later in this book, the way to relieve that suffering is in part helping them (or yourself) to let go of those attachments, which is not always the easiest of tasks.

But attachment, while it may be the cause of conflict, is only part of the story. For a real conflict to exist, the Three Poisons need to arise in the situation as well. And to fully understand what the Three Poisons are and how they arise, we need to understand a bit about how the human brain works, and what happens when it mixes emotions and fears with perceptions.

The Triune Brain

As I worked my way through writing this chapter, I was followed by a nagging question – if attachment and grasping characterizes all of our activities as humans, and if because of that we live in a state of more or less continual ignorance, then what distinguishes that basic state from the Three Poisons as they express in a state of conflict? The Three Poisons – greed, anger/hatred, and delusion – are certainly quite similar to the basic Buddhist concept of *trishna* – which has both a positive aspect of what I want (which would relate to greed) and a negative aspect of what I don't want (relating to hatred) – and to the omnipresent ignorance that our *trishna* fosters (related to delusion). But after much contemplation, the difference between basic *trishna/ignorance* and the Three Poisons as expressed during conflict became clear to me:

During conflict, the Three Poisons are like trishna and ignorance on steroids.

As noted, in the absence of enlightenment, *trishna* and ignorance are already prevalent. As the Buddha said in the Pali Canon, we are all "hindered by ignorance and fettered by craving."[18]. But in conflict situations, because of the kinds of physiological and psychological sequelae that arise, all of the tendencies of our ordinary states are magnified.

Much of this has to do with the nature of the human brain, a magnificent amalgam of the evolution of our species. I remember as a child learning the phrase "ontogeny recapitulates phylogeny" and feeling very mature and brilliant for being able to repeat it out loud. It was, of course, just a fancier way of saying that in the development of each of our embryos *in utero* could be seen the evolutionary history of how our species developed, so that the embryo would first resemble that of a fish, then a chicken, then a canine, then a man. While the "recapitulation" theory, as proposed by Ernst Haeckel in the 1860's, has since been largely discredited, we do have vestigial evolutionary elements woven into our physical structures and into our brains. In fact, our brains recapitulate the evolution of brains in other species as well.

Your brain has three major systems within it, thereby justifying the "triune brain" moniker for it coined by neuroscientist Paul MacLean

---

18 <u>In the Buddha's Words</u>, Bhikkhu Bodhi (2005), Wisdom Publications, Page 218, from the *Samyutta Nikaya* 15:3; II 179–80.

in the 1970's. First, there is the reptilian brain, which regulates the homeostatic features referred to in Maslow's lowest "physiological needs" tier – things like hunger, basic sexuality, and body temperature -- and basic survival response to positive and negative stimuli, as well as some of the aspects of the "safety needs" tier. Responses in this part of the brain tend to be more or less instinctual, meaning that conscious or mindful control of them is more difficult to achieve than responses in the other parts of the brain.

Next is the mammalian brain or "limbic system" (*limbus* is Latin for "rim", since the mammalian brain grows around the rim of the reptilian brain), which adds different types of abilities and responsive possibilities to that of the reptilian brain. First, it adds the ability to learn, and to remember what it has learned. Secondly, it adds the element of emotion to the mix, which is why lionesses can be affectionate with their cubs, but lizards generally can't with their offspring. The fact that he has a limbic system intact allows my dog Aiko to remember what to do when I need to control his behavior, because he is able to be loyal to me. The limbic system would correspond to the third Maslowian tier of "love and belongingness needs", as well as some of the loyalty-based security needs like that of protecting the family or maintaining territory/property.

The fact that we have added the mammalian brain to the reptilian does not, however, mean that the reptilian brain has in any sense been deactivated:

> "Although the mammalian brain grew over the top of the reptilian brain, it did not assume complete control. MacLean emphasized that the mammalian brain is very tightly connected to the reptilian circuits and can function only within their constraints. As the Buddha pointed out in his teaching, it is our primal reaction to feelings of pleasant or unpleasant that draws us into emotional states of craving or aversion."[19]

---

19 Buddha's Nature: A Practical Guide to Discovering Your Place in the Cosmos, Wes Nisker (1998), Bantam Books, Page 96.

2. The Nature Of Conflict

Not only do we have emotional and belongingness needs and responses, and reptilian instinctual responses underlying those, but over the past few million years we have developed the third and final part of our brain, the neomammalian or primate brain, which is much larger and more developed in humans than it is in other mammals. This part of the brain, concentrated in the pre-frontal lobes or neocortex, gives humans all the things that Aiko and the lizards don't have – the ability to plan, to develop morality, to play computer games, to study, to enjoy art, to be a Buddhist, to be a hired assassin, etc. It also gives the individual a consciousness that can be aware of itself and develop the concept of an "I", which in Buddhist theory and psychology is another cause of suffering for us all (more on that later). On Maslow's hierarchy, the primate brain would control all of the esteem and self-actualization needs.

And again, the newer part of the brain – which gives us as well the ability to justify and rationalize our behavior – is still subject to control and needs from the other two parts of the brain. In other words, we can use our words and (perhaps feigned) belief in our own apparent logic and "rightness" to try and explain away and excuse the fact that we are acting anything but logical or "right" in many situations, since the motivations for the behavior come from below the radar of our human intellect or awareness. Or as Joseph Chilton Pearce puts it, we're using the human part of our brain mostly to make excuses for the behavior generated by our reptilian and mammalian brains.[20]

It follows, of course, that our actions and perceptions are therefore the fused result of brain activities in all three parts of the brain. So our concept that we are rational people doing things for logical reasons is inaccurate – we are complex animals acting as a result of our physiological, emotional, and cognitive needs, and subconsciously but actively molding our perceptions to provide the justification for those needs and the ability to satisfy them. This situation is made more prone to conflict because of the way certain parts of the limbic system operate in the face of any perceived threat.

---

20   Buddha's Nature: A Practical Guide to Discovering Your Place in the Cosmos, Wes Nisker (1998), Bantam Books, Page 98.

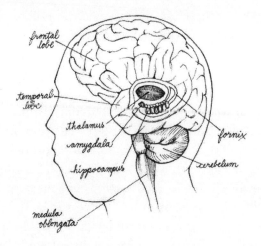

The drawing above is of the limbic system, which as we have noted is the "emotional" add-on part of the brain that appeared evolutionarily after the reptilian brain, but before the evolution of the human neocortex. Towards the center of the limbic system is an almond-shaped (actually, a pair of them on matching sides of the brain) structure called the amygdala. Arching around it is a structure that looks a bit like a bracelet, called the hippocampus.

The human brain, like that of many other species, is "on edge" most of the time, because evolutionarily that made the most sense – it allowed us to survive the dangers and potential threats in the natural landscape by keeping a constant, anxious vigil on our surroundings. The Buddha understood this well when he said that one of the three basic characteristics of human existence is unsatisfactoriness (more on that later as well). The amygdala goes beyond this generalized uneasiness and generates fear responses and other negative emotions in response to current events. And not only does it generate these emotional responses, but it has a memory for the feelings and emotions that arose in previous events that it perceived as perilous which it resuscitates whenever a new experience even remotely similar to the original event occurs.

Unfortunately, the emotional events that go into the formation of the amygdala's memory are not recent or pleasant, since they are deposited there before the "logical" adult brain forms. In fact, the amygdala is one of the first parts of the brain to fully develop, and is therefore a repository for memories of any early life traumas. Because of this, the danger signs that trigger the amygdala to send out distress calls are not subject to conscious control (at least, not at first) and generate involuntary preconscious emotional responses before the thinking brain can correct or analyze them.

The amygdala also plays an important role in the generation of anger as well as of fear. Whether the anger is "held in" and not expressed, or outwardly expressed or even allowed to develop into rage and violence, in either case there is activation in the amygdala and the right prefrontal cortex. Since the right prefrontal cortex is associated with negative emotions and depression (whereas the left prefrontal cortex relates to positive emotions like Compassion and joy), the amygdala actually joins forces in these situations with the part of the brain that fosters and maintains negative frames of mind.

And it not only engenders negative frames of mind, but it also helps them stay alive:

> "Not only does the amygdala hijack the brain, it can also hold it hostage: the adrenal and cortical stimulation caused by a strong emotional arousal can linger in our system for days... After the amygdala is aroused to deal with one problem, even though the initial cause for arousal may be handled or dismissed, the entire system stays of maximum alert long thereafter, looking for more threats or problems upon which to fixate, creating a state of continued anxiety."[21]

As we shall discuss later in this book, the onset of a conflict – when the Three Poisons are aroused and flare up – is this initial adrenal and

---

21 Buddha's Nature: A Practical Guide to Discovering Your Place in the Cosmos, Wes Nisker (1998), Bantam Books, Page 128.

cortical stimulation, which creates a "Refractory Period"[22] when it is most difficult to resolve the conflict because there is not yet any possibility of mindful dialogue or compassionate behavior.

Of course the amygdala doesn't act in a vacuum – it works in tandem with other parts of the brain, many of which are simultaneously involved in each mental event. So as the amygdala is generating emotions and the physical responses that go with them:

a) the hippocampus is providing a memory of the contexts that the individual is familiar with. So if someone reaches their hand towards you, you'll know (hopefully) not to block-and-attack if the hand belongs to your girlfriend or mother;

b) the ventromedial cortex portion of the frontal lobe (which is in the center and on the underside of the frontal lobe in the diagram above) is providing some control of the emotions being generated. But of course this is prefrontal control of a limbic event, which depends to some extent upon how the individual is perceiving what is going on around him or her; and

c) unfortunately, the amygdala is communicating directly with the back part of the brain where visual input gets processed. In other words, what we think we're seeing (as well as hearing, etc.) is being directly influenced and changed by the emotional response we have to the situations. This means that it is fairly easy to maintain an anxious and faulty perception of the events going on about us because we are changing them as they are experienced.

Obviously we won't go into a full-scale discussion of neuroscience here, but the simple facts recited above hopefully suggest why we

---

22 In neuroscience, the "Refractory Period" is a brief period where due to an initial stimulation a nerve is unable to respond to a second stimulus. In conflict situations, it's where the Poisons are so strong that they largely preclude the introduction of Compassion or logic into the situation.

don't always react calmly to conflict situations, don't always see things they way they actually are, and why we don't always get back to an even-keel right away. The very aspects of the human brain that allowed us to survive to populate the entire planet are the same ones that prime us for conflict. Put another way, our survival apparatus makes us continually ripe for the rise of the Three Poisons.

The Three Poisons

Depending upon the school of Buddhism you are most drawn to, there will be some term or other for the Three Poisons, which are also often called "destructive emotions" or "mental afflictions". Although the moniker "Three Poisons" was actually coined by the Mahayana Buddhists (the Buddhism prevalent in Japan, China, and Korea, which was an historical offshoot of the original Theravadan Buddhism of India, Ceylon, etc.), the original term for the poisons in Pali (the language of the Theravadans) is *kilesa*, "defilement", "corruption" or "poison". While the earliest Thervadan texts didn't use the term "Three Poisons", the Pali text quote from the Buddha at the beginning of this chapter shows that in the very earliest Buddhist writings three such *kilesas* were already recognized as preeminent – greed (*lobha kilesa*), hatred (*dvesha kilesa*), and delusion (*moha kilesa*). These same would be carried forward into the Mahayana schools, where they are called by their Sanskrit name *klesha*. Later still, in the Vajrayana schools of Tibet, they were named *nyon-mong*. In all three traditions, they refer to the same basic concept:

> "These three *kilesas* specifically refer to the subtle movement of mind (*citta*) when it initially encounters a mental object (in Buddhist conceptions of the mind, 'mental object' refers to any object which the mind perceives, be it a thought, emotion or object perceived by the physical senses.). If the mind initially reacts by moving towards the mental object, seeking it out, or attaching to it, the experience and results will be tinged by the *lobha kilesa*. Unpleasant objects or experiences are often

met by aversion, or the mind moving away from the object, which is the root for hatred and anger to arise in relation to the object."[23]

From these original three, the list of destructive emotions got expanded by various schools of Buddhism – in fact some Buddhists scriptures refer to eighty-four thousand different kinds of negative emotions, though they do not actually describe them all which is good since I won't then have to list them.[24] A very common amplification of the list is a five-poison menu: 1) greed, 2) hatred, and 3) delusion, with lesser poisons 4) pride and 5) jealousy on their heels.

A classic Theravadan formulation of an expanded poisons list is the "Six Main Mental Afflictions"[25], each of which is readily cognizable in both personal, inter-personal and geo-political conflict situations:

1) *Attachment or Craving.* In every conflict, each side has things it wants and thinks it needs. In an internal conflict, the "voices" at war in the individual will each have things it wants, and things it doesn't. In a divorce situation, one spouse may want freedom or to be freed from the weight of living in discord from the other, whereas the other may be afraid of the impending changes and crave things that make him or her feel secure. In the Middle East, Israel wants security from its neighbors, and Palestine wants autonomy and recognition;

2) *Anger (which includes hostility and hatred).* Most conflicts generate feelings of hostility and anger between the factions or participants. For example, in a divorce the spouse who has been left often feels hatred and anger for the departing spouse. The departing spouse may feel anger as well – first, because of the unresolved issues from the marriage, but also to cover feelings of guilt or failure on his or her part for having

---

23   http://en.wikipedia.org/wiki/Kilesa
24   Destructive Emotions, Daniel Goleman (2003) Bantam Books, Page 78.
25   These were originally articulated by Vasubandhu in the 4th century in a work called the Abhidharma-kośa. http://en.wikipedia.org/wiki/Kilesa

abandoned the relationship. In the political arena, part of the cycle of escalation of conflict is the anger and mistrust of the other side that each side develops, resulting in a hardening of negative attitudes toward the other side;

3) *Arrogance or Pridefulness.* The abandoned spouse's pride has been wounded because of feelings of humiliation at being left. The departing spouse pride has also been activated in the conflict – i.e. feelings of being unappreciated and misunderstood during the marriage are repaid by an exaggerated sense of self on his or her part. So arrogance and pridefulness actually have two aspects. First, there is the positive aspect of asserting the supremacy of the self and its needs over others. But there is also the aspect of protecting the threatened sense of self;

4) *Ignorance or Delusion.* As we shall see later in our discussion of the Wheel of Becoming, ignorance is the root cause of the cycle of birth and death that the Buddha said generates and delineates our suffering. Conflict thrives in the culture of ignorance, because through our ignorance we justify our belief in the rightness of our position in the conflict. The Palestinians see the Israelis as oppressive monsters, who in turn see the Palestinians as terrorists and lunatics. The abandoned spouse sees her ex as a selfish monster, who in turn sees her as a selfish self-pityer. In each of these cases, a more balanced view would show that the other side is usually acting as people naturally do in their given situation, which would start moving the conflict from stalemate to healing;

5) *Afflictive Doubt.* Afflictive Doubt is "not merely a vacillation but a doubt that involves veering away from reality," [26] In classical Buddhism afflictive doubt is doubt in the veracity and efficacy of the Buddha's teaching and methods (thus leading to a failure to perceive reality correctly), but more generally also means neurotic doubt or uncertainty that hinders approach to the truth. Doubt can come in many forms. If I'm suffering from an internal conflict, I could doubt that I

---

26   Destructive Emotions, Daniel Goleman (2003) Bantam Books, Page 102.

have the ability to solve it, or that I am worthy of having it solved in the first place. People embroiled in conflict can so doubt the capacity and integrity of the other side that they are unwilling to work towards resolution themselves. Thus, one nation will refuse to negotiate with another because it is "untrustworthy". Participants can also have undue skepticism about the resolvability of a conflict, and thus waver and refuse to act decisively to end it. To some extent, resolving conflict always involves the faith to take the first step towards resolution;

6) *Afflictive Views.* Afflictive views are the ones that grow out of the basic Three Poisons and prevent one from seeing the true nature of the situation – "I am good, and they are bad", "all Palestinians are terrorists", "my business partner is greedy", etc. Whereas ignorance is a basic condition, afflictive doubts and views are the ones that I build to enshrine my ignorance – as well as my hatreds and desires – into some sort of cognizable, hardened "position".

In the classical Theravadan psychological text, the *Abhidhamma*, which was composed during the three centuries after the Buddha's death, the basic Three Poisons were expanded into a list of ten "defilements" as follows: 1) greed; 2) hate; 3) delusion; 4) conceit; 5) wrong views; 6) doubt; 7) torpor; 8) restlessness; 9) shamelessness; and 10) recklessness. [27]

Further, Buddhist schools also discussed *derivative* mental afflictions that derive from the basic three, which are different "flavors" contained in the basic Three Poisons. A Theravadan formulation of these follows:

---

27   http://en.wikipedia.org/wiki/Kilesa, based upon Rhys Davids & Stede (1921-5), p. 217; and, Nyanatiloka Mahathera (1988), *Buddhist Dictionary*, Kandy: Buddhist Publication Society, entry for "kilesa," retrieved 2008-02-09 from "BuddhaSasana" at http://www.budsas.org/ebud/bud-dict/dic3_k.htm

Twenty Derivative Mental Afflictions

Anger
1. Wrath
2. Resentment
3. Spite
4. Envy/Jealousy
5. Cruelty

Attachment
1. Avarice
2. Inflated Self-Esteem
3. Excitation
4. Concealment of One's Own Vices
5. Dullness

Ignorance
1. Blind Faith
2. Spiritual Sloth
3. Forgetfulness
4. Lack of Introspective Attentiveness

Ignorance + Attachment
1. Pretension
2.. Deception
3. Shamelessness
4. Inconsideration of Others
5. Unconscientiousness
6. Distraction[28]

Here, certain mental afflictions are more relevant to inner conflict (such as Spiritual Sloth and Lack of Introspective Attentiveness). Others relate much more clearly to inter-personal situations -- all of the ones that relate to Anger and Attachment, plus some of the

---

28   Destructive Emotions, Daniel Goleman (2003) Bantam Books, Page 106.

ones related to "Ignorance + Attachment" (particularly Pretension, Deception, and Inconsideration of others).

Ultimately, though, all of these variations on the "poison list" boil back down to the original Three Poisons, kind of the way color wheels of infinite variety can be constructed out of the three primary colors. If you look at the list of five, pride is an attachment to concepts about yourself, and jealousy is attachment to what you see others having that you want plus hatred of them for having those things instead of you. So we've still really reduced the list back to the basic Three Poisons. Similarly, if you look at the *Abhidhamma* ten defilements, wrong views are a form of delusion, doubt is attachment to ambiguous beliefs, torpor is negative attachment (aversion) to required effort, restlessness is aversion to the status quo, shamelessness and recklessness are both attachments to sensual pleasure plus delusion about the effects of that attachment on oneself and others. Once again, we're back to the original three. So in what follows, I'll use the term "Three Poisons" to mean the original three plus all the derivative mental afflictions in the other lists.

Conflict grows out of the Three Poisons because once they arise, there is no longer Mindfulness (internal or inter-Mindfulness) of the true nature of the situation and of the compassionate needs therein, and because the parties to the conflict have shifted into psychological modes where clarity of perception and ability to empathize are greatly reduced. When one works with conflict regularly, one can "feel" the presence of the Three Poisons, because they tend to create an emotional charge which is not there when the Poisons are absent. Part of learning to work with conflict is to get sensitive to these intimations, so that one can start to identify which ones are at work and start to transform them.

You may be thinking in reading this that the Three Poisons are labeled as "bad" in classical Buddhism, or considered morally "wrong" in that they foster conflict with others, and lead to violence, etc. Actually, this is not the case. Buddhism generally follows a fairly simple rubric in analyzing situations or phenomena, which tends to be non-moralistic and looks rather to see whether something is positive or negative for the spiritual awareness of the individual. As the Buddha once stated, he knew only two things – the cause of suffering, and the way to relieve that suffering. Under that rubric, the mental afflictions or Three Poisons are viewed as afflictive (not *bad*) because they prevent the individual from perceiving reality the way it is, thus keeping him or her on the Wheel of Suffering and separated from nirvana, which is the unconditional state that arises from a true perception of the nature of reality.

The destructive emotions prevent the apprehension of true reality in two ways. First, they prevent proper discernment of the actual nature of the immediate situation, which is the one that gave rise to the destructive emotions in the first place. If you get angry with your boss, then the anger creates misapprehension of reality in your dealings with her, and prevents you from feeling Compassion for her in the situation. Second, and more important, they tend to make one have a false view of all of reality, which prevents one from proper discernment in other situations as well. So, after becoming deluded in dealing with your boss all day, you go home and yell at your spouse and your kids, and perhaps even develop a permanently jaundiced view of the way the world is because your perception of reality in general has become poisoned.

From the perspective of resolving conflict, the problem with the Three Poisons is much easier to state – they make things weird and resistant to settlement. They arise at the same time as the conflict situation, and they entangle and amplify it as they so arise. They also tend to make the individual participant(s) in the conflict feel isolated and powerless to change, which makes it harder to resolve since he/she/they are not "present" to their own feelings and what's going on around them. Let's look at an example of how that might arise:

a) <u>internal conflict</u> – most inter-personal conflicts start with some sort of internal conflict. So, for example, assume that a divorced mom needs for some reason to live in one city, while her child needs to go to high school in another city, thus necessitating that the child live with the other parent through much of the school year. Before this issue ever turns into any kind of conflict between the mother and the child or the ex-spouse, the mother may generate internal destructive emotions within herself through being conflicted about what she should do. Her actual conflicted situation might in this case be: should I change jobs, fight to make my child change schools, or accept the situation as it is? During this process, Poisons will arise. First, there may be craving or grasping for her child, which she will feel *even while her child is with her* during vacations. Then there may be anger at the world for creating the situation and at her ex-spouse for "getting the better" of the situation. Finally, there may be hatred of the ex-spouse which is just a reawakening of all the feelings she went through during the divorce. As and if these arise her cognitive grasp on the situation will be influenced by her fears and desires, reducing her ability to see what's "really" going on.

b) <u>inter-personal conflict</u> – many internal conflicts develop into inter-personal ones, because the conflicted individual needs some way to act out or relieve the conflicted feelings that develop. So in the case above, the mom might easily start creating conflicts with others because she's already feeling poorly herself. Unbalanced by the Poisons of craving, anger, and hatred, she may easily get into a conflict with her child, who she may accuse of favoring the dad and of not caring for the mom. Then, she may call the dad and accuse him of trying to come between her and her child, and threaten to take him to court to try to get increased custody of the child during the school year.

The result of these actions would, of course, likely be the spread of destructive emotions throughout the family microcosm. The child might become hateful towards the mom -- who she may say is acting like a real bitch - but also develop fear and anxiety from having been put in the middle of her two parents, both of whom she loves and from whom she seeks and needs approval and care. So her perceptions would shift because of her anger and insecurity – she could end up seeing her mom as bad, and be hypersensitive to every word either parent says for signs of future mishap. The ex-husband, feeling innocent of any wrong–doing, may become angry and hateful towards the mom, because the wounds of the divorce will reopen for him as well. But he might also feel fear for his daughter and her well-being, and fear that he will lose her or that she will somehow be taken away and stop loving him. He may also feel some sadness and attachment to feelings of failure about having gotten divorced, so that he will have the discomfort of guilt (i.e. hatred of self because of attachment to a concept of what one *should* be). Because of all this he could end up becoming defensive, seeing the mom as the attacker, and he and the child as victims.

The situation has now ripened into a "conflict" because we now have the necessary ingredients to make a conflict – in other words, the first three stages of the Eightfold Path To Resolve Conflict:

1) a **Situation** has caused attachment – the "tale of two cities" scenario has generated first the mom's internal anxieties, and then her attachment to being with her child – resulting in an intra-family conflict;

2) which has aroused one or more of the **Three Poisons** – each of the three family members is now angry, hateful, and fearful of loss, and thereby deluded as to the true nature of the situation;

3) which will now persist through a **Refractory Period** (in other words, the period of time it takes for the conflict to calm down enough to start resolving) leading to stasis – the parties will either start to resolve it on their own or with a mediator once the initial outburst of the destructive emotions has subsided and reached a steady state.

This then would be the conflict situation that would present to a mediator trying to resolve it, should the family go to mediation. The mediator will likely be struck by two contrary realizations almost immediately. First, she will understand that the *factual* situation is actually fairly common and amenable to resolution on a practical level. So, using weekends and school vacations and the like, she can easily suggest scheduling and communication techniques that would fashion a workable reconciliation of all the parties' needs.

Second, however, she will feel the presence of the Three Poisons and see them expressing through the situation, and realize that until these can be worked with and released or somehow transformed into something else, the workable reconciliation is likely going to stay out of reach.

In other words, situations would usually be pretty easy to resolve except that people always screw them up! They continually wind up at the third stage of the Eightfold Path To Resolve Conflict – the impasse at the end of the Refractory Period. Of course, the "third stage" can be anything that occurs before the resolution process, including armed conflict. Until the process has reached a stage where the destructive emotions are at least somewhat stabilized it is very difficult to start the actual resolution process, because no one is ready to start re-evaluating or looking truthfully at their own role in the conflict.

But once the situation has reached a workable impasse, the mediator can do a lot to start the transformation process. First, she can create an attitude of trust and (albeit perhaps begrudging) hope in the possibility of "life after conflict." She can create "inter-Mindfulness" in the family by having them each express their perceptions and feelings in such a way that the others can hear them, and thereby open their own awareness up to a greater sense of the true dimensions of the situation. And she can help each of the family members touch the core of Loving Kindness and Compassion that dwells within them, which is where the seeds of transformation really dwell.

The question then is how can the mediator and the family use Buddhist techniques to complete the other five stages of the Eightfold Path To Resolve Conflict? To answer that question, we need to understand a bit more about how those Buddhist techniques came about. To do that we will look at the role of conflict in the life of the Buddha, and in the psychology of the Dharma he created.

3. CONFLICT AND THE LIFE OF THE BUDDHA

"I am a Khattiya, warrior-noble stock. I was reborn into a Khattiya family. I am a Gotama by clan. My lifespan is of short length, is brief and soon over, one who lives long now completes the century or a little more. A king, Suddhodana by name, was my father. A queen, Maha Maya by name, was the mother that bore me. The royal capital was the city of Kapilavastu" [29]

Buddhism is not ordinarily thought of as a conflict resolution process. At the most basic level, it is a system meant to provide relief from the phenomenological suffering built into the human condition, a system of philosophical perspectives, psychological techniques, and ethical precepts intended to reduce spiritual suffering and allow one to ascertain more clearly the nature of reality.

It is, of course, a "religion" as well, though not in the sense that we normally presume in the Judeo-Christian tradition. In that tradition,

---

29   http://www.lakehouse.lk/budusarana/2007/03/03/Budu18.pdf, esoteric web publication, also *Digha Nikaya* 14, condensed translation by Late Ven. Bhikkhu Nanamoli's "The Life of Buddha"

religion has to do with a greater Being who creates us and/or controls our destinies. In Buddhism, while even the earliest writings seem to acknowledge the existence of gods and demons, and while the derivative Mahayana and Vajrayana traditions have expanded the idea of a heavenly realm for the Buddha (or Buddhas) and bodhisattvas to reside in, these considerations are really beside the point since the extinguishment of suffering is brought about by the efforts and awareness of the individual and not through the machinations of any divine *personae*. The Buddha regularly refused to answer ontological or cosmological questions.

But as we said in the introduction, because conflict is endemic and universal, and is itself the cause of much suffering in most of our lives, Buddhism by necessity deals with it in its teachings. And, although a great deal of Buddhist practice relates to the individual rather than the group, even at that level the techniques must address how the individual deals with the conflicts that arise in his or her life as they live it. Those same conflicts - at least some of them – must have been active in the life of the Buddha himself, since he made no claims to be other than a human being who was simply *awake*. So what follows is a discussion of the Buddha's life in light of the conflicts that arose for him or for those around him, and the lessons we can glean from how they were dealt with.

One problem in discussing the Buddha's life is the sheer volume of material written about it, and the various provenances of that material. The history, teachings and stories of the Buddha were transmitted orally for about a century after the Buddha's *paranirvana* (death) around 486 BC, and then carried in the form of inscriptions on palm leaves in three baskets for another 130 years or so, until about 250 BC when the monk son of the Mauran Emperor Ashoka of Sri Lanka oversaw the transcription of the Pali Canon [30] (source materials for the Theravadan Buddhists written in the Pali language), which is the first written record of the Buddha's life and words. Other scriptures and sutras (sayings and stories of the Buddha) that the Mahayana Buddhists rely on, however, were originally written in Sanskrit in the

---

30   Essential Buddhism, Jack Maguire (2001), Pocket Books, Pages 43-4. The *Pali Canon* is the earliest written compendium of the Buddha's teachings.

Buddha's native India. The originals of these were largely destroyed throughout the centuries, notably by Islamic invasions throughout India during the 8th through the 12th centuries, but not before many had been translated into either Tibetan or Chinese and spirited away to monasteries in those countries.

In addition to problems of provenance, there are embellishments to the Buddha's biography made over time through the religious fervor of his followers. As Joseph Campbell has noted, the enlightenment of the Buddha and the crucifixion of Jesus constitute the two single highest moments in Oriental and Occidental mythologies, respectively -- the Buddha was reborn on the Tree of Enlightenment, and Jesus transpired on the Tree of Redemption.[31] Campbell identifies each as a *hero* who "ventures forth from the world of common day into a region of supernatural wonder: fabulous forces are there encountered and a decisive victory is won: the hero comes back from this mysterious adventure with the power to bestow boons on his fellow man."[32] Because of the Buddha's heroic status and preeminence in the religious life of Asia, his life story has been mythologized much as Christ's life has been in the West. For example, each ended up in scriptures with a virginal mother, impregnated by divine will in one form or other. In fact, each one's history is embellished so richly one suspects that the needs of the embellishers have assumed as much importance as the lives of the luminaries.

Certainly the modern tendency is to downplay the mythologizing and try to portray the Buddha's life as just that – a life, with majestic and admirable qualities certainly, but still just the life of an individual. But we should also remember that the mythological ascriptions can be viewed as symbolic of the meaning of actual events, or of the importance attributed to them. So, in the following narrative, I do not always separate possible fancy from presumed fact, letting you the reader instead decide what to believe, and what to winnow out. Actually, I like the hyperbole, in any event.

---

31   The Hero With a Thousand Faces Joseph Campbell (1949), Princeton University Press, Page 33, Footnote 37.

32   The Hero With a Thousand Faces Joseph Campbell (1949), Princeton University Press, Page 30.

The First Conflict – Suddhodana's Dilemma

The Buddha was born Siddhartha Gotama in the Shakya Kingdom in Southern Nepal and Northern India in 566 BC (though he may have been born some 60 years or so after that, with the uncertainty due again to the time-delay in committing events to writing). Buddha's father Suddhodana was a Khattiya (warrior-noble stock), and the king or chieftain of the extended realm of the Shakya and/ or Gotama clan. The King was a worldly man, proud of his kingdom and eager to maintain or extend it. His wife Maya (or Mahamaya) was a beautiful and celibate woman, whose interests were in the spiritual and emotional realms as opposed to the world of power and politics.

One night, Maya was visited in her sleep by a beautiful, six-tusked white elephant, who rubbed her side with a golden lotus and thus conceived Siddhartha. The karma of the Buddha's final reincarnation had been thus set in motion. When Maya told Suddhodana about the visitation, he summoned his advisors, who told the King that the newborn, destined for greatness, would have to choose between a materialistic life of worldly power and a spiritual life of renunciation. One of the advisors, Kondanna, who would later become the first of Buddha's disciples to attain enlightenment, stated that the child would be a Buddha – an awakened person[33]. For Suddhodana, himself a worldling, the choice between the two paths was easy -- Siddhartha would be a worldly prince.

As the birth date neared, Maya traveled towards her parent's home to give birth, as was the custom at the time, but departed too late to achieve that aim. Before they got there, they stopped at a beautiful park of *sala* trees in the town of Limbini, in the Kapilavastu district of Nepal near the Indian border:

> "Queen Maya was standing beneath the most ancient and luxurious tree, gazing upward into its crown, when a transcendent sensation all over her body told her the birth

---

33   The Buddha and His Teachings, Narada Mahathera (1988), Vipassana Research Publ., Pages 11-2.

was beginning. The tree bent down a branch to her, and she grasped it and smiled.

Suddenly, a host of wonders occurred all at once. From the sky fell white and golden lotus petals. From the now-trembling earth rose the fragrant scents of jasmine and sandalwood. From the air resounded the lilting music of bells, lutes, and ethereal voices. And from the right side of Queen Maya, without causing any pain, emerged the baby.

Gods appeared and bathed the infant in heavenly dew, then set him down on his feet. Fully conscious, he took seven steps forward. In advance of each step, a lotus blossom sprang up to support his foot. Then, pointing one hand up toward the sky and the other down toward the ground, he announced in a loud, clear voice: "Behold, I am all between heaven and Earth! In this lifetime I shall awaken!" The miraculous baby then assumed the normal state of a newborn and was named Siddhartha, which means "every wish fulfilled."[34]

Upon her return to her palace in Kapilavastu, birth celebrations were held for the prince. During these celebrations, a holy man named Asita Kaladevala traveled from his mountain hermitage to see the baby. He looked at the baby for a while, and then began crying, to which Suddhodana and his entourage responded with alarm, asking if this meant a misfortune would befall the child. Asita spoke thusly:

> "This prince will reach the summit of perfect enlightenment, he will turn the wheel of the Dhamma, he who sees what is exceedingly pure (i.e. Nibbâna), this (prince) feels for the welfare of the multitude, and his religion will be widely spread.
>
> My life here will shortly be at an end, in the middle (of his life) there will be death for me; I shall not hear the Dhamma of the incomparable one; therefore I am afflicted, unfortunate, and suffering."[35]

---

34 Essential Buddhism, Jack Maguire (2001), Pocket Books, Page 4.
35 Sutta Nipata, III 11, http://www.ishwar.com/buddhism/holy_sutta_nipata/book03/book03_11.html

The first conflict in Siddhartha's life was set in motion at the time of his birth, but it was not yet so much his conflict as it was his father's. It was the conflict between what Suddhodana desired for his son and that which he feared would come in the way of fulfilling that wish. Here are the Three Poisons at work – for his father was ignorant about the extent of his ability to shape the future, attached to what he wanted, and fearful that what he didn't want would occur. Suddhodana tried to deal with this conflict by ensuring that his son would follow a worldly path. He did this by attempting to keep Siddhartha innocent of the suffering of the world while at the same time keeping his son's circumscribed life filled with pleasures of the senses – "three palaces and forty thousand dancing girls to keep his mind attached to the world"[36] – in addition to educating him mentally and physically for accession to the throne.

By all accounts Siddhartha excelled at all of the activities he engaged in – he was intelligent and athletic, good-looking and charming. He was so impressive at everything he put his hand to that he engendered another type of Poison – jealousy – in the heart of his cousin Devadatta, who would harbor destructive emotions for his cousin throughout his life, erupting into serious conflicts with the Buddha in their later years.

When Siddhartha was 16, he married his same-age cousin Yasodharā, and lived the life of a royal householder in their three palaces for the next 13 years. During these years, Siddhartha's frustration with the royal bird-cage life constructed by his father continued to increase. Luckily for him, Yasodharā was of like mind to Siddhartha, for while she shared the trappings of a royal life with him, she also was concerned with deeper, spiritual issues, and did charity work with poor citizens of the realm from her own sense of care and Compassion for them.

In Siddhartha's 29th year, the gods intervened on Siddhartha's four sojourns outside the palace chauffeured by his charioteer, Channa, thereby revealing to him the Four Signs (for old age, disease, death, and

---

36 The Hero With a Thousand Faces Joseph Campbell (1949), Princeton University Press, Page 56.

renunciation). On the first sojourn, one of the gods fashioned himself into a "decrepit old man, broken-toothed, gray-haired, crooked and bent of body, leaning on a staff, and trembling"[37]. Siddhartha had not before seen one such, and queried the charioteer what it was. When the charioteer informed him of old age, and that Siddhartha would himself someday reach that condition himself, Siddhartha returned to the palace ready to retire from the world. On Siddhartha's second trip outside the palace, the gods fashioned a diseased man for him to see. Once again, the prince returned in agitation to the palace. On the third trip, the gods fashioned a dead man for Siddhartha to see, leading once more to agitated seclusion on his part.

The fourth and final sign was the one that launched Siddhartha on his path to Buddhahood. For on this trip Siddhartha saw a monk Channa told him had "retired from the world". The charioteer (his tongue loosened by the gods) went on to praise the life of renunciation, leading shortly to the prince's decision to renounce his secular life, and to forge instead a life of abstinence and spiritual seeking.

And soon after these Four Signs Suddhodana's dilemma came to a head, for Siddhartha went to him to seek his permission to leave and follow a religious path. As with so many such conversations where a parent has very strong desires for his/her offspring which the child does not wish to oblige, the conversation did not go well. Siddhartha asked to be allowed to take up the life of a mendicant, and his father said no. Suddhodana told him that the kingdom and he required Siddhartha's continued presence. He told his son to follow the time-honored tradition of becoming a spiritual seeker in his later years after the "householder" period was over, which Siddhartha agreed to do only if Suddhodana could insure him against old age, illness, and death, which he obviously could not oblige. In other words, they argued. His father had the palace guards escort Siddhartha back to his palace, after which he tried to further entice and engulf Siddhartha with worldly pleasures.[38]

---

37 The Hero With a Thousand Faces Joseph Campbell (1949), Princeton University Press, Page 56-7.

38 *Buddharacita*, Asvaghosa, (Edited and Translated by Edward B. Cowell) http://www.ancient-buddhist-texts.net/Texts-and-Translations/Buddhacarita/Buddhacarita.pdf, verses 28-39.

Siddhartha's way of dealing with this conflict was the well-recognized strategy of *avoiding it by withdrawing from the locus of the conflict*. For one night soon after his conversation with Suddhodana, while the palace was in the midst of celebrations over the birth that very day of Siddhartha's son Râhula, he made his pivotal choice – to leave his encircled material life, and set off on a renunciate life. Mounting his majestic steed Kanthaka, the fall of whose hooves were silenced by the gods, and accompanied by the ever-faithful Channa, he rode away through the night, stopping only in the morning after passing over the border into the neighboring kingdom. There he shaved his head, changed from princely garb to that of a monk, and walked away from Channa and the horses as they turned back towards the palace.

The Years of Wandering

Thus began Buddha's six years of wandering, wherein he studied with many spiritual teachers, including the two most renowned of his day, to understand the great secret of life and death. These teachers taught him in particular about *samadhi*, the one-pointed concentration of mind developed through eight successively deeper meditative stages called "absorptions". The Buddha would later incorporate a hierarchy of absorptions into his own Mindfulness practice, though based upon different criteria and goals than those of his teachers.

First, he spent an extended period at the forest retreat of Alara Kalama, near the town of Anupiya. Alara taught Siddhartha to reach the absorptive level known as the "realm of limitless space", and then the "realm of limitless consciousness", and finally the "realm of no materiality", yet was unable to help the Prince-turned-monk to allay the anxieties and fears caused by the human condition itself. So, though Alara asked Siddhartha to become his successor, Siddhartha declined, and set off on his way once more.

After a further period of wanderings through the kingdom of Magadha, which had a tradition of spiritual teachers, and studying with many of them, Siddhartha found his way to the forest retreat of Master Udakka Ramaputtra, who was renowned throughout Magadha for his deep spiritual knowledge. Master Udakka taught him to attain the absorption of "neither perception nor non-perception", and like Alara asked Siddhartha to stay and become his spiritual heir. Once again the Prince declined, for the questions of suffering, life and death, and of liberation from suffering, remained unanswered and called him to further explorations.

Yet now he had reached a difficult position, for he had trained and excelled with the two most prominent spiritual teachers of his time, yet remained dissatisfied. For at the end of these years he knew still that he had not fulfilled his mission, and that there were further steps beyond *samadhi* that he needed to explore. He sought the answers in depths of self-denial and asceticism[39], became known as the "Great Ascetic", and gathered about him the "Band of Five" disciples (one of whom was Kondanna, who had prophecied baby Siddhartha to become a Buddha to Suddhodana after the child's birth) who shared in his skeletal self-denial while he spent his time "trying to tie the air into knots".[40]

Here, a river appears in the story – the Nairanjana River, tributary to the Ganges, near the village of Uruvela in Maghada where a sacred fig or pipal tree (later to be called the "Bo" or "Bodhi" Tree, the tree of enlightenment) was located. Siddhartha had come from the mountains to the north to beg for food, but collapsed from weakness and self-imposed starvation by the banks of the river. As the Great Ascetic lay starving to death, he heard three notes played by a boatman's three-stringed instrument. While one note was too shrill, and another too loosely twangy, the middle note played just right. Thus was born in him the concept of the "Middle Way" – a way of not too much self-denial, nor hedonism, but of the proper blend of materialism and self-denial to permit spiritual advancement. Then, he passed out.

As he lay passing in and out of unconsciousness, Sujata, the daughter of the local village leader, passed by carrying milk curds and other food to leave at the Bo tree as an offering to the forest gods.

---

39   When the Iron Eagle Flies Ayya Khema (1991), Wisdom Publications, Page 129.

40   Essential Buddhism, Jack Maguire (2001), Pocket Books, Page 24.

Seeing Siddhartha in his near-death state, she instead lifted his head and held the milk to his lips, letting him drink first one cup and then a second.

Revived, and convinced now of the rightness of the Middle Way, Siddhartha took up residence at the base of the pipal tree near the river, and once again began his meditation, though now without the ascetic edge he had pursued before. He also gathered around him a group of the local children – of all castes[41] – including Sujata, who would bring him food in the afternoon and listen with the other children to his as-yet unperfected teachings.

Several weeks later, after regaining his strength, he reached a state where he knew that his quest had reached the stage of fruition, and went into a deep meditative state wherein his liberation occurred on four watches (or periods) of one night during which he had first to deal with the temptations and challenges of the god Mara, the Evil One. Mara presented three challenges to Siddhartha – those of sensuality (in the form of lascivious dancing women), fear (demons and the raining of stones and fire), and threat (deriding Siddhartha as unworthy of his attainment), yet each was turned back by the immoveable prince, and by the earth itself which informed Mara that Siddhartha was the rightful heir to his place at the base of the tree of enlightenment. Mara withdrew in defeat.

With Mara gone, Siddhartha recalled all of his past lives (550 of which are now contained in a book called the *Jataka*) during the first watch of the night. On the second watch, he realized the law of karma, which "denotes the wholesome and unwholesome volitions and their concomitant mental factors, causing rebirth and shaping the character of beings and thereby their destinies."[42] On the third watch, he realized the links between birth, death and rebirth, and

---

41 In the Buddha's Words, Bhikkhu Bodhi (2005), Wisdom Publications, Page 112. In the Buddha's time, the caste system in India was much simpler than it later became. There were four basic castes – *Brahmins* (priests), *Khattiyas* (nobles, warriors, and administrators), *vessas* (merchants and agriculturalists), and *suddas* (menials and serfs).
42 When the Iron Eagle Flies Ayya Khema (1991), Wisdom Publications, Page 214.

the suffering that characterizes this "Wheel of Life" (the doctrine of "Dependent Origination"). It was during this watch that Siddhartha realized the Four Noble Truths:

- the truth of *dukkha*, "suffering, illness, and the unsatisfactory nature and general insecurity of all conditioned phenomena".[43] Simply put, that life is suffering.

- the truth of *trishna*, the craving or grasping that creates *dukkha* by wanting life to be other than it is. Again simply, that suffering comes from attachment.

- the truth of *nirvana* – that is, that there can be an extinction of *dukkha* by returning to Original Mind.

- the truth of the Noble Eightfold Path, that nirvana is attained through: 1) right understanding; 2) right thought; 3) right speech; 4) right action; 5) right livelihood; 6) right effort; 7) right Mindfulness; and 8) right meditation.

As dawn broke during the fourth watch of the night, Siddhartha achieved his enlightenment, and became the Buddha, or the "Awakened One", and spoke these words about the ignorance (the "jailer") he had now transcended:

> *"O jailer, I see you now. How many lifetimes have you confined me in the prisons of birth and death? But now I see your face clearly, and from now on you can build no more prisons around me."*[44]

In the forty-five years that followed the night of his enlightenment, the Buddha traveled and taught throughout Northern India, forming

---

43   When the Iron Eagle Flies Ayya Khema (1991), Wisdom Publications, Page 211.
44   Old Path White Clouds Thich Nhat Hanh (1991) Parallax Press, Page 121. This is just one version of what the Buddha spoke upon his enlightenment – other versions refer to "the builder" rather than "the jailer", but all versions acknowledge the limiting effect of the "self" and ignorance in human life.

several communities ("sangha") of *bikkhus* (renunciate monks) – supported by his lay followers from the surrounding vicinities – where his teachings were taught, practiced and developed (the collectivity of his teachings is called the *Dharma*, with the non-capitalized word *dharma* also referring to the laws and workings of the universe).[45] It was partly due to the fact that the Buddha was able to refine and expand his teachings and the philosophy and practices they embodied over such a long period of time that Buddhism has endured as such a complete study of human consciousness and the behavior it engenders. We shall look at that schema of human consciousness more fully in the next chapter.

But there were still conflicts that the Buddha had to deal with during his remaining years as well. The conflict with his father Suddhodana remained to be resolved, and the life of a religious leader with thousands of disciples in sangha communities across northeastern India would generate its own conflicts.

Reconciliation with Suddhodana and Siddhartha's Family

Siddhartha left his royal life in a state of conflict with his father. He also left behind his wife Yasodharā and their newborn son, Râhula, when he fled Kappilavastu. To many people, there is an element of seeming selfishness or irresponsibility to his leaving behind a wife and child that is inconsistent with the idea of an immaculate religious leader. However, those are cultural perceptions based upon our Judeo-Christian concept of marriage, and hardly suit the realities of royalty in Northern India at the time who regularly had multiple wives, concubines and separate families. Indeed, when Siddhartha argued with his father and was escorted back to his quarters, Suddhodana sought to placate him by sending a group of women to the palace to entertain him. The earlier historical texts refer to these women as Siddhartha's "wives."[46]

---

45   Essential Buddhism, Jack Maguire (2001), Pocket Books, Page 235.

46   The Buddha-Carita, Asvaghosa (trans. Edward B. Cowell 1895), Page 61, http://www.ancient-buddhist-texts.net/Texts-and-Translations/ Buddhacarita/index.htm

Siddhartha left Kapilavastu partly because the court life was suffocating him, but also because he was convinced that he had a spiritual destiny which he absolutely had to follow. Following that destiny was how he resolved his internal conflict. The question then was how could he resolve the conflict with his father, and mend the leaving of Yasodharā (his "true" wife) and his son? He was able to do this with four primary ingredients – a) time, b) absolute integrity of purpose, c) Mindfulness, and d) Compassion.

The time aspect of the resolution is the approximate eight years between his flight from Kapilavastu and fully reuniting (albeit in an entirely different format) with his wife and son and reconciling with Suddhodana. The use of time by Buddha in reconciling conflicts we shall see again in dealing with sangha-related conflicts later in his career. Usually this involved not actively dealing with a conflict until changes in the situation created the conditions for reconciliation. Using the language of our Eightfold Path To Resolve Conflict, it meant allowing the Refractory Period to play itself out.

The Buddha's awakening occurred six years after he rode into the night on Kanthaka. When he heard of his son's enlightenment, Suddhodana began to send delegations to entreat him to return home, the first nine of which the Buddha effectively refused by ordaining the messengers as bikkhus (monks). The tenth delegation, which was Kaludayi, a childhood friend, and the ever-faithful charioteer Channa, was responded to positively. So, about a year after his enlightenment, when he already had more than twelve hundred bikkhus living and studying with him at a monastery in Venuvana (Bamboo Forest) north of the capital Rajagaha in the northern state of Maghada, he accepted the invitation from his father to return to Kapilavastu. He traveled in springtime with three hundred of his bikkhus to visit his family, whom he had not seen for seven years.

Suddhodana invited his son and the traveling sangha to the palace for the meal, after which the Buddha expounded upon his teachings to the gathered audience. Over the following days, several members of the royal family joined the sangha -- his cousins Ananda and

Anuruddha, his half-brother Nanda, and his cousin Devadatta who would later become his enemy and try to kill the Buddha.

The Buddha also met with Yasodharā and was introduced to his son, Râhula (whose name means "fetter"), who was ordained and become the first novice monk of Buddhism at the age of seven. Rahula would spend the rest of his life (he died at the age of 51, at around the same time as his mother) as a part of the sangha and become one of the Buddha's ten most senior disciples.

But this ordination did not sit well with Suddhodana who, while impressed and inspired and ultimately transformed during the visit by his son, spoke thusly to the Buddha about the ordination of his grandson, and expressed his feelings about the significant defection of the male part of his family to the Buddha's sangha:

> "Lord, when the Blessed One gave up the world, it was a great pain to me; so it was when Nanda did the same; my pain was excessive when Râhula too did so. The love for a son, Lord, cuts into the skin; having cut into the skin, it cuts into the hide; having cut into the hide, it cuts into the flesh, … the ligaments,…the bones; having cut into the bones, it reaches the marrow and dwells in the marrow. Pray, Lord, let their reverences not confer the pabbaggâ ordination on a son without his father's and mother's permission."[47]

The Buddha thereon did pass such a rule for future ordinations of young bikkhus, but he did not release Râhula from his vows.

The Buddha returned to Kapilavastu the next year to see Suddhodana again, after a messenger arrived to tell him his father was on his death-bed. In fact, the Buddha spent the King's last moments of life with him, ensuring that Suddhodana died enlightened:

---

47   Mahavagga, First Khandaka 54(5), http://www.sacred-texts.com/bud/sbe13/sbe1312.htm

"The king lay mournfully on his couch. He was gasping for breath. Death was very near. Yet he smiled when he saw his son. And the Master spoke these words:

"Long is the road you have traveled, O king, and always did you strive to do good. You knew nothing of evil desires; your heart was innocent of hatred, and anger never blinded your mind. Happy is he who is given to doing good! Happy is he who looks into a limpid pool and sees his unsullied countenance, but far happier is he who examines his mind and knows the purity thereof! Your mind is pure, O king, and your death as calm as the close of a lovely day."

"Blessed One," said the king, "I understand now the inconstancy of the worlds. I am free of all desire; I am free of the chains of life."

Once again, he paid homage to the Buddha. Then he turned to the servants, assembled in the hall.

"Friends," said he, "I must have wronged you many times, yet never once did you show me that you bore malice. You were kind and good. But before I die, I must have your forgiveness. The wrongs I did you were unintentional; forgive me, Friends."

The servants were weeping. They murmured: "No, you have never wronged us, lord!" Suddhodana continued:

"And you, Mahaprajapati (*the woman who became queen and raised the Buddha after Maya died*), you who were my pious consort, you whom I see in tears, calm your grief. My death is a happy death. Think of the glory of this child you brought up; gaze at him in all his splendor, and rejoice."

He died. The sun was setting.

The Master said:

"Behold my father's body. He is no longer what he was. No one has ever conquered death. He who is born must die. Show your zeal for good works; walk in the path that leads to wisdom. Make a lamp of wisdom, and darkness will

55

vanish of its own accord. Do not follow evil laws; do not plant poisonous roots; do not add to the evil in the world. Like the charioteer who, having left the highroad for a rough path, weeps at the sight of a broken axle, even so does the fool, who has strayed from the law, weep when he falls into the jaws of death. The wise man is the torch that gives light to the ignorant; he guides mankind, for he has eyes, and the others are sightless."

The body was carried to a great funeral pile. The Master set fire to it, and while his father's body was being consumed by the flames, while the people of Kapilavastu wept and lamented, he repeated these sacred truths:

"Suffering is birth, suffering is old age, suffering is sickness, suffering is death. O thirst to be led from birth to birth! Thirst for power, thirst for pleasure, thirst for being, thirsts that are the source of all suffering! O evil thirsts, the saint knows you not, the saint who extinguishes his desires, the saint who knows the noble Eightfold path."[48]

So was the conflict between Suddhodana and the Buddha finally resolved, eight years after Siddhartha renounced his royal life, leaving only Yasodharā without resolution as to a continuing relationship with the Buddha. That matter was resolved shortly thereafter, however, when Yasodharā became a *bikkhuni* (female monk), being ordained as part of a large group of women from Kappilavastu who had followed Mahaprajapati to demand the rights of women to join the sangha. Yasodharā spent the rest of her life in the sangha until her death at the age of 78, two years before the Buddha, having gained a reputation in the sangha as the bikkhuni with the most supernatural abilities.

So the ancient Pali texts show that, though Suddhodana and Yasodharā suffered a great deal emotionally from Siddhartha's decision to renounce his royal life, both ultimately reconciled with that decision and followed in the Way he had forged. Râhula, whose

---

48   The Life of the Buddha, A. Ferdinand Herold [1922], http://www.sacred-texts.com/bud/lob/lob42.htm

sufferings if any are not recorded in the texts, also followed that path and was thereby reconciled with his father's decision as well. All three died before the Buddha as *arhants*, the Theravadan equivalent of a bodhisattva:

> "a spiritual practitioner who had—to use an expression common in the tipitaka—"laid down the burden"—and realised the goal of nirvana, the culmination of the spiritual life (*brahmacarya*). Such a person, having removed all causes for future becoming, is not reborn after biological death into any samsaric realm."[49]

What lessons does this intra-family conflict of the Buddha hold for us, whether in our own lives or in situations we mediate? One might think that there are no lessons at all for us in this tale, since it occurred long ago in the life of the Buddha, a towering historical figure. Such a thought would be faulty, though, for there are many valuable lessons for us in how these situations devolved.

The situation between Siddhartha and his father would seem to have been irreconcilable, which makes it much like many of the conflicts each of us must deal with. Suddhodana wanted Siddhartha to be male heir to a worldly throne, while the Buddha was magnetized to a spiritual life. Just as a spouse may want his or her mate to stay in a marriage when the mate has chosen to leave, or a business woman may want to continue working with her partner when the partner has taken a new job and is leaving the business.

The point is – things happen, and certain goals that we have for the others in our lives are not always going to work out. Conflict in human life is often the necessary concomitant to growth and development of the people and institutions involved. The resolution and reconciliation of conflict isn't necessarily about coming up with a simple, happy answer that forms a perfect, superficial match to the instant situation. The Buddha didn't have to say "Okay, Dad, I'll stay and be King, and be the Buddha on the weekends only", anymore

---

49   Wikipedia, http://en.wikipedia.org/wiki/Arhant

than a departing spouse would say "Okay, honey, I'll just stay here to make it okay for you, and live a separate, hidden life on the side so I don't go nuts living this way."

Reconciliation in these cases actually means having each person learn to accept the things that are ineluctable, grow as they must and allow the other person to do so as well, be aware of the feelings and ideas that arise as a result, and have the Loving Kindness and Compassion for him- or herself and the other person(s) involved to allow each to achieve Equanimity and peace with the result.

And that's just what the Buddha did in his relationship with Suddhodana, as well as with his wife and son. The Buddha's gift to his family –his teaching, for the development of which they had each sacrificed greatly – was exactly what he gave back to his family (and his followers) to help each of them accept what they must and dispel any inner conflicts that had arisen for them as a result. This gift – his awakening and development of the Way to teach his followers – was the fruit of the transformation that he needed to make, but also provided his family with the requisite tools needed to reconcile the conflicts that arose for them as a result of his need for transformation.

Dealing with Conflicts within the Sangha

The Buddha's following grew quickly after his enlightenment, for a variety of reasons in addition to his spiritual attainments. One significant reason was that his teaching ended up being sponsored by wealthy and/or royal backers in several of the states of northern India, because the sponsors were so deeply impressed by the Buddha and his teachings (and perhaps because they knew his family and were from the same upper class as he).

First, King Seniya Bimbisara of Maghada – who had tried to get the Buddha to come join him as a co-ruler of that state before the Buddha's awakening – invited the Buddha and all 1250 of his bikkhus to come to his palace in Rajagaha for a welcoming celebration soon after the Buddha's awakening, at the end of which he donated to the Buddha a beautiful 100-acre bamboo forest called Venuvana as a grounds for the sangha's first monastery. There would shortly be eighteen Buddhist centers in Magadha state. Another one of them was Ambavana, a mango grove donated to the Buddha by Ambapali, Bimbisara's chief consort, which would later become the first monastery for bikkhunis.

Soon afterwards, a wealthy merchant named Sudatta from the kingdom of Kosala convinced the Buddha to come to the capital of that kingdom, Savatthi, and preach the Dharma. While they were in Savatthi, Sudatta began to search in earnest for a local monastery for the sangha, and found a beautiful park that had been given by the king of Kosala, Pasenadi, to his son Prince Jeta. Sudatta asked Jeta if he could buy the park for the Buddha, and Prince Jeta jokingly said he would only sell it to Sudatta if the latter would pay Jeta however much gold it took to cover the property.

Sudatta, to Jeta's amazement, agreed to these terms, which according to local custom meant Jeta had to sell it to him even if he had been joking. Sudatta's wagons of gold dutifully showed up at the property the next morning, and covered more than half of the property before Jeta agreed to forego the rest of the gold. This monastery became known as Jetavana (after Jeta, of course), and would gradually become the location of the rainy season retreat for the Buddha and his top bikkhus every year.

There were many other such locations sprouting up simultaneously. In short, very quickly after his awakening, the community of bikkhus, and of lay persons who took the Three Refuges (the Buddha, the Dharma, and the Sangha) mushroomed into a large conglomerate of monasteries spreading across northern India, and included thousands and thousands of persons.

And, as with any community, this meant a geometric expansion of opportunities for interpersonal conflict to arise. The Buddha's primary concern and work was, of course, to teach the Way to as many people as possible. That does not mean that he did not have to deal with conflicts as they arose, or that the sangha community being "spiritual" would in any way lessen the ferocity of such conflicts.

The Dirty Basin Incident

The Dirty Basin Incident is a great example of three distinct aspects of conflict resolution. First, it shows how incredibly petty the triggering events for what turn into full-blown conflicts often are (or at least appear to be). Second, it shows how difficult conflicts can be to resolve during the "Refractory Period" when the Three Poisons are running amuck in the participants to the conflict. Third, it again demonstrates how the judicious use of time or patience is often of great benefit in resolving a conflict.

During the ninth rainy season after his awakening, the Buddha was staying near the monastery at Ghosita, which was named for a lay disciple who funded the opening of three monasteries near Kosambi in the state of Vatsa in northwestern India. By this time the leaders of each sangha community had specialized into certain functions because of the complexity of community life. Two of these specialized functions were *sutra masters*, who were charged with memorizing the teachings of the Buddha, and *precept masters*, who were in charge of enforcing the code of conduct to be followed by the novices and bikkhus living at the site. A dispute arose between a sutra master and a precept master in the following fashion:

> "Their argument stemmed from a small event, but ended up creating a sharp division in the sangha. A sutra master forgot to clean out the wash basin he had used and was charged with a violation of a lesser precept by a precept master. The sutra master was a proud person and contended that since he had not intentionally left the basin dirty, he was not to blame. Students of each bikkhu took the side of their own teacher, and the argument escalated. One side accused the other of slander, while the other side accused their opponents of acting foolishly. Finally, the precept master publicly announced the sutra master's transgression and forbade him from attending

the biweekly precepts recitation ceremony until he formally confessed before the sangha."[50]

The situation got so serious that the entire Ghosita sangha was polarized by it, save for those monks who refused to take sides, and they were not able to make any headway because of the anger and attachments of the two camps of polarized monks. One of the non-partisan bikkhus finally went to see the Buddha, and told him that the sangha had become dysfunctional and needed his intercession.

Now the Buddha was not by choice a mediator -- he was the teacher who taught the Way. On the other hand, he *was* the Buddha, and the spiritual leader to all of the partisan bikkhus involved in the dispute. One might think, then, that his intervention would be sufficient to quell the destructive emotions involved in the situation and return the sangha to a state of harmony.

Unfortunately, one would have to think again. The Buddha went to see the precept master and the sutra master, and asked them to put aside their differences. They would not. So he then summoned the entire sangha to the monastery's meeting hall, and said three times: "Bikkhus, give up quarrelling and using rough words, and have no disputes." Each time, one or other of the bikkhus would reply in the same fashion:

> "Venerable sir, the lord of the Teaching, be unconcerned, keep away! May the Blessed One abide in pleasantness here and now! It's we that will be known in this quarrel, dispute and using rough words"[51]

In other words, they told the Buddha to mind his own business. So the Buddha did what any mediator does when he realizes that the parties are definitely not yet ready to let go of their poisoned attachments to their positions – he moved on to other things. He

---

50   Old Path White Clouds Thich Nhat Hanh (1991) Parallax Press, Page 301.

51   Majjhima Nikaya III (128), http://zencomp.com/greatwisdom/ebud/majjhima/128-upakkilesa-e.htm

picked up his begging bowl and did his daily begging for food in Kosambi, and then recited the following verses:

> "The foolish do not consider the general opinion,
> The fact, there will be nothing, when the Community is split.
> Forgetful of the main aim and carried beyond
> They do not listen to the words of the wise.
> I'm scolded, beaten, defeated and carried away,
> The hatred of those that bear such grudges are never appeased.
> I'm scolded, beaten, defeated and carried away,
> The hatred of those that do not bear such grudges are appeased.
> In this world hatred never ceases with hatred
> With non hatred it ceases, this is the ancient lore.
> Some do not know that we have to go from this world.
> They that know it, appease their misapprehensions
> Those that cut limbs, destroy life, carry away horses, cattle and wealth
> And even ruin the country, they too turn round. Why shouldn't it happen to you?
> If you gain a clever friend, a wise co-associate,
> Overcoming all troubles, live with him mindfully.
> If you do not gain a clever, wise co-associate,
> Like the king that leaves behind his rulership and country
> Go alone like an elephant to the Maatanga remote.
> Living alone is superb, there should be no association with fools
> Living alone, unconcerned no evil's done.
> Like the elephant living in the Maatanga remote."[52]

And on that note, the Buddha picked up his begging bowl and left Kasambi for eighteen months, to allow the bikkhus at Ghosita the opportunity to resolve their own mess, as they had requested. In his words he went off to first be alone, and then visited a groups of monks that were living in peace with each other. After that, he spent the tenth rainy season since his awakening alone under a sal tree in Rakkhita Forest, near Parileyyaka, where he was watched over

---

52   Majjhima Nikaya III (128), http://zencomp.com/greatwisdom/ebud/majjhima/128-upakkilesa-e.htm

by his friend, the elephant Parileyya, "like the elephant in Maatanga remote.".

He then made his way back to Jetavana, where he had not been seen for the past fourteen months. He was informed there by his cousin Ananda that the Ghosita monks had fallen on hard times since they themselves had no teacher or access to new teaching by the Buddha, and found themselves rejected and without the support of the lay people from the community who were upset that they could no longer see or hear the Buddha. This was a very great problem for the Ghosita monastery during the rainy season, because the weather prevented the monks from doing their daily begging in the local communities and they therefore depended very heavily on the support of the lay community. [53] And it again shows the wisdom of the Buddha avoiding a more active intervention in the conflict – he stayed true to his purpose as a teacher, he allowed the "Refractory Period" to find its own natural ending (although it took longer than might have been desired), he allowed the mad monks to learn firsthand the negative results of their poisonous feelings, and he allowed them to on their own derive a way to transform those poisons into Compassion for each other.

Finally, monks from both Ghosita factions came to Jetavana to settle their dispute with the help of the Buddha. During that process, the sutra master acknowledged having committed an infringement which then made it technically possible for the precept master to reinstate him as a member of the community. Each party admitted to either pride, anger, or whatever other emotions or Poisons had hindered them from reconciling.

They also spent four days with the Buddha's senior disciples fashioning a dispute resolution process to be used by sangha members when disputes arose, which is still codified in the final items of the precepts for bikkhus in both southern and northern Buddhist traditions. These "Seven Practices of Reconciliation" are:

---

53 Life of the Buddha : Middle Years Stories & Teachings, http://www.
 wisdom-books.com/FocusDetail.asp?FocusRef=18

1. ***The Practice of Face To Face Sitting.*** With both sides of the conflict present, the entire community hears the dispute. This practice limits private conversations about the conflict, where people are more likely to choose sides and are thereby more likely to create further discord and tension.

2. ***The Practice of Remembrance.*** During this meeting of the whole community, both parties in the conflict try to remember everything from the beginning that led up to the dispute and then sustained the dispute. Presenters should speak with as much accuracy and clarity as possible and should include evidence and witnesses if they are available. In this way the community attempts to gather adequate information about the dispute.

3. ***The Practice of Non-Stubbornness.*** The community expects the disputants to reach reconciliation, resolving the conflict. The community encourages them to renounce stubbornness.

4. ***The Practice of Voluntary Confession.*** The community encourages each party voluntarily to admit her or his errors in speech or action. Each person should take as much time as necessary to speak about each error, no matter how minor it should seem. Did the harmful speech or action occur because of clear intention, or did it happen from ignorance or an unsettled heart? Admitting one's own errors encourages the other party to do the same and helps to bring the dispute toward reconciliation.

5. ***The Practice of Decision by Consensus.*** After hearing both sides and being assured of the wholehearted efforts by both sides to reach a settlement, the community reaches by consensus a verdict about the dispute.

6. ***The Practice of Accepting the Verdict.*** After the community reaches a verdict, it is read aloud three times. If no one in the community voices disagreement with it, the community considers the verdict final. Neither party in the dispute has the right to challenge the verdict once it has been reached by consensus. The have agreed beforehand to place their trust in the community's decision, and they will abide by it.

7. ***The Practice of Covering Mud with Straw.*** During the gathering the community appoints a senior member to represent each side in the conflict, someone to whom the community will listen with respect. These senior people listen carefully and say little, but when they do speak their words carry special weight. Their role is to soothe, to heal wounds, to call forth reconciliation and forgiveness, and through their words and personal example to help the disputants to release bitterness and petty concerns. They also help the community to reach a verdict acceptable to both sides. These elders serve like straw covering mud, allowing everyone to pass over the mud without dirtying their clothes. [54]

The Seven Practices of Reconciliation are thus a sort of hybrid between mediation and arbitration, in that the disputants use certain techniques to try to get "unstuck" from their attachments and detoxify their Poisons, while the community of non-disputants uses a consensus vote to reach a decision. So, unlike mediation, it does not depend solely upon the voluntary arrival at a resolution by the actual parties to the conflict. Yet unlike arbitration, there is a definite slant towards having the parties admit their own roles in the development of the conflict, so they can let go of their attachments and destructive emotions and thereby help restore harmony in the community at large. And it is a good example of "inter-Mindfulness", which we shall discuss later in this book, in that the parties concerned get to say out loud in a somewhat "neutral" setting their own perception of events and to then hear the perceptions of the other side, which tends to show the transience and flaws of each perspective, and thus bring the parties closer to a shared understanding of what actually occurred.

The lessons for us as individuals and/or as mediators in the Dirty Bowl Incident are legion, but different than those in the Buddha's

---

54   The seven are reprinted from http://www.cs.unm.edu/~richards/sangha/buddha_on_community.html, which draws heavily and often verbatim from Old Path White Clouds Thich Nhat Hanh (1991) Parallax Press, Page 311-13,

family conflict. That situation was a "transformation" conflict in which one party by necessity transforms as he or she must, and those around him or her try to resist or interfere with the transformation because of their attachment to their own views. The Dirty Bowl is more of a classical Three Poison "vanilla" conflict, with two sides becoming venomous at about the same time, and resisting outside attempts to resolve the conflict during the Refractory Period.

The Buddha probably assumed the monks would listen to him when he first told them to stop quarreling. After all, each of the monks had taken formal "refuge" in the Three Jewels (the Buddha, the Dharma, and the Sangha) to join the monastery, thereby agreeing to follow the teachings of the Buddha. So he was within his rights as "monarch" of the monastery to tell them to stop. Instead, they told him to stay out of the matter. The first lesson herein for mediators (which most know well already) is that until the parties have some openness to discussing resolution, it is extremely difficult to make them do so.

Even the Buddha had little power at that moment when the Poisons were coursing full strength through the situation – as he said, he was "scolded, beaten, defeated and carried away". He chose therefore to go into solitude to avoid being in "association with fools," but also acknowledged in leaving the innate possibility for those fools to see a better way: "those that cut limbs, destroy life, carry away horses, cattle and wealth, and even ruin the country, they too turn round. Why shouldn't it happen to you?"

By leaving, the Buddha allowed the Refractory Period of the warring monks to play itself out, and also allowed the "karmic seeds" of their actions to bear fruit. And here's the second lesson mediators can cull from the Dirty Basin Incident – the passage of time will itself often create the conditions for resolution, either fortuitously or in reaction to the forces unleashed by the Poisoned events. Which is what happened to the Ghosita factions – the conflict started with the Buddha's request that the monks cease fighting falling on deaf ears, but eighteen months later those same ears approached the Buddha for help to mediate their dispute.

And the concept of time leads us to the third Dirty Basin lesson, for only time ultimately tells us the "result" of a conflict, which becomes clear only after the energetic and karmic lines emanating from the dispute have woven their real mosaic. What started as an egotistical spat between the precept master and the sutra master ultimately morphed into the "Seven Practices of Reconciliation", which has been helping countless monks the world over resolve their conflicts for more than 2,500 years. It is by working with conflict as it unfolds through time that its real value is revealed.

Finally, "Seven Practices of Reconciliation", though a hybrid process, is a retrospective affirmation of many of the techniques and practices used by mediators and conflict resolution professionals at present. The fact that these same tools – facing each other, listening to each others' remembrance of how a conflict developed, admitting our errors, and letting go of stubbornness – were developed long ago by a group of saffron-robed monks trying to deal with their own problems, and then again independently by modern-day mediators, is a powerful endorsement of their efficacy and appropriateness for their intended purpose.

The Buddha as Statesman – the Incident at River Rohini

In the fifteenth year after his awakening, the Buddha had the opportunity to mediate a land-use dispute between the kingdoms of Sakya, which was the kingdom of his father's family, and Koliya, from whence came his mother and many of his cousins, including Ananda and Devadatta. The dispute concerned water rights of the two kingdoms.

The Rohini River lay between Kapilavastu and Koliya, and was the sole source of irrigation water for the farmers in the two kingdoms whose produce supported the two capital cities. In that year, there was a drought and the water level had dropped quite low, so that there was not adequate water for everyone's needs. As a result, each of the two kingdoms planned to build a dam on the river in such a location that all water would be diverted to that kingdom. When each side found out about the other's plans, they began shouting across the river at each other, then throwing rocks, and then accusing each other of things that had nothing to do with the current situation. Finally, armies from the two sides lined the river, preparing for battle.

The Buddha – who had family members on both sides of the river – knew he must intercede in order to avoid bloodshed. In the classical (more mythical) version of the story, the Buddha appeared to the parties in the sky, in perhaps the earliest recorded case of air shuttle diplomacy:

> "As the Teacher surveyed the world at dawn and beheld his kinsmen, he thought to himself, "If I refrain from going to them, these men will destroy each other. It is clearly my duty to go to them." Accordingly, he flew through the air quite alone to the spot where his kinsmen were gathered together, and seated himself cross-legged in the air over the middle of the River Rohini."[55]

The more modern versions of the story simply have the Buddha coming to discuss the matter with the two sides, rather than floating in the air above the river. In all versions, he first has trouble finding out what the dispute actually concerns. Everyone he asks about it says they don't know what the conflict is actually about (even though they're standing there in full battle garb ready to kill each other) and passes the buck, until the Buddha finally finds out from the slave-laborers that the issue is about *water*. So the Buddha discusses the matter with each King:

> 'Then the Teacher asked the king, "How much is water worth, great king?" — "Very little, reverend sir." — "How much are Khattiyas (warrior/nobles) worth, great king?" — "Khattiyas are beyond price, reverend sir." — "It is not fitting that because of a little water you should destroy Khattiyas who are beyond price." They were silent. Then the Teacher addressed them

---

55   Buddhist Stories from the Dhammapada Commentary, The Wheel Publication No. 73 (Kandy: Buddhist Publication Society), http://nt.med. ncku.edu.tw/biochem/lsn/AccessToInsight/html/lib/authors/burlingame/ wheel324.html

and said, "Great kings, why do you act in this manner? Were I not here present today, you would set flowing a river of blood. You have done what should not be done. You live in strife, I live free from strife. You live afflicted with the sickness of the evil passions, I live free from disease. You live in eager pursuit of the five kinds of sensual pleasure, but I live free from eager pursuit." So saying, he pronounced the following stanzas:

We live indeed so happily
Unhating amidst the haters;
Among those who hate
We dwell free from hate.

We live indeed so happily
Unailing amidst the ailers;
Among those who are ailing
We dwell free from illness.

We live indeed so happily
Ungreedy amidst the greedy;
Among those who are greedy
We dwell free from greed."[56]

Because of the intervention, the two sides did not go to battle, and were able to reach an accord about water usage. And, importantly for our purposes here, the incident shows that different measures are called for by the risk of irreparable harm present in the situation. For unlike the Dirty Basin Incident (and, indeed, unlike his conflict with Suddhodana), where the Buddha chose to let the disputants' Refractory Period play itself out on its own timetable, at the River Rohini he made all possible haste to intervene to avert open conflict.

A simple way to state this rule is: if someone will die because of a conflict, or some other deep and irreparable harm will occur, then

---

56 *Buddhist Stories from the Dhammapada Commentary*, The Wheel Publication No. 73 (Kandy: Buddhist Publication Society), http://nt.med. ncku.edu.tw/biochem/lsn/AccessToInsight/html/lib/authors/burlingame/ wheel324.html

you intercede immediately, without waiting for the parties themselves to cool off. Thus, at River Rohini we have the Buddha saying to himself: "If I refrain from going to them, these men will destroy each other. It is clearly my duty to go to them."

It is the same realization that the young Thich Nhat Hanh and his fellow Buddhist monks realized years ago in Viet Nam. Instead of hiding in their monasteries, they would go out as teams to rebuild the villages that had been bombed, listening with an open heart to the opinions and concerns of both sides as they encountered them, yet never taking sides. Because of their refusal to take sides, many of the Buddhists were killed in the mistaken belief that they were from "the other side". But this risk was necessary to make a stand for reconciliation and peace:

> "The situation in the world is still like this. People completely identify with one side, one ideology. To understand the suffering and fear of an enemy nation, we have to become one with him or her. To do so is dangerous – we will be suspected by both sides. But if we don't do it, if we align ourselves with one side or another, we will lose our chance to work for peace. Reconciliation is to understand both sides, go to one side and describe the suffering being endured by the other side, and then go to the other side and describe the suffering being endured by the first side. Doing only that will be a great help for peace."[57]

While the realization of the necessity to intervene in an aggressive-stage conflict was the same for both the Buddha and Thich Nhat Hanh, the Buddha's interevention was somewhat different, and is the first example of *substitution* or *antidote* that we shall discuss in this book. For rather than relate to each of the kings in the Rohini conflict the suffering being or to be endured by the other side, the Buddha had

----

57 Being Peace, Thich Nhat Hanh (1987) Parallax Press, Page 70. I have substituted the word "enemy nation" for "Soviet Union", as was done in the version of the paragraph reprinted in Ordinary Magic, ed. John Welwood (1992), Shambhala Press, Page 246.

each king consider the suffering that he and *his* people were going to suffer as a result of the conflict. In doing so, he did two things at once: a) he substituted the lives of each side's own Khattiya warriors for the sought-after water in the minds of the two sides; and b) he shifted each of the parties towards Loving Kindness and Compassion for those lives, which introduced an antidote to neutralize the anger and hatred it was feeling for the other side. These two techniques are valuable tools for anyone working towards the resolution of conflict.

The Buddha Deals with Devadatta's Jealousy and Treachery

Jealousy is not one of the stated Three Poisons, though it is listed as No. 5 on both the expanded list of five Poisons and on the list of Twenty Derivative Mental Afflictions. It's a simple but especially venomous mixture of two of the original Three Poisons, since it's a greed for what someone else has, and a hatred of them for having it instead of you. For anyone who has felt it, it's a pretty yucky way to feel. And it's really bad when you have to live with it for a long time, as did Devadatta, whose entire life was lived in the shadow of the Buddha's. He is the dark side or Darth Vader of the spiritual path of the Way, someone very talented who followed it part of the way, and then was led down the dark side by his own pride and ambition.

Devadatta was the son of King Suppabuddha and his wife Pamita, who was Siddhartha's aunt. Since Devadatta's sister was Yasodharā, he was both a cousin and brother-in-law of the Buddha. He was also the brother of Ananda, who would become the Buddha's chief assistant for the last 30 years of his life (due in part to Ananda's remarkable aurographic memory for the Buddha's spoken teachings). Siddhartha, Ananda and Devadatta, along with other royal relatives within the palace household (Bhagu, Kimbila, Bhaddiya, and Anuruddha) were all educated and trained in various arts together.

And, unfortunately, Siddhartha was a very tough person to try to measure up to, if that was what one had in mind. He was heir to the throne, his birth was hailed as a remarkable event, he was remarkably attractive physically, and he seemed to excel at everything he tried. So even though Devadatta was himself a formidable character, and in fact stronger than the yet-quicker Siddhartha, if one wanted to be jealous,

Siddhartha was a good person to focus that energy on. And that's what Devadatta did, starting at a young age. There are two animal-related incidents of conflict between the two during their youth. The first involved a swan, the second an elephant.

When Siddhartha and Devadatta were still boys, Devadatta shot down a swan while the two were out walking in the country. As the swan fluttered wounded to the ground, both boys ran to find where it landed. When Siddhartha arrived first, he held the bird gently and pulled out the arrow from its wing. Then he applied leaves on the wound to prevent further bleeding, and stroked the wounded bird. Devadatta was very angry and said the swan belonged to him, since it was his arrow that had brought it down. But Siddhartha insisted that since the bird had not been killed, it belongs to whoever found it first, and would not let Devadatta kill it. The boys then went back to the court counselors who discussed the merits of the two boys' positions – in the end a court wise man sided with Siddhartha and let the bird go free.[58] In other words, the conflict was resolved in the time-honored manner of having it decided by a (hopefully) neutral trier-of-fact or judge.

Later, when they were young men, there was a martial arts contest in which they both competed. Devadatta was reputed to be as strong as five elephants, but Siddhartha was quicker and used better techniques, and succeeded in winning the contest. When the white elephant that was the prize to the victor was brought around, some of the texts say Devadatta, out of envy, killed it, and that the carcass blocked the city gates until Siddhattha had it removed.[59] Others say that Devadatta dropped the elephant to its knees by injuring a soft spot on it trunk, after which he was scolded by Siddhartha who nursed the wounded elephant back to its feet and rode it on a victory lap around Kapilavastu.[60]

When the Buddha visited Kapilavastu after his enlightenment and preached the Dharma at the palace, Devadatta was converted together

58 Pali Canon Studies, Ryuei Michael McCormick (2006), http://nichirenscoffeehouse.net/Ryuei/Devadatta
59 http://www.palikanon.com/english/pali_names/d/devadatta.htm
60 Old Path White Clouds Thich Nhat Hanh (1991) Parallax Press, Page 55.

with his friends Ananda, Bhagu, Kimbila, Bhaddiya, Anuruddha, and their barber, Upāli. He later sought out the Buddha at Anupiyā and entered the Order as a bikkhu, after which he showed great spiritual abilities through his meditation:

> "Soon after becoming a monk, Devadatta attained the five types of supernatural powers that can be developed through meditation. These five were: supernatural mastery of the body, the divine ear (clairaudience), mind reading, past life recall, and the divine eye (clairvoyance). For a long time, Devadatta was a respected member of the Sangha. Unfortunately, his jealousy and envy prevented him from attaining any genuine insight or liberation, and his supernatural powers only increased his arrogance."[61]

The fact that he had been such a talented and productive member of the sangha and a good monk would be referred to as a mitigating factor by the Buddha after Devadatta had committed many very serious offences against him later. However, the fact that Devadatta and other monks developed supernatural powers was of little interest to the Buddha, since he said that such were irrelevant to purpose of the Dharma which is the eradication of suffering. But the arrogance and pride attached to these powers, as well as his lifelong competition with Siddhartha, finally led Devadatta to try to gain more power and renown, starting in the 37th year of the Buddha's teaching career:

> "The occasion was this. Once when Devadatta was alone in retreat this thought arose in his mind: "Who is there whose confidence I can win over and thereby acquire much gain, honor and renown?" Then he thought: "There is Prince Ajatashatru[62]. He is young with a glorious future. Suppose I win over his confidence? Much gain, honor, and renown will accrue to me if I do so."

61   Pali Canon Studies, Ryuei Michael McCormick (2006), http://nichirenscoffeehouse.net/Ryuei/Devadatta
62   King Bimbisara's son.

So, Devadatta packed his bed away, and he took his bowl and outer robe and set out for Rajagaha, where he at length arrived. There he discarded his own form and assumed the form of a youth with a girdle of snakes, and in that guise he appeared on Prince Ajatashatru's lap. Then Prince Ajatashatru was fearful, anxious, suspicious and worried. Devadatta asked: "Are you afraid of me, prince?"

"Yes, I am afraid. Who are you?"

"I am Devadatta."

"If you are Devadatta, Lord, then please show yourself in your own form."

"Devadatta discarded the form of the youth and stood before Prince Ajatashatru, wearing his patched outer cloak, bowl and robes. Then Prince Ajatashatru felt prodigious confidence in Devadatta owing to his supernormal powers. After that he waited on him evening and morning with five hundred carriages and five hundred offerings of milk-rice as a gift of food. Devadatta became overwhelmed with gain, honor, and renown. Ambition obsessed his mind, and the wish arose in him: "I will rule the Sangha of monks." Simultaneously with the thought his supernormal powers vanished."[63]

The Buddha's monks were very concerned about Devadatta's control over Ajatashatru, particularly since Ajatashatru built a monastery for Devadatta at Mount Gayashirsha, but the Buddha told them not to worry about it, since Devadatta's desire for gain, honor and renown would actually diminish his spiritual wholesomeness as well as his power, and ultimately of itself cause his own self-destruction and undoing. But it seems clear that by this point the Buddha must have known there was an impending show-down in the power struggle within the sangha, and that his behavior towards Devadatta may have been motivated at least in part by that knowledge.

---

63   Pali Canon Studies, Ryuei Michael McCormick (2006), http://nichirenscoffeehouse.net/Ryuei/Devadatta, adapted from Life of the Buddha, Edward J. Thomas (2000), Dover Publications, Page 257.

Devadatta shortly attempted to gain power over the sangha. He went to a dharma talk by the Buddha where, before three thousand disciples, including kings and other dignitaries at the Bamboo Forest, he stood up before the congregation, and told the Buddha he should hand over control of the sangha to him. There are different translations of how the conversation went, but a sample version is Horner's translation, in which Devadatta said:

> "Lord, the Lord is now old, worn, stricken in years…It is I who will the lead the Order of monks"[64]

The Buddha's reply was that Devadatta should desist from such questioning, and not aspire to govern the sangha. Devadatta asked again, and received the same answer. When he asked yet a third time, he got the following reply from the Buddha:

> "I…would not hand over the Order of monks even to Sāriputta and Moggallana[65]. How then could I to you, a wretched one to be vomited like spittle?"

This was a very powerful public denunciation of Devadatta. He was horrified to have been rebuked in public in front of monks and dignitaries (not seeing, of course, that his request to the Buddha in public was itself inappropriate). He arose and left the assembly. The Buddha then stated to the assembled meeting – including King Bimbisara, Ajatashatru's father – that the sangha publicly denounced Devadatta, and would no longer bear any responsibility for any of his acts or deeds. The sangha then carried out a formal Act of Information against Devadatta, informing the laypeople of Rajagaha that Devadatta's actions were now completely dissociated from the Buddha and the sangha, which was afterwards circulated in Rajagaha by Sāriputta and a group of monks.

---

64   The Book of the Discipline: Vinaya-Pitaka Cullavagga, trans. I. B. Horner (1966), Vol 5, p. 264.

65   The Buddha's top two disciples.

The statement by the Buddha at the denunciation is one of the only places in the canons and sutras where he seemingly acts in a way that you or I might. If I were the head of a group and someone like Devadatta suggesting that he take my place, I can easily see myself getting angry and saying something like "why would I let a creep like you take my place?" But in that event, I would be acting under the influence of the Poison of anger (and also possibly grasping, to keep my position).

This, of course, is not the way a Buddha is expected to act, though I cannot make that presumption with regard to what actually underlay or motivated the Buddha in the situation. But after the issues with Devadatta arose, the other spiritual leaders in Magadha did make such a presumption, assuming thereby that they had detected the Buddha's weak spot – that he was not, in fact, a perfect Perfect One. In fact, Nigrantha Jnatiputra (Mahavira), the founder of the Jains and a contemporary of the Buddha in Maghada, sent one of his students to trip the Buddha up on this very issue after the denunciation and some follow up conversations had been had by and between Devadatta and the Buddha and his monks. In the *Abhaya Sutra*, Nigrantha tells the student, Prince Abhaya (another of King Bimbisara's sons, not heir to the throne):

> "Come now, prince. Go to the contemplative Gotama and on arrival say this: 'Lord, would the Tathagata[66] say words that are unendearing & disagreeable to others?' If the contemplative Gotama, thus asked, answers, 'The Tathagata would say words that are unendearing & disagreeable to others,' then you should say, 'Then how is there any difference between you, lord, and run-of-the-mill people? For even run-of-the-mill people say words that are unendearing & disagreeable to others.' But if the contemplative Gotama, thus asked, answers, 'The Tathagata would not say words that are unendearing & disagreeable to

66   Means both "one who has thus *gone*" (*Tathā-gata*) and "one who has thus *come*" (*Tathā-āgata*) – as well as, some have argued, "one who has gone *to* That" (*Tat-āgata*). Still others assert that the name means "one who has found the Truth". It is the name the historical the Buddha often used when referring to himself. http://en.wikipedia.org/wiki/Tathagata

others,' then you should say, 'Then how, lord, did you say of Devadatta that "Devadatta is headed for destitution, Devadatta is headed for hell, Devadatta will boil for an eon, Devadatta is incurable?" For Devadatta was upset & disgruntled at those words of yours.' When the contemplative Gotama is asked this two-pronged question by you, he won't be able to swallow it down or spit it up. Just as if a two-horned chestnut were stuck in a man's throat; he would not be able to swallow it down or spit it up. In the same way, when the contemplative Gotama is asked this two-pronged question by you, he won't be able to swallow it down or spit it up."[67]

The Prince, in furtherance of Nigrantha's request, did set up a meeting with the Buddha, at which meeting the Prince had his baby son in his own lap. The translator of the sutra suggests this was so he could pinch the baby and terminate the audience if he felt it was not going well. The Prince had not, however, reckoned on how formidable the Buddha was at the art of persuasion, for the Buddha was able to convince him of the rightness of his words to Devadatta when he came to the Prince's house the next day:

"As he was sitting there he said to the Blessed One, "Lord, would the Tathagata say words that are unendearing & disagreeable to others?"

"Prince, there is no categorical yes-or-no answer to that."

"Then right here, lord, the Nigranthas are destroyed."

"But prince, why do you say, 'Then right here, lord, the Nigranthas are destroyed'?"

"Just yesterday, lord, I went to Nigrantha Nataputta and... he said to me... 'Come now, prince. Go to the contemplative Gotama and on arrival say this: "Lord, would the Tathagata say words that are unendearing & disagreeable to others'?"...

67   Abhaya Sutta, trans. Thanissaro Bhikkhu (1997), http://www.accesstoinsight.org/tipitaka/mn/mn.058.than.html

Just as if a two-horned chestnut were stuck in a man's throat: he would not be able to swallow it down or spit it up. In the same way, when the contemplative Gotama is asked this two-pronged question by you, he won't be able to swallow it down or spit it up.'"

Now at that time a baby boy was lying face up on the prince's lap. So the Blessed One said to the prince, "What do you think, prince: If this young boy, through your own negligence or that of the nurse, were to take a stick or a piece of gravel into its mouth, what would you do?"

"I would take it out, lord. If I couldn't get it out right away, then holding its head in my left hand and crooking a finger of my right, I would take it out, even if it meant drawing blood. Why is that? Because I have sympathy for the young boy."

"In the same way, prince:

[1] In the case of words that the Tathagata knows to be unfactual, untrue, unbeneficial (or: not connected with the goal), unendearing & disagreeable to others, he does not say them.

[2] In the case of words that the Tathagata knows to be factual, true, unbeneficial, unendearing & disagreeable to others, he does not say them.

[3] In the case of words that the Tathagata knows to be factual, true, beneficial, but unendearing & disagreeable to others, he has a sense of the proper time for saying them.

[4] In the case of words that the Tathagata knows to be unfactual, untrue, unbeneficial, but endearing & agreeable to others, he does not say them.

[5] In the case of words that the Tathagata knows to be factual, true, unbeneficial, but endearing & agreeable to others, he does not say them.

[6] In the case of words that the Tathagata knows to be factual, true, beneficial, and endearing & agreeable to others, he has a sense of the proper time for saying them.

Why is that? Because the Tathagata has sympathy for living beings."

"Lord, when wise nobles or priests, householders or contemplatives, having formulated questions, come to the Tathagata and ask him, does this line of reasoning appear to his awareness beforehand — 'If those who approach me ask this, I — thus asked — will answer in this way' — or does the Tathagata come up with the answer on the spot?"

"In that case, prince, I will ask you a counter-question. Answer as you see fit. What do you think: are you skilled in the parts of a chariot?"

"Yes, lord. I am skilled in the parts of a chariot."

"And what do you think: When people come & ask you, 'What is the name of this part of the chariot?' does this line of reasoning appear to your awareness beforehand — 'If those who approach me ask this, I — thus asked — will answer in this way' — or do you come up with the answer on the spot?"

"Lord, I am renowned for being skilled in the parts of a chariot. All the parts of a chariot are well-known to me. I come up with the answer on the spot."

"In the same way, prince, when wise nobles or priests, householders or contemplatives, having formulated questions, come to the Tathagata and ask him, he comes up with the answer on the spot. Why is that? Because the property of the Dhamma is thoroughly penetrated by the Tathagata. From his thorough penetration of the property of the Dhamma, he comes up with the answer on the spot."

"When this was said, Prince Abhaya said to the Blessed One: "Magnificent, lord! Magnificent! Just as if he were to place upright what was overturned, to reveal what was hidden, to show the way to one who was lost, or to carry a lamp into the dark so that those with eyes could see forms, in the same way has the Blessed One — through many lines of reasoning

— made the Dhamma clear. I go to the Blessed One for refuge, to the Dhamma, and to the Sangha of monks. May the Blessed One remember me as a lay follower who has gone to him for refuge, from this day forward, for life."

Not only does the Buddha end up converting Nigrantha's student to the Way, but he tells him the underlying reason for the words to Devadatta was Compassion (other translations of the sutra use the word "compassion" rather than "sympathy"). So, rather than anger being the basis of his behavior towards Devadatta, the Buddha says that his words are uttered as they are because he has "sympathy for living beings", which would include Compassion for Devadatta himself.

Devadatta tried again to cause a schism in the sangha, this time by proposing at a mass sangha meeting behavioral precepts that were more stringent than those the Buddha prescribed. The proposed new precepts were:

1) bikkhus would have to live in the forest, and would be censured if they lived in a village;

2) bikkhus would have to beg only for food, and would be forbidden to take meals in homes as guests;

3) bikkhus would have to wear robes made of rags, and would be censured if they wore a robe;

4) bikkhus would have to dwell in tree-roots, and would be forbidden from dwelling in buildings; and

5) bikkhus could not eat meat or fish for any reason, even if put into their begging bowl.

The Buddha refused to agree to these, saying that while any bikkhu was free to follow these if he so chose, they were too stringent to demand of the entire sangha all the time. Devadatta thereafter, with the help of his top monk Kokalika, convinced 500 of the newly-ordained bikkhus to leave the Buddha's sangha and join his at the monastery at Mount Gayashirsha, on the grounds that the Buddha's precepts were too lax to be effective.

The Buddha's response to this was not anger or grasping, but one based on Compassion for the young monks who had been led off. He told Sāriputta and Moggallana that these newly-ordained monks had not had enough information to make an informed choice as to where they wished to train, and that they deserved to be informed properly about the Dharma before making such a decision. He therefore sent Sāriputta and Moggallana to Gayashirsha to preach the Dharma to the monks, which they did. At the end of the lecture, after they had "raised the image of the dharma" in the young monks' minds, they said they were returning to Bamboo Grove and invited the monks to return there with them, which the young monks did *en masse*. So the second attempt at creating a schism in the sangha was foiled without resort to violence or poisonous behavior by the Buddha or his followers.

With his attempts at controlling the sangha in shambles, Devadatta resorted to more desperate attempts to gain power, all of which clearly demonstrate that, as the Buddha had stated, Devadatta was not qualified to lead the sangha. For he now went to Ajatashatru to persuade him to try to kill his father, Bimbisara, and thereby ascend to the throne of Maghada. Devadatta's rationale was that with an ally as king of Maghada it would give him a better platform from which to gain control of the sangha. Ajatashatru at first demurred, but Devadatta convinced him that to wait was to risk dying without ever gaining power.

Ajatashatru was caught in the attempt, and admitted that he had been put up to the matter by Devadatta. The guards brought him before a mortified and mystified Bimbisara for instructions as to how to deal with his son. The king asked his son why he had done such a thing, to which the reply was that he did it because he wanted to be king immediately. Remarkably, and mistakenly, Bimbisara agreed to step down immediately and give the throne to his son.

Devadatta again meddled in court matters at this point, convincing Ajatashatru to put his father in jail to prevent him from attempting to regain the throne. Bimbisara was put into a cell, where he was gradually and eventually starved to death, with his wife dying soon thereafter. The Buddha and his monks, unable to have them freed because of the political situation, tended to them through this process to ensure that they attained enlightenment before they died.

With his puppet now in power, Devadatta amped up his play to get power over the bikkhus by trying to have the Buddha assassinated. The first attempt was made by having a group of Ajatashatru's soldiers go to Vulture Peak (another of Buddha's meditation centers in Magadha, given to him by Bimbisara). The plan was as follows: one man would go up to the top and kill the Buddha. He would in turn be killed by the next two men waiting down the hill, who would be killed by the next four down the hill, who would be killed by eight more waiting further down, who would be killed by sixteen more waiting at the bottom. In this way it was planned that no direct evidence of Devadatta's involvement with the actual assassination of the Buddha would remain.

Once again, however, the Buddha's formidable presence and persuasiveness were not properly reckoned with, for the first soldier could not bring himself to attack the Buddha, who sensed the intruder's presence and called out to him. The soldier admitted his aims, and repented of them, after which the Buddha expounded on the Dharma to him. The Buddha then told him that he was sure the man would be killed if he left Vulture Peak by the route he had been instructed to follow, so the man left by another path. After a while, the two soldiers whose job it was to kill the first soldier came up to the peak to find him, and were also converted by the Buddha, which scenario was then repeated with all the remaining soldiers. Devadatta's first assassination attempt was defused by the Buddha's compassionate acceptance of the men sent to kill him, and their transformation from killers to spiritual seekers.

Devadatta decided now to take matters into his own hands, since he was unable to rely on others to get the job done. Not long after the failure of the soldier assassins, he climbed to the top of Vulture Peak and waited for the Buddha to return from alms-seeking. As the Buddha walked uphill, Devadatta hurled a large boulder down the mountain towards him, but before it got to him it got stuck between two spurs of stone in the hillside. Only a boulder fragment continued towards the Buddha, piercing his foot:

'Then he looked up and said to Devadatta:"Misguided man, you have made much demerit; for with evil intent, with intent to do murder, you have drawn the blood of a Perfect One."

Then the Blessed One addressed the monks thus: "Monks, this is the first deed with immediate effect on rebirth that Devadatta has stored up, in that with evil intent to do murder, he has drawn the blood of a Perfect One."[68]

Other than noting the bad karma attendant to his actions, the Buddha did nothing to retaliate against or otherwise foster the state of conflict with Devadatta. In fact, strictly speaking there was no conflict, since the Buddha was seemingly not acting out of a poisoned state of mind.

The Buddha was injured and bedridden for some time from his foot injury, but eventually recovered. When he was again able to go on his morning begging rounds in Rajagaha, Devadatta implemented his last attempt at the Buddha's life by having the keepers of a mad elephant named Nalagiri release him onto the street where the Buddha was begging. Though his monks pleaded with the Buddha to remove himself from the street, he refused, telling them that a Perfect One does not die and enter nirvana due to violence on the part of another. He walked to the middle of the road and awaited as Nalagiri charged towards him, using Loving Kindness to defuse the situation:

"Then the Blessed One encompassed the elephant Nalagiri with thoughts of loving-kindness. The elephant lowered his trunk and he went up to the Blessed One and stood before him. The Blessed One stroked the elephant's forehead with his right hand and addressed him with these stanzas:

---

68   Pali Canon Studies, Ryuei Michael McCormick (2006), http://
      nichirenscoffeehouse.net/Ryuei/Devadatta, adapted from Life of the
      Buddha, Edward J. Thomas (2000), Dover Publications, Pages 261-2.

O elephant, do not attack a tusker,
For it is hurtful to attack a tusker;
There is no happy destiny beyond
For one who kills a tusker.
Have done with vanity and recklessness;
The reckless have no happy destiny.
So do you act in suchwise that you go
To a happy destination."[69]

So again, rather than feed into a conflict situation, the Buddha was able to convert it to something else, this time through the power of Loving Kindness. This was done also in part out of Compassion for the citizens of Rajagaha, who might themselves have been injured by Nalagiri had the Buddha not stopped him from rampaging through the city. He did thereafter scold the elephant keepers, telling them not to allow the elephant out because it could hurt other people – he did not scold them for endangering him.

In fact, other than the perhaps questionable public denunciation, he had never engaged in any conflict-based responses to the many things that Devadatta wrongly did to him. He had merely said that Devadatta's actions would themselves cause his downfall.

Which is what indeed occurred. Around the time of the Nalagiri incident, which was very public knowledge in Rajagaha and led to great disfavor of Devadatta by the populace, Bimbisara, and then his wife Queen Vaidehi, both died, which in turn led to remorse on the part of Ajatashatru (who took refuge with the Buddha and became a lay follower) and to him severing ties with Devadatta. So Devadatta was now isolated from the sangha and the local community, and had lost all access to powerful patronage as well. He became ill, and presided over his dwindling group of disciples at Gayashirsha until his death a few years before the Buddha's. There are numerous versions of how Devadatta died and/or the outcome of that death:

---

69   Ibid, adapted from <u>Life of the Buddha</u>, Edward J. Thomas (2000), Dover Publications, Page 264.

a) In the *Ekottaragama Sutra*, he smeared poison on his fingernails, and then tried to get to the Buddha at the Jetavana Monastery to kill him. Prior to getting there, however, the earth opened up and swallowed him, sending him to the Avici Hell to suffer misery for thousands of lifetimes;

b) The Pali commentaries say that he fell ill for nine months, then repented and asked to be taken to the Buddha, but that before he got there the earth swallowed him up and sent him to Avici hell. They also state that in the future he will be released from his suffering and be a "private-Buddha" named Atthisara;

c) In the *Lotus Sutra*, the Buddha states that he himself attained Buddhahood in his present lifetime because of teachings a previous incarnation of Devadatta gave his incarnation in a former life, and that in a future reincarnation Devadatta would become the Buddha of that age. [70]

d) In more modern writings, the ill Devadatta went to see the Buddha, who received him at his hut on Vulture Peak. Devadatta, who had been transported on a stretcher due to his poor health, said "I take refuge in the Buddha", upon which the Buddha placed his hand on Devadatta's forehead. Later that evening, Devadatta passed away. [71]

In reviewing the entire saga of the Buddha's relationship with Devadatta, certain themes or concepts present themselves as instructive for mediators and others involved in conflict:

First, as we saw in the Suddhodana and Dirty Basin conflicts, time itself is a factor in the resolution, and one which shouldn't be overlooked as a "tool" in determining how to resolve a conflict. We see this in the Buddha's acknowledgement that Devadatta's actions would lead to their own derailment, followed by his patience in

70 Pali Canon Studies, Ryuei Michael McCormick (2006), http://nichirenscoffeehouse.net/Ryuei/Devadatta
71 Old Path White Clouds Thich Nhat Hanh (1991) Parallax Press, Page 539

allowing events to evolve naturally through time. Indeed, if we take the "modern" version of Devadatta's demise as the true one, all conflict between the Buddha and him effectively ended when on his deathbed he took refuge in the Buddha. But that fails to take account of the many people who suffered as a result of the conflict – King Bimbisara and his Queen, both of whom died at the hands of their son, Prince Ajatashatru, who in turn had to suffer the remorse at causing his own parents' deaths once he regained his senses. Unlike the Dirty Basin Incident, this conflict left death and suffering in its wake.

Which brings us to the second lesson of the Devadatta conflict – not all conflicts can be successfully resolved before more suffering arises. Which doesn't mean that the mediator should lose faith in his or her craft, or that he or she should stop trying to alleviate suffering for those involved in the conflict. Rather, it means that they should be cognizant of the limitations inherent in certain conflicts.

Devadatta seems to have defined himself by the very activities that led to the conflict with the Buddha, and by the Poisons that drove him. It's a little like the story I read about a peace negotiator who went to try to resolve an ongoing conflict between the government and a rebel group headquartered in the mountains outside the capital city. When the negotiator proposed a seemingly logical resolution to the issues between the government and the rebels, the rebel leader said something like: "Are you kidding? This conflict is my career!"

But the Buddha's activities in the face of an intractable conflict generated by a relentless foe are instructive, for he lessened suffering by focusing Compassion and Loving Kindness where it would be effective. So, when Devadatta tried to cause a schism in the sangha by spiriting away the 500 newly-ordained monks to Mount Gayashirsha, or when the soldier-assassins invaded Vulture Peak, the Buddha used Compassion for their welfare to change the conflict situation (or, at least, that part of the conflict situation) into a resolved one. When Bimbisara was imprisoned and the Buddha unable to have him freed, he made sure that his teachings were available to enlighten Bimbisara before he died. Afterwards, he counseled Prince Ajatashatru on how to deal with his remorse. With the elephant Naligiri, we see a similar effect of Loving Kindness. So even in situations where one or more of the main instigators of the conflict are not subject to persuasion, or where their Poisons are so systemic and ingrained that they continue to resist transformation into Sublime Abodes, the work of creating peace and Compassion can still be a fulfilling and challenging role for the mediator.

The Last Days of the Buddha

During the last few years of his life, the Buddha, Ananda, and groups of bikkhus worked their way northward from Vulture's Peak in Rajagaha to Kusinara, where the Buddha would die eight years after the start of the problems with Devadatta and forty-five years after his Awakening. When they reached Vesali, about half way between Rajagaha and Kusinara, the Buddha informed Ananda that he would die in three months' time.

At the end of the three months, they arrived at the mango grove of Cunda, a poor blacksmith in the town of Pava. Honored by the visit, Cunda invited the Buddha and all of his traveling retinue to a meal at his house the next day. The meal that Cunda prepared had "choice food, hard and soft, prepared in his abode, together with a quantity of *sukara-maddava.*"[72]. *Sukara-maddava* is a confusing term, since it can mean either the tender parts of a pig or boar (found dead, since if it had been killed for the meal the Buddha would not have eaten it), but could also refer to the mushrooms, truffles, yams, tubers or bamboo shoots that are enjoyed or walked upon by such animals. We will never know with any surety which of the food types was prepared, but we do know that the Buddha told Cunda to serve the *sukara-maddava* to him only, and to serve the rest of the food to his bikkhus, After eating his food, the Buddha spoke as follows to Cunda:

> "Whatever, Cunda, is left over of the *sukara-maddava*, bury that in a pit. For I do not see in all this world, with its gods, Maras, and Brahmas, among the host of ascetics and brahmans,

---

72   Digha-Nikaya 16, Part IV:17, http://www.accesstoinsight.org/tipitaka/ dn/dn.16.1-6.vaji.html.

gods and men, anyone who could eat it and entirely digest it except the Tathagata alone." [73]

Immediately afterwards, the Buddha fell violently ill, presumably with dysentery. Despite being sick and in great pain, he told Ananda that they would leave immediately towards a grove of Sala trees near the town of Kusinara. In order to get there, they had to cross the Hiraññavati River, which is the third and final river we mention in this chapter, and was the last river that the Buddha would ever see or cross. Prior to crossing to the northern side, the Buddha expressed concern to Ananda that Cunda would feel remorse for having given the Buddha his last meal, so he told Ananda to give Cunda the following message (no doubt within earshot of others):

'It is a gain to you, friend Cunda, a blessing that the Tathagata took his last alms meal from you, and then came to his end. For, friend, face to face with the Blessed One I have heard and learned: "There are two offerings of food which are of equal fruition, of equal outcome, exceeding in grandeur the fruition and result of any other offerings of food. Which two? The one partaken of by the Tathagata before becoming fully enlightened in unsurpassed, supreme Enlightenment; and the one partaken of by the Tathagata before passing into the state of Nibbana in which no element of clinging remains. By his deed the worthy Cunda has accumulated merit which makes for long life, beauty, well being, glory, heavenly rebirth, and sovereignty."'[74]

From there, the Buddha and his retinue crossed the river to the Sala Grove, where he lay between twin sala trees which broke out in full bloom though it was not the flowering season. He died shortly thereafter (after anointing his final convert, Suhadda, and delivering

---

73   Digha-Nikaya 16, Part IV:19, http://www.accesstoinsight.org/tipitaka/dn/dn.16.1–6.vaji.html

74   Digha-Nikaya 16, Part IV:56, http://www.accesstoinsight.org/tipitaka/dn/dn.16.1–6.vaji.html

some final discourses to his collected, grieving bikkhus). He then delivered his final exhortation before passing into nirvana:

> *"Handa dani bhikkhave amantayami vo: Vayadhamma sankhara appamadena sampadetha,"* which translates roughly as:

> *"Behold now, bikkhus, I exhort you: All created things are impermanent. Strive on with diligence"*.

And so we all strive, in part by learning to live with and resolve the internal and interpersonal conflicts that beset us. We'll look next at the "psychology" of Buddhism, to see what clues are provided therein for those efforts.

4. Buddhist "Psychology" and the Genesis of Conflict

The brahmin Aramadanda approached the Venerable Mahakaccana, exchanged friendly greetings with him, and asked him: "Why is it, Master Kaccana, that khattiyas fight with khattiyas, brahmins with brahmins, and householders with householders?"

"It is, brahmin, because of attachment to sensual pleasures, adherence to sensual pleasures, fixation on sensual pleasures, addiction to sensual pleasures, obsession with sensual pleasures, holding firmly to sensual pleasures that khattiyas fight with khattiyas, brahmins with brahmins, and householders with householders."

"Why is it, Master Kaccana, that ascetics fight with ascetics?"

"It is, brahmin, because of attachment to views, adherence to views, fixation on views, addiction to views, obsession with views, holding firmly to views that ascetics fight with ascetics."[75]

As Westerners, we have mostly been raised to consider the self, and its perfection, as the path to psychological health. And that bias is incorporated into the writings of the seminal "teachers" of western psychology. Thus, when Freud developed his schema of the id ("a

---

75   In the Buddha's Words, Bhikkhu Bodhi (2005), Wisdom Publications, Page 35, from the *Ariguttara Nikaya* 2: iv, 6, abridged; I 66.

primitive chaos, a cauldron of seething excitement"[76]), ego (the "officer in charge" or perhaps the *mediator* between the id and the superego), and superego (the sense of right and wrong that controls the officer), these were viewed as parts of a distinct entity known as the *self*, which while conflicted could be perfected as a self. And while Jung theorized that an unknowable transcendent Self underlay the limited ego and could be accessed through archetypal images (the shared images of the collective mind) emerging in the subconscious mind, "like most western psychologists he could not allow for egoless awareness as a developmental step beyond ego"[77].

This firmly entrenched belief in the "self" informed both Freud's and Jung's notions of what underlay "Eastern" religious concepts as well. Jung viewed the enlightenment experience as a development of the self with "Buddha-Nature" or godliness added – not as an actual relinquishment of the self altogether.[78] Freud also believed that the development of a stronger "self" lay at the core of Asian religious practice:

> "It can easily be imagined, too, that certain practices of mystics may succeed in upsetting the normal relations between the different regions of the mind, so that, for example, the perceptual system becomes able to grasp relations in the deeper layers of the ego and in the id which would otherwise be inaccessible to it. Whether such a procedure can put one in possession of ultimate truths, from which all good will flow, may be safely doubted. All the same, we must admit that the therapeutic efforts of psycho-analysis have chosen much the same method of approach. For their object is to strengthen the ego, to make it more independent of the super-ego, to

---

76 *An Outline of Psychoanalysis*, Sigmund Freud (1940), trans. James Strachey, Norton, http://webspace.ship.edu/cgboer/freudselection.html

77 *Toward a Psychology of Awakening*, John Welwood (2002), Shambhala Press, Page 41.

78 Jung's Foreward to Introduction to Zen Buddhism, Daisetz Teitaro Suzuki (1964) Grove Press, Page 14.

widen its field of vision, and so to extend its organization that it can take over new portions of the id. Where id was, there shall ego be...It is reclamation work, like the draining of the Zuyder Zee."[79]

And so we in the West all have our issues, and delve at length with alternating dread and relish into the intricacies of our pasts and the effects therein of and on the lives of others, to see if we can somehow clean and repair the damages to the self brought on by our narcissistic wounds. Alternately, we utilize the tools and techniques of Western psychology to differentiate our "selves" from others, often compensating for our loneliness and isolation by fomenting conflict or trying to dominate others.

But Freud, Jung, and the many other founders of western psychology saw only what they saw. All of their schema are, like Buddhism, approaches to the vastness of the field of consciousness, and none can actually embrace or fully codify what is essentially unknowable and infinite. I remember listening to an "earth scientist" on NPR one morning, saying that when scientists study a single spoonful of dirt, they find items and organisms and processes unknown, really almost beyond identification. If we can't know a lump of soil, we probably can't "explain" human life, nor expound any one single rubric to describe completely how the human mind and spirit or their possible perfections work. But we can learn to recognize the strengths inherent in each formulation. While Freud and Jung gave us a doorway into a new world in the early 20th century, 2500 years earlier the Buddha did it in a way intrinsically different than western psychology and religiosity.

Unlike western psychology, which holds that the healing and polishing and strengthening of the self is the way to wholeness, in Buddhism the basic idea is *there is no self!* That's right – the very thing you were hoping to fix isn't even there. But the things that make you think there's a self are, and since you cling to those things you cling to the idea of a self, which then itself causes you suffering. The Buddha

---

79   An Outline of Psychoanalysis, Sigmund Freud [1940], translated by James Strachey. N.Y. Norton

used an analogy to the leashed dog to illuminate the effects of our attachment to the illusory self:

> "Suppose, monks, a dog tied on a leash was bound to a strong post or pillar; it would just keep on running and revolving around that same post or pillar. So, too, the uninstructed worldling regards form as self…feeling as self…perception as self…volitional formations as self…consciousness as self.…He just keeps running and revolving around form, around feeling, around perception, around volitional formations, around consciousness. As he keeps running and revolving around them, he is not freed from form, not freed from feeling, not freed from perception, not freed from volitional formations, not freed from consciousness. He is not freed from birth, aging, and death; not freed from sorrow, lamentation, pain, dejection, and despair; not freed from suffering, I say."[80]

And the thing that keeps the dog running and revolving is the human mind. In Buddhism, the underlayment for our life is the human mind itself. The *Dhammapada*, which is a collection of four hundred twenty-three aphorisms drawn from the Pali Canon, has as its very first couplet:

> *"Everything has mind in the lead, has mind in the forefront, is made by mind. If one speaks or acts with a corrupt mind, misery will follow, as the wheel of a cart follows the foot of the ox.*
>
> *Everything has mind in the lead, has mind in the forefront, is made by mind. If one speaks or acts with a pure mind, happiness will follow, like a shadow that never leaves."* [81]

---

80   In the Buddha's Words, edited by Bikkhu Bodhi (2005), Wisdom Publications, Pages 278-9, quoting from Samyutta Nikaya 22:99; II 149–50.
81   Dhammapada: Sayings of Buddha, (trans) Thomas Cleary (1995), Bantam Books, Pages 7-8.

A different translation of the opening lines of the same aphorisms has it that *"Mind precedes things, dominates them, creates them."*[82] Whatever the translation, it appears that perception and realization are not directed outward>inward, but rather in concentric circles outward from the human mind. In this model of human consciousness, then, health would extend similarly concentrically from the individual within him- or herself outward, and not be imposed externally and/ or discursively via a therapeutic toolkit or religious imperative.

So…what is this mind? Is the mind the issues we mentioned, or the thoughts of good or bad or advantage that could arise at any moment? Is it a receptacle, conduit, or cipher?

Actually, in its natural state, Buddhism holds that the mind ("Original Mind") is pure, and within itself already at peace. It is *sunyata*, or empty. But it is all too easy to unbalance and disturb out of its state of peaceful purity because of its proclivity to attach to passing thoughts and feelings and to structure itself in reaction to these "mental formations". So, in fact, the mind which is essentially peaceful is virtually never at peace, and its fundamental purity nearly always sullied. The practice of Buddhism is significantly involved with returning to an awakened or enlightened state that allows Original Mind to re-emerge from the cloud under which it has been hidden– the cloud of "self". Our perennial problem is that we cover the "nothing" of Original Mind with the somethings of the "selves" we mistakenly believe ourselves to be, and then have to deal with the problems created by the cover-ups. But the actual experiencing of calm, clear mind is an event of innate happiness. It is the unconditioned state of nirvana (or *nibbana* in Pali).

It is difficult for Westerners to accept certain ideas that are integral to Buddhism. For instance, the idea that life is *dukkha* or suffering leads many people to consider Buddhism depressing and pessimistic. The concept of *anatta* (lack of self, "corelessness") is similarly anathema to the Occidental mind. For we as a culture revel in and idealize the self. Our psychology is geared towards the healing and polishing

---

82   The Heart of Buddhist Meditation, Nyanaponika Thera (1954), Weiser
     Publications, Page 21

of it, and our popular culture (at least in America) is geared to the embellishment and strengthening of the individual "self" against those of others, so that one can stand out in a crowded field of selves. A philosophy that holds that there is indeed no "self", then, would appear inimical and dangerous in such a culture.

Yet that is what Buddhism holds – that the self is a construct created by the needs of attachment, yet which is actually without any real substance. For the "self" gives us the illusory feeling of certainty and control in an existence that Buddhism says has three essential characteristics: *anicca* – impermanence; *dukkha* – unsatisfactoriness; and *anatta* – corelessness or lack of self.

And, so whereas western psychology would have you perfect a self of its issues, Buddhism aims to have one get beyond the fixed self altogether, so that one may see reality – and one's place in it – clearly. In fact, Buddhism holds that there is no real fixed self to get beyond.

This doesn't mean that one suddenly forgets his or her identity, or walks about like someone in the grip of dementia. We need a socially constructed identity to function in the world. If the attendant at the airline ticket counter asks me for my ID, I'm not going to say that I have no self – I give her my passport! I have a name, and address, a history, and plans for the future. As Douglas Berggren, my college philosophy professor, was wont to say, humans are remarkable that they are always planning for a future they aren't certain to ever arrive at. But it would be unrealistic and unworkable to claim on a day-to-day basis to have no self. We need and have social identities, allowing us to view ourselves as members of families, groups, endeavors, and societies throughout the limited time-span of our existences.

But the concept of the self also connotes permanence, as do the concepts of the individual in many religions. In fact, the Hinduism in which Siddhartha Gautama was raised posits the concept of *atman*, a personal self that transmigrates through multiple reincarnations. In Christianity, the soul survives independent of the mortal frame, and ultimately unites with God. But not in the Buddhist cosmology – here the self is a convenient illusion without a lasting spiritual or metaphysical existence.

What we mistakenly call the "self" is in Buddhism the result of the ever-shifting mix of the five *khanda* (Pali) or in Sanskrit *skhanda* (both of which literally mean "heaps"), and which in English are usually named the "five aggregates". The Buddha's references in the leashed dog simile to the uninitiated regarding "form as self... feeling as self...perception as self...volitional formations as self... consciousness as self" are references to the five skandhas, which are referred to elsewhere throughout the Pali Canon. The five skandhas are:

1) *body (or form)* -- the body is the realm of matter, and consists of the six organs that Buddhism asserts comprises the bodily sensation – the eyes, ears, nose, tongue, body, and mind (Buddhism is dissimilar to western thought in considering the mind a part of the body). If you think that people don't confuse their bodies with their "selves", you haven't been reading enough gossip or glamour magazines!

2) *feeling (or sensation)* -- feeling or sensation is how each of these six organs is experiencing reality at any given moment, not the kind of feelings we mean when we say "I feel happy" or "I feel hungry". The word for this aggregate in Sanskrit and Pāli is *vedanā*, traditionally translated as either "feeling" or "sensation", and generally refers to the pleasant, unpleasant and neutral sensations that occur when any of our six body organs come into contact with external sense objects.[83] For example, as I write this paragraph sitting in my chair, my flanks feel the pressure of the chair, my eyes alternately see the computer keyboard and screen and the periphery around them, my ears hear the birds singing in the tree outside my home office and the click-clack of the computer keys, my nose feels the breath entering and leaving through the nostrils, and my tongue tastes the tea I am drinking. The totality of these comprise the feelings or sensations that I have at any moment.

3) *perception* – perception (called *sañña* in Pali) is the way I recognize and label the data and feelings (discussed in 2, above)

---

83   http://en.wikipedia.org/wiki/Skandha

that the body (and mind, since it is part of the body) presents to me at each moment I am conscious. As the Buddha said of this aggregate:

"And why do you call it 'perception'? Because it perceives, thus it is called 'perception.' What does it perceive? It perceives blue, it perceives yellow, it perceives red, it perceives white. Because it perceives, it is called perception."[84]

So when certain visual stimulus hits my eye and gets processed in my brain, I say "traveling coffee cup" or "photograph" or "scotch tape dispenser". All of this – this act of labeling sensory input -- occurs with remarkable rapidity, so that it is virtually impossible in most situations to separate the feeling/sensation from the perception that I attach to it.

4) *mental (or volitional) formations* - "mental formations" or "volitional formations" are the "slants" or "takes" that I impose upon the perceptions that have in turn developed out of the feeling/sensations I have in each moment, including mental habits, thoughts, ideas, opinions, compulsions, and decisions triggered by a sensory input or event. These are more complicated than perceptions, for here the historicity of my consciousness imposes subjective value on those perceptions. Perhaps I would rather be having a drink and playing pool with a friend than writing right now. There is the concentration on the writing task at hand, but also the other mental impressions that intrude on that concentration. Did I make my daughter's lunch for school tomorrow? What will really transpire on that event that started to unfold at work as I was leaving the office today? Why doesn't my daughter make her own lunch? And why does one of the actors in that work drama I mentioned inspire a bit of dislike and distrust in me? These mental formations are powerful, for the very

---

84 Khajjaniya Sutta, from the Samyutta Nikaya 22.79, trans. by Thanissaro Bhikkhu, http://www.accesstoinsight.org/tipitaka/sn/sn22/sn22.079.than. html

reason that they attach to perceptions unconsciously (at least for now) and "below the radar" of my controlled self, so that they color the very nature of the perceptions themselves.

The Pali word for these formations is *saṅkhāra*, which can mean either 'that which has been put together' (in other words, the unconsciously generated mental states) or 'that which puts together' (mental activities that generate future karmic effects, the 'karmic seeds'). This fourth aggregate, *saṅkhāra-khandha*, is the mind's faculty and tendency to put together formations which act as causes for real-world effects later than they are created in the unconscious.[85]

5) *consciousness* – consciousness is the organizer and overseer of the perceptions, and the part of us that thinks it's in charge of the mental formations. It is most readily the aggregate that causes a sense of an illusory "self" since it is aware of itself.

In the Pali Canon, the Buddha makes it clear that each of the skandhas is "subject to clinging" – in other words, each of the parts of your consciousness automatically tends to cling or attach (either through attraction or repulsion) at all times, until the mind is trained to let go of that clinging.

The mental formations are the truly fertile ground for folly. In western psychology, they lead to "neurotic" behavior – cyclical, self-damaging behavior that arises time and time again in similar situations, without any seeming control by the conscious mind – and to psychopathology in general. The way to deal with them in psychological therapy is to learn their origins, and hopefully to re-experience the emotions that underlay the development of those formations, so that the self can be improved by learning to live with the ghosts of that past.

In Buddhist thought, while all the aggregates are suspect since they are all the product of attachment, the mental formations are doubly suspect since they primarily lead to the arising of Three Poisons –

---

85   Wikipedia, http://en.wikipedia.org/wiki
     Sa%E1%B9%85kh%C4%81ra#cite_note-4

greed or craving, anger or hatred, and delusion or ignorance.[86] As we discussed in Chapter 2, these are the three basic ingredients of conflict. Greed or craving characterizes the things that we want or need or move towards, in both the positive and negative sense – the desire for what you don't have, or to hold on to what you do have. Anger and hatred are the feelings that arise towards those who stand in the way of your greed and craving, who prevent you from achieving what you believe to be your due. And delusion is the consciousness that shapes itself around the feelings of desire or revulsion to justify your attachment to the outcome you want to materialize, that validates your slant on the phenomenal world as "right."

Conflict (like all suffering) is caused by attachment. The Venerable Mahakaccana, one of the Buddha's senior disciples, refers to two kinds of conflict-generating attachment at the beginning of this chapter – that of the worldling, and that of the renunciate. For the worldling, it is sensual pleasures to which one attaches. Sensual pleasures here would constitute a broad range of things, not just sexual behavior. That car you want, a piece of cake, drugs, money, more sex, respect from co-workers, to be rid of a person you dislike – basically anything in the sensate world. And the attachment can be positive or negative, for one can be as attached to his dislikes as his passions. If you dread driving to work on the freeway in the morning, you are attached to that ride. If you envy someone else's achievements, you are "sensually" (i.e. attached through your *senses*) attached to that person. You are *trishna* or grasping. And you will note that all of these types of trishna are mental or volitional formations, which illustrates the statement above that this fourth aggregate is a breeding ground of the Three Poisons.

For the *bikkhu* or monk or nun, the attachment arises somewhat differently. For here, at least on the surface, many of the distractions and enticements of the "real world" are eliminated. No traffic jams, or messy love triangles, not too much noise. And, since they've already accepted the Dharma, they are by faith conflict-averse. Life revolves

---

86 Since all the concepts in Buddhism are translations out of Pali or Sanskrit, there is variance to how the terms are translated. In this paper I try to find a "middle way" in interpreting the terms whenever possible.

around meditational practices, and work meditation. But they still have their "views", perhaps including a vision of what they want or think they have already gotten from the practice, and their analysis of other practices and faiths. You might easily judge others, even your fellow communal *bikkhus*, based on your views. You and they could have conflicts over views of how best to reach enlightenment. Views are, of course, also mental or volitional formations. One need only remember the Dirty Basin Incident to imagine how a renunciate community can be derailed by the Three Poisons.

In Buddhism, the way to deal with these poisons is to mindfully transform the Three Poisons of greed, hatred and delusion into the Four Sublime States of Loving Kindness, Compassion, Appreciative Joy, and Equanimity, thereby liberating the person or persons to let go of the conflict. This is done generally by following some of the "active" (as opposed to the "ethical") steps of the Noble Eightfold Path – to develop Right Understanding by using Right Thought, Right Effort, Right Mindfulness, and hopefully Right Meditation.

Right Thought is thinking in a way that is healthy and conducive to harmony within and without, so that one's thoughts do no harm to oneself or create conflict with others – by practicing right thought, you align yourself to the possibility of letting go of the conflict. Right Effort is the commitment to "engage in all of life's activities in the manner that best suits the situation, oneself, and everyone else involved".[87] Right Mindfulness is the awareness of what one is doing, feeling and thinking in each moment so that one does not act unconsciously towards him- or herself and the others around one. It is being "present" in one's own life. Right Meditation is contemplative practice that leads to the attainment of liberation, which presupposes that the Three Poisons have been eradicated. By using some or all of these, Right Understanding comes -- seeing things as they really are, which necessitates letting go of the preconceptions and misconceptions that cause us to suffer and inflict suffering on others.

For our purpose of illuminating the relationship of these steps to the conflict resolution process, it's better to outline the process

---

87   Essential Buddhism, Jack Maguire (2001), Pocket Books, Page 94.

in a slightly less classical format. *In a nutshell, through Mindfulness you first become keenly aware of what is taking place inside of you in the conflict situation, then you convert each of the negative responses into a positive one.* The Mindfulness can be either personal – such as when I meditate to learn what feelings or Poisons I have developed about myself or a situation I am in -- or inter-personal, in which case a group that is in conflict will work together to develop Mindfulness ("inter-Mindfulness") about their shared situation, by discussing what is not working in the conversation and learning what might be done to improve it.

Once you (singular or plural) have become mindful of the situation, you use the truth that appears thereby and also perhaps appropriate techniques to convert the Poisons into their opposites. In other words, you may need to find ways to convert the relevant Poisons into more positive states in addition to being mindful. Buddhism generally posits three ways to deal with negative emotions: antidote (activating the opposite of the Poison), liberation (allowing it to dissolve by looking straight at it and realizing its intrinsic "emptiness"), and utilization (winnowing out the positive aspects of the Poisons and utilizing them to resolve the conflict). We will review and expand upon these later on in this book.

In the process of stopping the poisonous feelings, whether using additional techniques or not, the very nature of Mindfulness will tend to convert them into Loving Kindness and Compassion. This should normally occur during the process of generating a resolution to the conflictual situation, after which the final stages of development of Appreciative Joy for what each person has gained through the process and Equanimity (inner peace) can occur. At that point, the last vestiges of the conflict will have dissolved.

Perhaps East and West are not really so different, in that both seek to alleviate suffering through awareness. And both must, by necessity, deal with the inherent existential problems of suffering and life and death, since those are universal – indeed, all our sufferings are but the minute deaths that assault us throughout our lives. But the discursive awareness of psychology is not the mindful awareness of meditation. And because Buddhism posits *anatta* (no self) as one of its core beliefs, the emphasis is more on clearing the consciousness than it is on perfecting the self, since the mental formations are ultimately as illusory as the self that supposedly created them.

The Buddha didn't say not to have the wants or views. They will arise, whether we want them to or not. Instead, he says conflict comes from being attached to them. The wants and views are themselves impermanent, like the self. They're like the clouds in the sky, forever shifting and reforming, never the same. But our human consciousness wants the self and the things it wants to be permanent, or true, or whatever, and so we see the world that way. Our view of reality becomes "clouded" over. For you and me the feelings and perceptions and volitions will arise, generated by inner compulsions and outer influences. They're not good or bad, they just are.

For the Buddha this type of arising perhaps didn't occur because he had experienced in a way few people ever do just how his mind and feelings worked. But most people (like me) are a bit slower on the uptake than he was. I'm still working on the lessons he already completed, polishing my Buddha-nature as it were. As the Zen saying goes "The Buddha way is unattainable – I vow to attain it".[88] There's work involved for us to understand and resolve conflict.

For feelings and perceptions and volitional formations to generate conflict, there must be a second quality -- some attachment to them. They must not only arise, but also do so in some way that we treat them and try to hold on to them as if they are "real" or permanent. If I don't try to hold on, they remain clouds in the sky, and will surely pass on. But by holding on to them, my mind changes them into what they are not. And then my situation is worse, because I have now to deal with something that isn't what I perceive it to be.

The two factors – the arising of the physical need and/or mental formation, and the attachment to it -- are foundations of conflict. And a Buddhist approach to resolving conflict has to deal with both of these aspects from both an internal as well as an external perspective.

---

88   Essential Buddhism, Jack Maguire (2001), Pocket Books, Page 77.

For all conflict is on some level intrinsically internal, because each of the parties is a "self" at war with itself – here, the Buddhist practices Mindfulness to dissolve the attachment. And externally as well, for while one can't always make the other party or parties to a dispute agree to practice Mindfulness, one can utilize techniques that will help the disputants to actually see what is happening – thereby creating an "inter-Mindfulness" -- and then help them find ways to let go of their attachment to destructive emotions and mistaken views of the situation.

Recognizing the need for this shift away from attachment is not unique to a Buddhist perspective. In one of the seminal works on negotiation, Getting to Yes, the authors from the Harvard Negotiation Project posit four basic principles for the resolution of conflict:

1) separate the people from the problem

2) focus on interests, not positions

3) invent options for mutual gain

4) insist on using objective criteria[89]

Inherent in the first and second of these is the concept of attachment, even though the Harvard methodology is a more-or-less rationalist approach to the resolution of conflict. For the "positions" of the parties are based on their feelings, perceptions, mental formations, to which they have become stuck. Speaking to the first principle, the Harvardian authors state "(w)e are creatures of strong emotions who often have radically different perceptions and have difficulty communicating clearly".[90] Here is echoed the Buddhist concept of poisoned communication and deluded perception. The second principle – focusing on interests rather than "positions" - is perhaps another way of acknowledging that peoples' attachments to their own feelings generate their adherence to positions, which cloud their eyes from seeing what their interests in the negotiations actually are.

---

89   Getting to Yes, Fisher and Ury (2d Ed, 1991) Penguin Books, Pages 10-11.

90   Getting to Yes, Fisher and Ury (2d Ed, 1991) Penguin Books, Page 11.

What distinguishes the Buddhist approach is its inherent recognition that the resolution of conflict is not primarily a rational undertaking, nor a mere realignment of the participants' thought processes and political positions. Instead, it is the process of taking errant perceptions and poisoned feelings and transforming them into expressions of Loving Kindness and Compassion that blossom in the heart.

For that is the progression of the opening that should and does occur through following the Buddhist path in the resolution of conflict – what begins in the minds of the disputants as an increase in awareness and Mindfulness can gradually open their hearts to Loving Kindness and Compassion, dissolving and transforming the conflict. And since the first step on that path to the resolution of conflict is the development of Mindfulness, that is what we shall explore next.

5. MINDFULNESS – STEP ONE TOWARDS RESOLUTION

This is the sole way for the purification of beings, for the overcoming of sorrow and lamentation, for the destroying of pain and grief, for reaching the right path, for the realization of Nibbana, namely the four Foundations of Mindfulness.

What are the four? Herein a monk may dwell practicing contemplation on the body… practicing feeling-contemplation on feelings…practicing mind-contemplation on mind… practicing mind-object contemplation on mind-objects, ardent, clearly comprehending and mindful, having overcome covetousness and grief concerning the world.[91]

"Mindfulness" is a very popular word these days. For some it has a positive connotation, that one is keeping a "head's up" on what's going on around them. For others, it negatively suggests someone who is stuck in their head and is thus unable to fully and viscerally enjoy their life.

---

91   The Heart of Buddhist Meditation, Nyanaponika Thera (1954), Weiser Publications, Page 139, quoting from the *Samyutta-Nikaya*, Verses 47,11. The *Nikayas* are the four major collections of the Pali Canon. These words are attributed to the Buddha as he sat under a different tree – the Goatherd's Fig Tree – in the fifth and seventh week after his enlightenment.

For the Buddhist, however, "Mindfulness" is a term of art, and is used to describe meditational techniques devised and recommended by the Buddha. They are particularly practiced by Theravadan Buddhists (the branch of Buddhism prevalent in Cambodia, Myanmar, Sri Lanka, and Thailand), and are also widespread throughout Europe and the United States.

Mind you, there is Mindfulness in all forms of Buddhist practice. Zen practice will center on zazen, which is a modified form of the Theravadan techniques. The Pure Land Buddhists pray to a Buddha in the Western Heaven. The Tibetans imagine the souls of departed Buddhist saints (or Boddhisattvas, as they call them).

Mindfulness is essentially impossible to define since it refers to events that occur within the consciousness of the person practicing the techniques − in an analogy offered by the Buddha, any words used to describe it or his other techniques are like fingers pointing at the moon, not the moon itself. If you really want to understand Mindfulness, you need to practice it. But since our medium here is words, we will have to use those fingers for the present.

Mindfulness is variously described as "bare attention", or as:

· mirror-thought, reflecting only what is actually happening
· nonjudgmental observation
· impartial watchfulness
· non-conceptual awareness
· present-moment awareness
· non-egotistical awareness
· awareness of change
· participatory observation[92]

Through the development of Mindfulness, the meditator learns to accept whatever arises in his or her consciousness without attachment, by watching it arise and dissolve, and also learns to recognize the underlying causes of these arisings. And because he or she sees that these arisings do all dissolve, they lose the appearance of permanence.

---

92   Mindfulness in Plain English, Bhante Henepola Gunaratana, (2002) Wisdom Publications, Pages 139-141.

Once their appearance of permanence is gone, there is no longer anything to which to "attach".

As noted in the *Nikaya* quotation at the beginning of this chapter, there are four foundations of Mindfulness referred to by the Buddha in his teachings – that of the body, that of feelings (in the sense of sense-impressions or feelings as in the second aggregate discussed in the previous chapter), that of mind (or *mind-states*, "the feeling-tones of the mind, the different colored filters through which we perceive the world"[93]) , and that of "mind-objects" (the way the mind actually works while experiencing its mind-states). While they all ultimately dovetail into the overarching "Mindfulness" that is continuous and full, each is a different aspect of that fullness. And each one has specific subjects of meditation and exercises to foster it.

The first, and most widespread in its practice, is Mindfulness of the body. Its popularity is perhaps due to the fact that the very first exercise taught by the Buddha – Mindfulness of breathing – is the simplest to explain and the most adaptable to a wide range of personal situations. Mindfulness of breathing can be practiced by anyone, anytime, anywhere. A simple technique for practicing Mindfulness of breathing is included later in this chapter.

In traditional *bikkhu* practice, there are further stages of this First Foundation. There is the Mindfulness of postures of the body (such as walking meditation, or being aware of the body itself as it sits, stands, or lies down), Mindfulness of parts of the body, feelings in the body, and even contemplation of dead bodies in the cemetery. One does not need to follow these, unless one wants to do advanced Buddhist practice. As long as you have been mindful of your breath, you've been mindful of your body, and you have succeeded in this foundation.

The second foundation is that of feelings, which of course in our world could mean anything. "I'm feeling it...", "Here are my feelings..." *ad nauseum*, so the word will mean whatever the speaker intends within his or her own lexicon. In classical Buddhism, and

---

93   Buddha's Nature: A Practical Guide to Discovering Your Place in the Cosmos, Wes Nisker (1998), Bantam Books, Page 120.

as discussed in the last chapter, it has a definite meaning. It means *sensation* or sense impression, not "feelings" the way we envision them. It means the basic way we experience impressions on the body or mind, before we build a "story" around them:

> "In the formula of 'Dependent Origination' (*paticca-samapudda*) by which the Buddha shows the conditioned 'arising of this whole mass of suffering', Sense Impression is said to be the principal condition of Feeling (*phassa-paccaya vedana*), while Feeling, on its part, is the potential condition of Craving, and subsequently, of, more intense, Clinging (*vedana-paccaya tanha, tanha-paccaya upadanam*)."[94]

Dependent Origination, which we will look at more closely later on, in one of its formulations shows the chain of events that lead from the arising of any phenomena to our (usually deluded) response to it. So sense impressions are important since they lead to more and more intense levels of attachment, which in turn leads to more suffering.

These feelings can be either pleasant, neutral, or painful, and can be internal or external. And to be mindful of them in this foundation, one notes just that and no more. For the Second Foundation of Mindfulness, one's job is not to respond to the feeling, but rather to recognize that it has arisen. Feeling in this sense is a critical area to which one should focus his or her attention, since it is the beginning of a conditioned reaction to those impressions. In fact, once Mindfulness of the body is established, the meditator will naturally begin to be aware of how he or she responds to the bodily feelings, and with Mindfulness of those they will be less likely to control his or her actions.

On the simplest level, the feelings will be simple responses to physical stimuli. For instance, if you're meditating and your knee starts to hurt, you note that your knee has a painful internal sensation – and that's it. For the Second Foundation of Mindfulness one is simply

---

94   <u>The Heart of Buddhist Meditation</u>, Nyanaponika Thera (1954), Weiser Publications, Pages 68-9

mindful of the sensation – if one has a response to it, like "I don't like this", one has moved past the Second Foundation and into the Third Foundation. For the sense-impression of the pain and the reaction to it are different. One can simply pay attention to the pain without an emotional response – to just watch the feeling in the knee without attaching any positive or negative response to it – or one can choose to "judge" the pain or fight it, in which case a whole new round of karmic cause and effect is initiated.

It is natural after meditating for a while to start to separate the bodily sensations from the responses we have to them. It is our choice how to respond to them. So we start to gain control over our feelings by seeing their causes, and by choosing whether to attach to them or simply acknowledge and identify them while realizing that they are not you or by seeing that, as my daughter Malia used to say, they are not "the boss of you".

And this same process occurs in our dealings with others. Buddhism doesn't suggest that we not have feelings, just that we know them when they arise, and not get attached to them as true in any way. If you're having an argument with your partner, girlfriend, or whoever else might be important in your life, feelings will arise. And they can either control the outcome of the communication, or be useful as one of the tools used to understand and transform conflict. If they arise without any Mindfulness on your or the other party's part that they are there, or of their nature, they will control and exacerbate the conflict. If, on the other hand, you see them for what they are – anger, hurt, resentment, or whatever – as they arise, they lose their power to control, and become simply factors in your interpersonal equation.

I recently had an argument about a seemingly minor issue with my girlfriend, which became heated. Actually, once the emotions (in this case, disappointment on one side and anger on the other) started to arise on both sides, they actually took over the communication, so that she and I were acting as *their* spokespersons. This went on for a while, during which time the thought "Gee, I'm acting out of anger" arose quite calmly in another part of my mind. My girlfriend (who also practices Mindfulness) was presumably going through a similar process, because at a certain point we both looked at each other and simultaneously burst out laughing. Not because the argument had been silly or meaningless, but because we both saw without saying so at about the same time how dramatic and amplified the conversation had become because of the emotions driving it, as opposed to the issues that underlay it.

In a Harvardian schema again, we had failed up to that point to separate the interests that we each had in furthering a loving, kind relationship, from the positions we had assumed, because we had failed to separate the feelings from the issues that generated them. But because feelings are entirely subjective and "self"-centered, until they are brought under the light of Mindfulness by both sides to the conflict, there is little hope of resolution, because they are running the show, sort of like the Wizard of Oz ran Dorothy's fate until he revealed himself from behind his curtain. Once that occurred, his power to control the situation evaporated, and he was just another Ozian with his own hopes, desires and fears. Similarly, the reason that the "conflict" between my girlfriend and me suddenly dissolved in laughter was because we both saw the feelings that were at play in the situation, saw how we had been whipsawed by them, and realized that they were no more "true" than the clouds in the sky.

The Third Foundation of Mindfulness is Mindfulness of the mind or mind-states. As originally formulated by the Buddha, the contemplation of the mind is by awareness of opposite states of mind, and knowing where one's present consciousness is within those opposites. The opposites are:

· mind with lust (or craving), and mind without lust
· mind with hate, and mind without hate
· mind with delusion and without delusion
· mind in a developed state, mind in an undeveloped state
· mind as surpassable, mind as unsurpassable
· the concentrated mind, and the unconcentrated mind
· the freed mind, and the unfreed mind

In addition to these "opposite" states of mind, there are two non-polar qualities of mind that one can focus "bare attention" on – the shrunken mind (one that is lazy or rigid, hesitant or slow, or unable to grow and change), and the distracted mind.[95] I'm sure the reader will be familiar with the distracted state of mind, because it is endemic in our harried modern life. And meditators know it well, since it makes it extremely difficult to do even so simple a thing as be mindful of the breath.

All of these states of mind can become transparent, like the feelings, if we simply observe them, and know them for what they are. And by seeing a state of mind for what it actually is – desire, revulsion, unfree, etc. – the mindful person can start to swing it from that state to its "positive" side, and thereby free himself from the yoke that the mind has snared him in.

Finally, there is the Fourth Foundation, the Mindfulness of "mind objects", which in the Buddha's discourses actually means Mindfulness of aspects of the Dharma that present themselves to the mind during meditation, and which are either to be overcome or sought by the monk (or worldling) in his or her practice. These are:

- *the five hindrances,* which are roadblocks that appear on the path to enlightenment, but which can be transformed into their own opposites. They are 1) sense desire; 2) anger; 3) sloth and torpor (laziness or aversion to following the chosen path); 4) agitation and worry; and 5) doubt (as to the value of the path or the Buddha's teachings).

- *The five aggregates of clinging,* which are the aspects of the life to which one would mistakenly impute some sort of permanence, and which were discussed in the previous chapter. These are 1) body or form; 2) feeling; 3) perception; 4) mental or volitional formations; and 5) consciousness. Each of these, in Mindfulness training, is seen ultimately to be impermanent, seen to arise, exist, and then pass away, therefore allowing one the freedom from attachment to it.

---

95   The Heart of Buddhist Meditation, Nyanaponika Thera (1954), Weiser Publications, Page 122, quoting from the Part III of the 22nd Text of the Long Discourses of the Buddha (Digha-Nikaya)

· *The six internal and external sense-bases*, which are the pathway through which stimuli reaches the mind, thus fettering the mind to perceptual reality. The six bases are: 1) the eyes (which know visible form); 2) the ears (which know sound); 3) the nose (which knows smells); 4) the tongue (which knows flavors); 5) the body (which knows touch); and 6) the mind (which knows the "objects" which arise therein). Again, through watching the arising, duration, and dissolution of each of these perceptions, the Mindfulness practitioner realizes that each is inherently impermanent, and therefore not something to which to become tethered.

· *The seven factors of enlightenment*, which are: 1) Mindfulness; 2) investigation of reality; 3) energy; 4) rapture; 5) tranquility; 6) concentration; and 7) Equanimity. These factors are also stages through which the Mindfulness practitioner will gradually progress as his or her practice deepens, and of which he or she should be "barely aware" as they arise.

· *The Four Noble Truths.* The truths of dukkha, trishna, nirvana, and the Noble Eightfold Path, which is the pathway to the extinction of suffering enunciated by the Buddha after his enlightenment.

It might appear, in looking at the Four foundations, that they are all distinct stages or parts of Mindfulness, separated by either time or experience into neat little compartments. That is not the case. They are all operating simultaneously, and each will present itself by arising (and then dissolving) at the appropriate times in your life. And all four will also present, at some time or other, during the simple act of meditating, as well as in other parts of your life.

Further, it might also seem that these classifications are of a different world, since they might appear to presume adherence to a religion/philosophy created by a spiritual genius some 2500 years ago. In the Buddha's time, *siddhus* (yogic renunciates) and *bikkhus* abounded, and it was an ordinary part of Indian society that people would renounce their mundane life and enter the wandering life of spiritual seeking. And it was not odd for yogis to concentrate or be mindful of parts of their bodies (even ones which would make us squeamish, like defecation), or of the decomposition of corpses. Perhaps, now, that seems strange, even in a world where we kill each other for advantage or political ideology, mass produce animals for execution and consumption, and have televised contests where people eat insects and live creatures for money. Every culture appears "normal" to itself, simply because its own norms and mores are the socially conditioned filter through which reality is viewed. Our rituals -- e-mails, mortgage payments, traffic jams, Judeo-Christianity – would be as odd to a bikkhu two millennia ago as his/hers are to us. But every culture is comprised of mortals seeking to understand their existential plight, and to deal with the problems and conflicts that make up that plight. And, really, all the four foundations – of body, feeling, mind, and mind object – exist at all times in all places, though perhaps in different cultural garb.

For example, you might be sitting down to do breathing meditation, but recognize that your mind is distracted. You're trying to keep your mind on your breathing, but there's a sense of *dis*ease and consternation in your chest, and a feeling of slightly increased heat around your face. Realizing that, for the moment at least, you're not able to keep focused on your breath, you start to examine the state of mental distraction itself. As you focus on the distraction, you notice that it has to do with something that happened yesterday, when you were passed over for a promotion at the office. You realize that you are angry about that, and feel animosity towards the boss who orchestrated the event. You also feel envy of the person who got promoted, and a craving for the respect and rewards that would have come with the promotion. There is some shame in having to tell your wife/partner that this has occurred, and some indignation that your true worth was not properly recognized in the situation.

On the other hand, you have other thoughts and feelings, as well as thoughts about feelings. You know, based upon your own experience, that the person who got the promotion, though not necessarily "better" than you, is a good person, one who will undertake her new responsibilities with integrity and energy. And – even though you feel some negative feelings about the person who "beat you out" – you know that she is just doing her best for her own career and family, and that her life is beset with all the same fragilities and sufferings as your own. And you know that spending your energy feeling resentment, anger, contempt, and shame is a bad path to follow, since it will only feed on itself and make you a smaller, more isolated person.

You may not be a bikkhu, but in that one sitting you actually have experienced all four of the foundations of Mindfulness referred to by the Buddha in the *Samyutta-Nikaya* quotation at the heading of this chapter. You have practiced Mindfulness of the body by concentrating (however successfully) on your breath. You have practiced Mindfulness of sense impression by noticing the actual feelings in your center and the facial heat, and by recognizing these as unpleasant and as "disturbances" of your normal bodily sensation. You have practiced Mindfulness of the mind by recognizing your inability to focus on your breath, and the disappointment, anger, frustration, resentment and shame that grew out of the physical responses to the promotion of your co-worker (for these are "unconcentrated mind", "mind with craving", "mind with anger", etc.). Finally, you have practiced Mindfulness of mind-objects, by recognizing that your responses to the event includes three of the five hindrances (can you determine which three?), and resolving to transform these hindrances by using Equanimity and Mindfulness (two of the seven Factors of Enlightenment) into Loving Kindness and Compassion, which are supreme virtues on the Noble Eightfold Path. So, while you may not be a "Buddhist", the simple fact of being "mindful" of the genesis and manifestations of any situation or conflict in your life has aspects of all four foundations of Mindfulness built right in.

A "Simple" Mindfulness Practice

As stated above, the simplest and most universally practiced type of Mindfulness practice is Mindfulness of the breath. You don't have to go to a monastery or class to get started, again due in part to the directness and simplicity of the practice. And what's so truly wonderful about this practice is that it is a gateway to all Four Foundations of Mindfulness, as shown by the example at the end of the previous section of this chapter.

You will want to be sitting upright to do this kind of meditation. Of course, the Buddhist texts don't mandate a sitting position, but as the nun Ayya Khema told one of her students who asked why she couldn't do the practice lying down, "(w)hen you wake up, you'll know why not!"[96] And the varieties of the sitting position are legion – some people sit in half or full lotus, some use meditation pillows or stools, some sit in chairs. Do whatever works for you – it's not necessarily more noble or better to choose a "spiritual" sitting position. As long as your back is vertical and more or less straight, you're fine.

Choose a quiet time and place if possible. Trying to meditate in a room with a TV on and other people talking is probably not a great idea. Early morning is good because the hustle and bustle of the day hasn't set in – early evening before dinner is also a popular time slot, since the metabolic slump of the mid-afternoon is on the rebound yet you're not so tired that it's time to go to sleep. Best not to meditate right after eating, because the digestive processes are distracting.

Once you've chosen your sitting position, the basics are simple – keep your eyes closed, and focus your attention on your breathing. Of course, "breathing" involves a lot of things. There's the entrance of the breath into, and exit of it from, your body through the nostrils. There's the filling and emptying of your lungs with air during the process. And there's the rise and fall of your stomach and abdomen during that same process.

---

96   When the Iron Eagle Flies Ayya Khema (1991), Wisdom Publications, Pages 115-6.

Probably the most common form of "breathing" Mindfulness concentrates on the rim of your nostrils as the air enters and leaves the body through the nose. So, with your eyes closed, sitting upright, you simply focus your attention on the contact of the air with the inner rim of your nostrils as you breath in and out. You don't control the breathing – in other words, you don't purposefully breath deeply or try to equalize the inward and outward breaths. One of the beauties of breathing is that you don't have to control it, since it's part of the autonomic nervous system not regulated by the conscious mind.

And that's it! You just sit with your eyes closed, and concentrate on your breathing for some predetermined length of time (Bhante Gunaratana suggests starting with 15 minutes in the morning, before you begin your day's activities). If you can, build up to thirty minutes twice a day, once early in the day, and once more before dinner or before going to sleep. Two sources with more detailed explanation of this type of meditation are included in the footnotes to this text.[97]

It sounds so simple. I mean, what could be easier? You just sit, and keep your mind easily focused on your breath. However, what you'll realize fairly quickly is that it's not really that easy, because of the powerful activities of the mind itself. The images of the mind from Hindu and Buddhist history and mythology are those of wild stallions attached to a chariot, pulling it in separate directions all at once, or a pack of wild monkeys. Put in modern psychotherapeutic language:

> "The path of mindfulness is the path of the eternal Now. All that exists is this present moment – right here, right now. But the ego lives in the past and future, spinning out fantasies and inhabiting a kind of virtual reality that is more akin to dreaming or being half asleep. Because of gross desires for things, people, sensory pleasure, and avoidance of pain,

---

97   The Heart of Buddhist Meditation, Nyanaponika Thera (1954), Weiser Publications and Mindfulness in Plain English, Bhante Henepola Gunaratana, (2002) Wisdom Publications, are both excellent "hands-on" guides to this type of Mindfulness practice.

consciousness becomes dull, tied to the fixed groove of sleepwalking". [98]

Or, in Buddhist lingo, we could simply say that the mind *attaches* to things, and goes on little voyages of its own volition while you're trying to do the simple activity of watching your breath.

So, almost immediately after you sit down to watch your breath, your mind will start taking these excursions. Your job is not to prevent that, but simply to watch it and note what occurs without judgment or self-criticism, and then bring the attention back to the breath as soon as you comfortably can. In the example above of the meditator who went through various kinds of Mindfulness about being passed over for a promotion, these mental and emotional gyrations occurred within the confines of a single meditation session. The fact that they occurred was neither "good" nor "bad" – it simply was. The meditator's "job" was to watch their arising and ebbing away, and to note without judgment the nature of the mental phenomena as they occurred.

As one practices this Mindfulness, through time, many changes will start to manifest. First, the level of extraneous activity in the mind will tend to decrease (though it may increase periodically during transition periods in your life), leading to a greater calmness and awareness both during the meditation sessions as well as in the rest of your life. Second, you will become aware of how your mind works – what things rile it, what things sooth it, what your concerns are, and the nature of your feelings about the various people and events in your life. Third, the events that take place around you in your life will become clearer and more transparent, because you will no longer be projecting as much of the contents of your psyche onto them – you will see them as they are, not as-they-are-with-you-added-in. Finally, and perhaps most importantly, you will learn that there is an infinite expanse or ground that exists around and between the breaths, from which ground the "seven factors of enlightenment" can take root and grow.

---

98   Integral Psychology, Brant Cortright (2007) State Univ. of New York Press, Page 111.

The obstacles to following this "simple" method of Mindfulness are widespread and common. And, because they are prevalent, there are antidotes for them.

First there is *doubt* (one of the five hindrances mentioned in the Fourth Foundation of Mindfulness). Quite simply, you might say to yourself -- "This is stupid and a waste of time! With all the things I've got going in my life, why am I sitting here trying to watch my breath?" The response to this is that you need to have some faith in the process, and give it time to see if it adds value to your life. Many great transformers and scholars of human consciousness – the Buddha, Gurdjieff, countless Zen masters, Gestalt therapists –have known Mindfulness practices to be of great psychological and spiritual benefit to their practitioners. So give it a chance, and see if it works for you.

Then there are *agitation* or *worry* (another of the five hindrances). Sometimes it's very difficult to stay focused on the breath when there are a great number of other, real-world concerns swirling about in your life. But if you can stay mindful of what the agitation and worries are, you can perhaps see them in a clearer light. If the agitation takes your mind off your breathing during meditation, try counting your breaths from 1 to 10 and back to 1, then 1 to nine and back to 1, and so on until you get back to just one. If you're so agitated that for the entire meditation session you can't get back to watching your breath, then let Mindfulness of the agitation be your practice – be a "witness" to it, and watch it dispassionately.

Then, here's *sloth* or *laziness* (another hindrance), the feeling that, well, you're just not in the mood to meditate right now! Whatever you do, don't guilt trip yourself about it! It's normal and natural, so just watch it, be mindful of what it feels like, and then when you're ready, get back to your meditation schedule. Your life and spiritual development are not a contest or a chance for you to berate yourself for lack of perfect desire. It's the trajectory of your life that's important, not the need to have the directions you choose be without short detours and lapses.

Finally, you might find that breathing meditation just doesn't suit you, period. But there are lots and lots of different types of Mindfulness practice to choose from – walking meditation, mantra meditation (such as Transcendental Meditation), visualization meditation, etc. – and any one of them might be the right one for you. So if the simple breath meditation isn't your cup of tea, do a bit of research and find some way to learn another way, or, better yet, find someone to teach you.

Mindfulness in Your Own Conflicts

In your life, there are many types of conflict that affect you personally. Primarily, there are your internal conflicts, and those with the people around you.

A few years ago, when I went to the first day of a class with Robert O'Donnell at Pepperdine, he began by pointing out to us that we are in a continual conversation with ourselves, and that we ought to look at that conversation to see how we've been treating ourselves. I hadn't really ever thought of it in that way before, since the cacophony of internal monkeys I had been carrying around in my head had always seemed normal to me.

In the days that followed, I started to listen or "watch" that internal dialogue. At the time, I was not practicing Buddhist Mindfulness, but the nature of what I did was the same. I simply stood aside as a witness, and watched my internal dialogue. It was an odd dialogue, with one "side" telling the other that what it was doing was wrong, or perhaps should have been done better, etc., and the other remonstrating with excuses or rationalizations.

Ultimately, I saw that I had two sides inside me having a discussion, and that, indeed, they were not very nice to each other. In fact, they were highly critical of, or defensive towards, each other. And I resolved to have them learn to talk to each other with less judgment, and with more love towards each other. And that is, in fact, what I have done since then, so that the war between the "sides" has been to a significant degree set aside, and my internal voice has become more often one voice instead of two.

Mindfulness training operates similarly with respect to our inner dialogues and treatment of ourselves. The contours and nature of our conversations with and treatment of ourselves becomes transparent, and thus the hidden players in that conversation are, like the Wizard of Oz, revealed from behind their curtains of mystery.

There are schools of thought that think that Mindfulness is not really the right methodology for dealings with our inner conflicts. They note that while Mindfulness can be useful for illuminating ordinary "neurotic" conflict, it is not a valid tool for dealing with more virulent forms of personality disorder, for which long-term psychotherapy or drug therapy is indicated. Second, they believe that Mindfulness' focus on the mind rather than feeling makes it an "incomplete" way to resolve entrenched internal conflict.[99]

Since I'm not a therapist, I am perhaps not in a proper position to disagree. I have had to deal with people in family, work, and mediation settings whose internal conflicts, as they presented themselves in the disputes, seemed deeper and more resistant to transparency than those of the other participants, suggesting that the conflicts were of such complexity that they were not amenable to self-correction (although I have seen some of these resolve, at least temporarily, within those same situations). Ultimately, perhaps, if the person in the conflict is psychotic or has a severe personality disorder, Mindfulness may be irrelevant.

The argument on the lack of emotion is less compelling. For most of us, thoughts and defenses cover our emotional responses to situations. Yet it is only to the extent that we are too attached to and ignorant of these cover-ups that we are out of touch with our emotions. Indeed, the second and third Foundations of Mindfulness as elucidated by the Buddha (Mindfulness of feelings and of the mind) deal with how our minds and emotions respond to and distort our being-in-the-world so as to separate us from Original Mind and a truer understanding of the nature of reality.

---

99   Integral Psychology, Brant Cortright (2007) State Univ. of New York Press, Page 123.

The process of Mindfulness, in fact, mirrors on an internal level the very way that the therapeutic process, or at least the first part of it, works. In therapeutic situations, of whatever persuasion, the first job is to illuminate what has been outside of the awareness of the patient, "making the unconscious conscious" in Freud's words. In most types of therapy, this is done face-to-face with the therapist, who will perhaps comment upon and guide the patient toward further exploration of the revealed patterns. Emotions reveal as part of that process, but only usually as the patterns begin to unravel.

But that's just what Mindfulness does as well! As one sits, and once again watches the mind spin away from the object of the practice (watching the breath, etc.), one begins to see the patterns that repeat in taking us away from our focus. One becomes aware of the physical and mental components of the patterns and, as they are allowed to exist without judgment or attempts to modify them, the emotions that underlay them reveal as well.

For example, I recently had an argument with a very close friend, which became heated, and resulted in us parting ways and not talking to each other for several days. I practiced Mindfulness during the separation – the normal routine of one-half hour each morning. Because of the intensity of the argument I had had with my friend, my mind kept drifting during the practice to parts of the argument, to the feelings of anger and frustration I had had, to resentment for my friend not "seeing" things properly, and so on. Each time it drifted to such thoughts or feelings, I would let it "play out" for a while, and would then bring it gently back to a focus on the breath.

After three or four days of this, something quite different arose in me, not so much during the meditation sessions at first, but rather in my innards as I went through my day. It wasn't a thought, or justification, or anything of that sort – it was a very clear and deep feeling of sorrow or sadness. This sorrow then became a part of my meditations, since I was feeling it clearly throughout, as the anger and frustration I had originally felt fell away. As I mindfully allowed the sadness to arise (and fall away) during these meditations, I understood that it felt similar to sadnesses I had felt earlier in my life, and that the anger and frustration here, as in those earlier situations, were defenses I used to cover up the hurt that I felt.

So, to this point, the Mindfulness process had worked very much as the therapeutic process would have. First, an issue of discomfort or dis-ease was raised to the level of consciousness. Then, it was allowed to express itself without editorial or moralistic intervention until it revealed its emotional basis, which in turn showed itself to "echo" events from the past. In other words, the present situation was seen to have reawoken "core" wounds from the past. But really, the process for any psychotherapeutic healing would have been the same:

> "Therapists of different orientations stress parts of this wounding proper to their own school, for example a classical Freudian will emphasize the loss of instinctual energies, a Jungian will emphasize the loss of imaginal capacities...But in all this the path of healing leads through two phases – the structural/relational and the somatic – before the psychological transformation culminates in the emergence of the authentic self". [100]

The Mindfulness process, then, has led through the first two phases, by allowing the structural and relational issues present in the conflict to emerge, and then revealing the underlying emotional (somatic) pain that elucidates the core wound being revisited.

The final phase is also the same in resolving our inner conflicts as it is in therapy – that is, the emergence of the authentic self (or in Buddhist terminology, a person who is neither deluded nor fettered by clinging). If I speak as one voice internally, then I am likely speaking with an authentic voice, having quelled the inauthentic ones. In my interpersonal conflicts, such as that with my friend, the second phase would appear to be somewhat different, at least at first blush. For in the resolution of conflict, the goal of this phase is to resolve or reconcile the conflict, and ostensibly not to "out" the authentic self.

---

100 Integral Psychology, Brant Cortright (2007) State Univ. of New York Press, Page 69.

But – are they really different? In my argument with my friend, that resolution occurred when we talked again. In that conversation, I told her that I had spent a great deal of time upset and angry at her because of the argument, but that those feelings had gradually morphed into sadness, which made me realize that, underneath our surface differences, I loved and cared for her.

That was my authentic self, at least in that moment and in that situation. The authentic self (which is not to be confused with the self that Buddhism says we don't have, but which is the peculiar "flavor" or "perfume" that each of us constructs throughout of our five aggregates in this lifetime) is continually being revised and reinvented, through the presence and integrity we bring to each situation and relationship in our lives. Since it is relational and continually in process, there is no static ground where we can say "there, now, I've found and captured my authentic self!" Authenticity from this perspective is the lifelong process of learning who we are, and how that person can express fully and honestly in all of our relations – both with ourselves internally, and with the others in our lives. So to the extent that we can resolve our conflicts honest as to our internal process, and with openness and candor towards those others, we are as authentic as can be hoped for. And that is just what the process of Mindfulness opens for us as an increased possibility.

Creating "Inter-Mindfulness"

Of course, when we work with our own internal conflicts, we decide to become mindful, and then can on some level "control" the process, which works as a sort of inner purge of all the things that cover our Original Mind. That process unfolds within us, as part of a very intimate internal dialogue. All sorts of things come up, become transparent in their impermanence or irrelevance, and then dissolve.

But when the conflict involves more than one person, that "internal-ness" and self-control of the process is gone – for now the mind that must be freed of its prejudices and misconceptions is a group mind. But that doesn't mean the process is really different – there is still the need to let what needs to arise to arise, to see through its lack of any inherent reality, and to get to the empty space beneath it. The difference is it will have to be done out loud or visibly, rather than in the mind of the individual. But it will still have the effect of reducing everyone's attachment to their own deluded perspective.

The ways to do this are legion. Here are just some of them:

a) you can agree to allow each person to say their perspective on the conflict, and the other or others agree to listen without responding for a certain period of time. After that, the other person will state not what his or her reply to the story is, but what he or she thinks they heard in it. Then it becomes the other person's turn. In order to do this successfully, it's best if each speaker agrees to talk about his/her feelings rather than what the other person did, and talk about what he or she would like to see occur rather than what the other needs to do;

b) you can agree that each person in the conflict will draw a picture of how they see the conflict, and then explain that picture to the others. Because it will tend to be visual rather than verbal, it is less likely to be seen as an attack by the other or others as an attack, and thus will create a shared perspective on the conflict rather than opposing views; or

c) you can have each person write a three-part story, with the first part being their version of the conflict, the second being what they think the conflict is from the other person's perspective, and the third being what a shared reconciliatory version of the story would be.[101]

In any event, use techniques that do not attack the listener, but allow them to see the other parts or views of the conflict they have not yet considered. It is in this way that "inter-Mindfulness" – that is, a shared Mindfulness of what is actually occurring – is fostered.

---

101 This technique was taught to me in class at Pepperdine by Kenneth Cloke.

Mindfulness in working with "Other Peoples' Conflicts"

In the 1980's, there was lots of talk, and even a feature movie, about "other peoples' money", the idea being that it was not only potentially lucrative but also much less risky to one's own well-being to work with such funds. Acting as a mediator or other neutral in other peoples' conflicts is similar, since there is less likely to be any damaging emotional involvement on the part of the mediator in the structure and outcome of the conflict.

Our own conflicts have an emotional charge that is usually and hopefully lacking for the mediator. That's because none of the mediator's Three Poisons have yet been activated. So, even when the communication between two persons about an issue upon which they disagree has become Poisoned, the relationship of a third person to their conflict will usually not be.

For example, you and I might sit down at a café to discuss America's foreign policy, and disagree about our right to militarily intervene in other countries. To the extent that the discussion remains emotionally neutral, even if we disagree, there is no conflict – there is merely debate.

If however, either of us gets emotionally involved, the debate will likely turn into conflict. From a Buddhist perspective, conflict would now exist because one or more of the Three Poisons have arisen, and will need to be quelled. An integral psychologist might point out, the conversation which had been originally conducted on the mental level will now be conducted on the central (relational) and lower (instinctual) emotional level. While the central emotional level will be primarily concerned with the relationship to the other, as seen through the filter of the totality of our past interpersonal and subjective experiences, the instinctual level is much more volatile, a level at which the question "can I eat it, mate with it, or kill it?"[102] comes into play. It's the engagement of the lower emotional level in the communication that brings it to the level of conflict, and

---

102 Integral Psychology, Brant Cortright (2007) State Univ. of New York Press, Page 16.

confounds us in the process. It's the reason that I, a normally rational and compassionate person, am suddenly getting angry and "hot under the collar" and why if I'm truly honest with myself I might acknowledge that in some dim part of my consciousness my friend's disagreement with me makes me wish him personal or bodily harm. I'm not necessarily a psychopath or bad person – that's just the way humans work.

But let's say that just now, a mutual friend approaches our table, and notices that we are both looking agitated and angry with one another. He sits down and asks us what the problem is, and we each heatedly explain our beliefs about American foreign policy to him.

If our friend decides to buy into either side – in other words, if he weighs in favor of or against interventionism by the US military – then he will be drawn into the conflict, because he will start to develop his own mix of the Three Poisons, and will be mixed into the Poisons of the side he favors to boot. If, on the other hand, he decides to stay out of the actual debate and instead focus his skills and attention on helping his two friends heal their relational rift by having them acknowledge the bodily sensations they've experiencing and feelings about each other during the confrontation, and their perceptions of how these feelings have aggravated the debate to a new and more aggressive level, then he will not become part of the conflict but, rather, make a stand for the end of it.

And that's one of the beauties of mediation – that the mediator, who is in a triangulated relationship with the disputants, is not instinctually or emotionally involved with the fruits or results of the conflict. Instead, the mediator can act with Mindfulness to help those who are instinctually charged by the dispute see what they are actually doing, and thereby assist in the process of defusing the conflict.

Mindfulness is a very powerful tool for mediators, because it allows the mediator to separate from two types of attachment that hinder the effective resolution of conflicts – the attachment to our own assumptions (or prejudices) about the participants in the process, and attachment to the "results" of the process.

The first type of attachment is quite insidious, since mediators by and large feel that they are neutral, and compassionate, and fair. I mean – why else would they be called to the task of helping others resolve their conflicts? And because the calling is noble, it is easy to fall into the belief that one's own character and perceptions are noble as well.

But judgment and discrimination are endemic and universal in the human condition, so the job of the mediator is not so much not to have them as it is to recognize and compensate for them. While the ultimate goal might be to not judge at all ("Judge not, lest ye be judged"), a more attainable goal is to see your judgments as they arise, see them for what they are, and let them float away like clouds in the sky.

I recently attended a Buddhist week-long meditation retreat which, like most such events, is conducted in silence. So for a week, I and fifty other people lived, ate, meditated, and did work meditation together. Even though I had never spoken to any of the other participants prior to the retreat, as the week went on, I noticed that I began to form judgments about the others – that one seems a bit "aggressive" in his demeanor, that one eats funny, that one appears overly unctuous in his attentiveness to the teacher, that one seems "nice" and "friendly", etc. Of course, when the retreat ended and we all got to talk while cleaning up the retreat grounds, each of these other people was revealed to be not at all as I had judged them. But the more important lesson to me in the process was seeing that the judgmental faculty – the innate, automatic process of classifying people into slots based upon their acceptability or lack thereof – is ongoing, and the Mindfulness process we practiced there was actually a useful tool to both see and contain those judgments.

Mindfulness works similarly for mediators. No matter how noble or well-meaning our intentions are as mediators, we are human, and our judgmental facilities will kick into gear in every mediation. If I enter a mediation with four participants, I will not see them each as an equal participant, but will instead feel resonance or dissonance with each individual to differing degrees. As Leonard Riskin notes, "…it seems reasonable to suspect that Mindfulness could help negotiators be more aware of certain deep assumptions, including those based on ethnicity or culture, and of psychological processes that can interfere with wise decision making, such as reactive devaluation, optimistic overconfidence, risk aversion, and anchoring."[103]

In addition to helping mediators see these prejudices, Mindfulness allows the mediator to insert what Riskin calls a "wedge of awareness" between the arising of the prejudice and the undertaking of any act that would follow from it, thus allowing for a more truly "neutral" role in the resolution of the conflict.

Mindfulness also allows the insertion of a wedge of awareness between one's "take" on how a conflict should resolve and one's actions during the mediation – in other word, it allows us to forego attachment to the results of the mediation, thereby giving us the freedom to allow the situations to resolve as they truly ought, as opposed to how we think they should.

One mediation – the Hateful Neighbor mediation -- I conducted clearly shows how the lack of Mindfulness can get in the way of allowing resolution. Several years ago – before I started practicing Mindfulness – I conducted a mediation between two co-owners of a two-unit residence in San Francisco. They had been at odds with each other since the day they each moved into their respective units, and I undertook to help them resolve their conflict.

The conflict had many parts, ranging from small items like where each would keep their garbage cans on the property, to more major ones, like the desire of one owner to build a deck off his rear bedroom which would cut most of the sunlight out of his downstairs neighbor's bedroom.

And I was quite attached to the idea that the proper resolution to the situation was to resolve all the sub-issues between the parties (of which there were about 46, if I recall correctly), and have them continue to co-exist in the building in harmonious friendship. And

---

103 <u>Mindfulness: Foundational Training for Dispute Resolution</u>, Leonard L. Riskin, Journal of Legal Education, Volume 54, Number 1 (March 2004).

for three days I worked diligently towards that goal (to which I was attached), resolving 45 of the issues, leaving only the deck issue, which I had saved until last so as to let them get used to agreeing on issues in general.

The last issue proved to be very obstinate, despite my efforts to have the parties redesign or reconfigure the deck, move the deck, forego the deck, and so on. Finally, the downstairs owner (who had been silent for quite a while at that point) turned to his neighbor and said, "you know, I hate you and always have, and would rather live in hell than let you have any kind of deck anywhere on our property. What I really want is to get as far away from you as possible, so please buy out my interest in the property."

Which is, in fact, what happened shortly thereafter -- the downstairs neighbor sold his interest to his upstairs neighbor. At the time, I was quite disturbed that I had somehow failed as a mediator, since the conflict had not in my mind been resolved through my efforts. Yet, as I thought about it more, I realized that the conflict had indeed been resolved – the parties are no longer in conflict, and the situation resolved as they ultimately decided. The downstairs neighbor moved back east and bought a house for he and his family, and the upstairs neighbor built himself a gorgeous deck before finding a new co-owner for the lower, now-darker unit.

What had really occurred was that I, as a mediator, had gotten attached to a concept of how the situation should resolve, which made me blind to the possibilities that actually existed in the situation. Yet had I been mindful of the process at the time, I could have seen my attachment for what it really was – an attachment, a preconception – and inserted a wedge of awareness between that arising and any attempt on my part to implement it.

So the practice of Mindfulness helps us in all three types of conflict. It helps us learn to recognize the inner voices that form the conflicted internal dialogue we have with ourselves. In our relationships with others, it helps us see and experience the actual nature of our behavior, and the feelings that underlie the events that transpire between us, thereby freeing us from the knee-jerk reactions that our immediate responses might otherwise lead us to follow. And in working with the conflicts of others, it helps us avoid attachment to our own inner prejudices, and to the results we might conjure up as "right" for those conflicts.

But there is another, overarching effect of Mindfulness, without which Mindfulness is somehow incomplete. For Mindfulness is ultimately the gateway to Compassion. Compassion completes Mindfulness, and it is compassionate Mindfulness that most effectively resolves conflict.

6. LOVING KINDNESS
AND COMPASSION

If we can see our own mistakes, and neither dislike them nor hate ourselves for
them, but simply see them and accept them, we may then resolve to change...
By accepting the difficulties in ourselves and seeing them clearly, we have the
beginning of an understanding of others. Other people have similar difficulties
– often identical ones. This is one of the great advantages and a unique factor
in the Buddha's teachings: he showed us that we are all made of the same
ingredients; we all have the same dukkha and we are all yearning for relief.[104]

Years ago, when I first heard about Buddhist (in that case, Zen)
practices, they seemed to me quite selfish (the judgment faculty at
work). As far as I could tell, people just zoned out through meditation,
and used it as a mask for their desire to be uninvolved with and
unconcerned about others. When I then learned that a most basic
tenet of the teaching was that life is suffering, I became even more
suspect of the whole practice, since it now seemed not only self-
centered but dismal as well.

Learning more later, my perceptions started to shift. I learned that
the Buddha – and the many Bodhisattvas who followed – intentionally

---

104 <u>When the Iron Eagle Flies</u> Ayya Khema (1991), Wisdom Publications,
    Pages 33-34.

put off their final nirvana and resolve rather to stay in this world and work for the relief of suffering for all sentient creatures. And I learned that Loving Kindness and Compassion for others are indeed the most noble virtues to which the Buddhist can obtain, along with Appreciative Joy and Equanimity. And it is toward these four virtues or "Sublime Abodes" that Mindfulness leads. It does this quite naturally, since love and Compassion are natural in a mindful state.

In fact, Buddhism is not selfish, but as an inner-to-outer study necessitates that the self (whatever that word is meant to describe) be understood and mastered in order to be in proper relationship with the other people in one's world. As Bhante Gunaratana says: "(t)he ultimate goal of our practice of meditation is the cultivation of these four sublime states of loving friendliness, compassion, appreciative joy, and equanimity".[105]

These four virtues can be divided into two sections, with one section (Equanimity or *upekkha*) being concerned with the nature of the individual, while the other section of three Virtues has to do with the way the seeker deals with or feels about himself and others. And each of these three – *metta* or Loving Kindness, *karuna* or Compassion, and *mudita* or Appreciative Joy – is the precursor of the next in order (as all three are together the precursor of Equanimity), for *metta* forms the basis from which Compassion develops, and Compassion forms the basis out of which Appreciative Joy is fashioned. *Metta* is the ability to love without requiring anything, and *karuna* is the ability through that love to understand and feel the suffering of another. *Mudita* is the ability to exult in the benefits and blessings that have accrued to another.

Metta (in Pali, or *maitri* in Sanskrit) is not the same as our western concept of love, which has often to do with attachment to another, and with an expectation that it will be in some form returned to us. This is not to say that such love is good or bad – just that it is not the kind of love that *metta* implies:

---

105 <u>Mindfulness in Plain English</u>, Bhante Henepola Gunaratana, (2002)
      Wisdom Publications, Page 181.

"Metta is a quality of our own heart...When we talk about metta in the Buddha's way, we are thinking of a warm and kind feeling towards others. It is not a matter of judging others – whether they are worthy of love, or willing to love us back, or become our friends and supporters, or even whether they want our love. It is strictly a matter of clearing out our negative reactions, which are often based on negative facts."[106]

In fact, Loving Kindness is intended by the Buddha to transcend transgressions against one by others, thus clearing out any negative reactions to those transgressions. In one of Buddha's discourses to his monks, he gave them the "Simile of the Saw", as follows:

"Monks, even if bandits were to sever you savagely limb by limb with a two-handled saw, he who gave rise to a mind of hate toward them would not be carrying out my teaching. Herein, monks, you should train thus: 'Our minds will remain unaffected, and we shall utter no bitter words; we shall abide compassionate for their welfare, with a mind of loving-kindness, never in a mood of hate. We shall abide pervading them with a mind imbued with Loving Kindness; and, starting with them, we shall abide pervading the all-encompassing world with a mind imbued with Loving Kindness, abundant, exalted, immeasurable, without hostility, and without ill-will.' That is how you should train, monks."

"Monks, if you keep this advice on the simile of the saw constantly in mind, do you see any course of speech, trivial or gross, that you could not endure?" – "No, venerable sir." "Therefore, monks, you should keep this advice on the simile of the saw constantly in mind. That will lead to your welfare and happiness for a long time."[107]

---

106 When the Iron Eagle Flies Ayya Khema (1991), Wisdom Publications, Pages 32-33.

107 In the Buddha's Words, edited by Bikkhu Bodhi (2005), Wisdom Publications, Pages 278-9, quoting from Majjhima Nikaya 21: Kakacupama Sutta; I 126-27, 129.

Which is similar to the words of Jesus in the Sermon on the Mount when he said to the multitudes:

> "Ye have heard that it hath been said, Thou shalt love thy neighbor, and hate thine enemy. But I say unto you, Love your enemies, bless them that curse you, do good to them that that hate you, and pray for them which despitefully use you, and persecute you..."[108]

As shown by the quote at the beginning of this chapter, Loving Kindness starts through mindfully becoming aware of our own selves, and learning to have a non-judgmental acceptance of who we are, and of the feelings and thoughts and actions we experience. "If we don't begin with ourselves, we have no way of actually, truly loving others".[109] Not that we will not grow and change and strive to become deeper, better people – just that the starting point for growth and change will be acceptance of ourselves, not judgment.

And as our non-judgmental love and kindness towards ourselves grows, it will of its own begin to spread in concentric circles to include others. Certainly it will include those for whom we have more readily recognizable attachments – lovers and families, co-workers and neighbors – but also those who are not so recognizable. So the person who cuts you off in traffic, or stands next to you at the grocery store, will soon be enveloped in your Loving Kindness. Finally, even the people like the bandits in the Simile of the Saw will be included, so that there are no people towards whom you feel no Loving Kindness.

Practices for the Development of Loving Kindness and Compassion

The question then is of course *how* to develop Loving Kindness in your life in sort of a general, abstract way, and also how to develop

---

108 King James Bible, World Publishing Company, St. Matthew 5:39.
109 When the Iron Eagle Flies Ayya Khema (1991), Wisdom Publications, Page 34.

it in the situations in which you are involved. The Buddha himself gave some reflections and meditations to his followers to help them develop Loving Kindness, such as the following "Discourse on Good Will":

> *May all beings be filled with joy and peace*
> *May all beings everywhere –*
> *The great and the ordinary*
> *The powerful and the oppressed*
> *The mean and the generous*
> *The healthy and the sick*
> *The old and the young*
>
> *May all beings everywhere –*
> *Seen and unseen*
> *Dwelling far off or nearby*
> *Being, dying, or waiting to become –*
> *May all be filled with lasting joy.*
>
> *Let no one deceive another,*
> *Let no one anywhere despise one another,*
> *Let no one out of anger or resentment*
> *Wish suffering on anyone at all.[110]*

To benefit from this reflection by the Buddha, one can simply stand or sit, and recite the reflection out loud, facing each of the four directions in turn. In fact, the Discourse continues:

> *"Just as a mother protects her child from harm,*
> *So within yourself let grow*
> *A boundless love for all beings.*
> *Let your love flow outward through the universe,*
> *In every direction –*
> *A limitless love, without enmity or hatred.*

---

110 The *"Discourse on Good Will"* from the <u>Sutta Nipata</u>, in a translation presented to a Thanksgiving meditation retreat at Spirit Rock Meditation Center.

> *If you strive for this wholeheartedly*
> *As long as you are awake – whether*
> *Standing, sitting, walking or lying down –*
> *Your life will be a blessing to the world."*

So the development of Loving Kindness is an active, rather than a passive, practice. In the Simile of the Saw, the Buddha exhorted his *bikkhus* to "pervade" the four directions with Loving Kindness. In the Discourse on Kindness he says the same thing – to have you love flow out in very direction, and to devote your mind to the development of it in all of your activities.

It is common for Buddhist authors and teachers to also offer variants of this "pervasion" process in their writings and teachings. A fairly common format provided by many Buddhist teachers and authors is to recite a mantra of Loving Kindness, applying it first to oneself, and then to those with whom one is closest, and then to increasingly remote degrees of persons. Bhante Gunaratana provides an example of such a meditation:

> *May I be well, happy and peaceful. May no harm come to me. May no difficulties come to me. May no problems come to me. May I always meet with success. May I also have patience, courage, understanding, and determination to meet and overcome inevitable difficulties, problems and failures in life.*[111]

The first round of this is directed at the "me". Next come parents, then teachers, relatives, friends, all persons, enemies, and finally all living beings. So the meditation allows one to start with the self and those who are already likely to kindle feelings of Loving Kindness, and then to spread those feelings to those who one would ordinarily not have such feelings for, even to such as one's enemies.

---

111 <u>Mindfulness in Plain English</u>, Bhante Henepola Gunaratana, (2002) Wisdom Publications, Page 91.

Ayya Khema provides a different structure for a similar set of exercises involving a contemplation followed by three guided meditations, which actually encompass three of the Four Sublime States – Loving Kindness, Compassion, and Appreciative Joy – while fostering the development of the fourth (Equanimity or Tranquility, which is developed to some extent whenever one practices these types of exercises).

In the contemplation, one concentrates on his breath for a few minutes, and then recites either silently or out loud:

> *"May I be free from enmity.*
> *May I be free from hurtfulness.*
> *May I be free from troubles of mind and body.*
> *May I be able to protect my own happiness.*
> *Whatever beings there are, may they be free from enmity.*
> *Whatever beings there are, may they be free from hurtfulness.*
> *Whatever beings there are, may they be free from troubles of mind and body.*
> *Whatever beings there are, may they be able to protect their own happiness."*[112]

So again, one starts by beseeching one's own happiness, followed by wishing the same for others. The meditator has now done an exercise to create and foster Loving Kindness.

Khema then proceeds to the first guided meditation, wherein after allowing the breath to settle, one opens to feeling Compassion in one's heart for one's own *dukkha* or suffering, whether past, present or future. Then one extends this feeling of Compassion to those physically proximate to one, to one's parents, to those emotionally close to you, to those with whom you have difficulties, and finally to those whose lives are more difficult than one's own. End this meditation by reciting to yourself "May all beings have Compassion for each other".

---

112 <u>When the Iron Eagle Flies</u> Ayya Khema (1991), Wisdom Publications, Pages 41-2.

Thereby, the meditator has now performed a meditative exercise for the development of Compassion.

In the second guided meditation, after allowing the breath to settle, one opens to feeling joy in one's own achievements and opportunities, and for the chance to be on a path that allows truth and wisdom to develop. Then one extends this feeling to those physically proximate to one, to one's parents, to those emotionally close to you, to your friends, to those with whom you have difficulties, and to as large a group of beings as you can imagine, before coming back once again to acknowledge your own joy. End this meditation by reciting to yourself "May all beings have joy in their hearts". Through this exercise, the meditator has developed Appreciative Joy – that is, an abiding and non-grasping joy in both what one has been given, and in the blessings bestowed on and/or earned by others.

In the third and final guided meditation, after again allowing the breath to settle, one imagines a beautiful white lotus flower opening in one's heart, from the center of which "comes a golden stream of light which fills you from head to toe with warmth and light and a feeling of contentment, and surrounds you with a feeling of lovingness and well-being"[113]. This golden light is allowed to expand outward, touching first those close to one physically, then your loved ones and family, then everyone in your work and home worlds, then those with whom you have difficulties, finally returning to yourself alone, where the white lotus will close and envelop the white light within. End this meditation by reciting to yourself "May all beings be happy".

Another form of meditation for the development of Loving Kindness and Compassion is the Tibetan practice of *tonglen* (which means "giving and taking" or "sending and taking"), which was developed by the Indian Buddhist teacher Atisha Dipankara Shrijnana in the 10th century AD (who went on to become one of the great influences on the development of Buddhism in Tibet, where he died), and later revived by the nineteenth-century Tibetan teacher Jamgon

---

113 <u>When the Iron Eagle Flies</u> Ayya Khema (1991), Wisdom Publications, Page 46.

Kongtrul, and more recently again popularized in the West by the Dalai Lama and Pema Chodron. *Tonglen* is a meditation technique that works with both universal suffering and individualized suffering.

At its most basic level, *tonglen* is the taking into oneself of all the world's suffering, and the giving back of Loving Kindness and Compassion. Osho describes this basic practice thus in his book on Atisha's methods:

> "Now he (Atisha) says: start being compassionate. And the method is, when you breathe in – listen carefully, it is one of the greatest methods – when you breathe in, think that you are breathing in all the miseries of all the people in the world. All the darkness, all the negativity, all the hell that exists anywhere, you are breathing it in.. And let it be absorbed into your heart…when you breathe in, breathe in all the misery and suffering of all the beings of the world – past, present and future. And when you breathe out, breathe out all the joy you have, all the blissfulness that you have, all the benediction that you have. Breathe out, pour yourself into existence. This is the method of compassion: drink in all the suffering and pour out all the blessings…And you will be surprised if you do it. The moment you take all the sufferings of the world inside you, they are no longer sufferings. The heart immediately transforms the energy. The heart is a transforming force: drink in misery, and it is transformed into blissfulness… then pour it out…Once you have learned that your heart can do this magic, this miracle, you would like to do it again and again. Try it. It is one of the most practical methods – simple, and it brings immediate results. Do it today, and see.[114]

The full-scale practice of *tonglen* has four parts, which Pema Chodron schematizes thusly:

---

114 The Book of Wisdom : Discourses on Atisha`s Seven Points of Mind Training, (2005) Osho, Tao Publishing, http://lojongmindtraining.com/Commentary.aspx?author=1&proverb=7

1) A flashing openness of *bodhicitta* (the wish to move towards enlightenment for the benefit of all sentient beings), where you direct yourself towards enlightenment and Compassion in the particular situation;

2) Working with the texture, breathing in dark, heavy, and hot, and breathing out white, light and cool (this is the part referred to by Osho in the quote above, which others call the "archetypal" aspect of *tonglen*);

3) Working with relieving a specific, heartfelt instance of suffering – the "personal" phase;

4) Extending that wish to help everyone, in the "universal" stage.[115]

Chodron states that *tonglen* must deal with both the personalized and the universal to be fully effective (being too theoretical without the personal, and too limited without the universal).

While it may at first blush appear a bit complicated, *tonglen* provides a good, comprehensive way to turn problem situations into expressions of Loving Kindness and Compassion. It can start with anything – either a pain or Poison that you feel in your life, or an awareness of suffering in the life of another. In fact, one of the really interesting things about the *tonglen* practice is the way it blends dealing with one's own pain with that of others, because working to develop Compassion for others often creates an awareness of blockages or hurt in your own life, or vice versa, which then themselves become the subject of the *tonglen* exercise.

For example, let's say that you're hurt and a resentful because your girlfriend (who is now your *ex*-girlfriend, of course) just broke up with you because she justifiably wanted more commitment and time than you could give her, but also feeling bad for how sad she's feeling about the breakup. You both love each other, but for whatever set of

---

115 <u>Start Where You are</u>, Pema Chodron (1994), Shambhala Classics, Page 43.

reasons it's just not working out. So the suffering in the situation is dual – yours and hers. In *tonglen* practice, you would do the following:

The first step, the *bodhicitta* phase, would be the flash of awareness that this *is* the situation, with an awareness of the Poisons that have and/or could get generated (resentment, anger, etc.) and an openness in your heart to work with and transform it and them. One good way to do this is the visualize that your heart has an ocean spreading out infinitely in every direction from it.

Now comes the "archetypal" phase, in which you will deal with universal suffering. Many commentators suggest that you visualize the suffering you breath in as thick, dense, black, hot clouds or smoke, and transform it in your heart into cool, luminous white light which you then exhale (incidentally, each round of this may extend over several breaths, and not be done within a single breath). So you might picture the suffering of the world as foreboding dark smoke clouds that fill the air above the heart-ocean, darkening completely the light. Once this darkness has reached its zenith, you breath it in and let it saturate every pore of your body, and then change it into cool luminous light and exhale it out every part of your body and breath to thereby transform the universal suffering into happiness and tranquility. While this might seem like a very theatrical exercise, I assure you it is quite powerful. Do it for as many cycles as you feel appropriate.

Following, you move into the "personal" phase where you will attempt to transform the suffering that your girlfriend and you are feeling. You could try to do just one or the other of you, but that would likely feel incomplete – if you just do you, you're not milking the situation for the Compassion you need to develop for her, and if you just do her, you'll fail to transform the attachments and hurt that still reside in you. So, for example, you could envision her suffering, breath it in, and breath it back out as the cool white light of Loving Kindness and Compassion for her. Then you would allow yourself to feel your own pain and suffering about the situation – including any resentment or anger or other negative feelings – and likewise transform them with your breath.

Finally, you enter the "universal" phase by extending your Compassion towards both yourself and your girlfriend through the knowledge that millions of people are suffering this same way as each of you, and by now including their suffering in the in-breath and out-breath you perform for you and her. In other words, you extend that awareness by breathing in the suffering of all people with hurt feelings or broken hearts everywhere, and exhaling the cool, white breath of relief, Loving Kindness and Compassion for them all.

Ultimately, any type of meditation or exercise which allows for the development of Loving Kindness – and thereby Compassion – is going to be beneficial to you and those around you. If the ones mentioned above don't seem to "click" for you, come up with your own. For sometimes, when one tries to adopt a meditative regime propounded by others, it has a somewhat contrived feeling, which is not what you want when you're trying to open up your heart chakra.

So…if none of the exercises listed above work for you, develop your own! That's actually how I started doing these types of exercises, which are somewhat different than Mindfulness exercises because they involve the creation of an inner process or dialogue, whereas Mindfulness is much more devoted to being a witness to autonomic or uncontrolled mental processes. I knew at the time that I wanted to start to explore Loving Kindness practices, but when I tried to follow the ones prescribed by the Buddhist authors, I wasn't satisfied because I couldn't remember the proper sequencing of the words, and I didn't want to recite from a book.

But it just happens that at the time every Tuesday night my daughter had a class that lasted an hour, where I dropped her off at 5:00 and picked her up at 6:00. I decided that, during the one-hour interim, I would do a Loving Kindness practice, rather than wait in the car or stop at a café. Instead, I went for a walk and practiced Loving Kindness meditation while I did so. I devised my own mantra for it, which goes as follows:

"May (fill in the blank) be loved.
May (fill in the blank) have peace and harmony both within and
with others.
May (fill in the blank) have a life filled with wisdom and
compassion.
(fill in the blank) is loved."

Normally, "fill in the blank" was at first me, and finally returned to me as well. But in the intervening walk (which was generally a total of 44 San Francisco blocks - 22 westwards and 22 eastward), I filled in that blank with as many types and groups of people and other sentient creatures as I could – Canadians, men, women, refugees, people I'm mad at or disappointed with, sea creatures from the Indian Ocean, songbirds from South America, my Aikido teacher and classmates – whatever! It doesn't matter who the group or type is, as long as the motivating feeling and resultant awareness is one of Loving Kindness and Compassion for the creatures around me, and an intentionality to create that Loving Kindness in my own heart.

The practice proved itself to be both easier and harder than I expected. It was easier because it worked – I still make mistakes and have "small" moments with people, but gradually the feeling of Loving Kindness enlarged within my emotional landscape so that I felt more for others, and had a greater Compassion for their suffering than I had previously. It was a bit difficult though, because just as in Mindfulness training the mind tends to wander, so after a one-hour stretch of practicing it while walking, I was ready for a break, because my meditative mind had gotten tired keeping the focus for so long.

Whatever format works for you is what is best, as long as you have some time and space to practice in. You can do it while sitting, lying, standing or walking (or running or doing a Stair Master), as long as you do it with a true intention to develop Loving Kindness and Compassion and to reap the benefits of living your life in a more loving fashion.

What's in It for You?

When I first read of these types of practices and reflections, they seemed a bit naïve or silly. "Namby-Pamby" was a word that came to my mind. I mean – what good was it going to do anybody for me to do silly recitations about Loving Kindness? But in fact it does a world of good, because our brains are *neuroplastic* and because different types of mental activities activate or emanate from different parts of the brain.

> *"A decade ago the dogma in neuroscience was that the brain contained all of its neurons at birth and it was unchanged by life's experiences… But the new watchword in brain science is "neuroplasticity," the notion that the brain continually changes as a result of our experiences – whether through fresh connections or through the generation of utterly new neurons…MRI studies find that in a violinist, for example, the areas of the brain that control finger movements in the hand that does the fingering grow in size. Those who start their training earlier in life and practice longer show bigger changes in the brain."[116]*

Traditionally, doctors and psychologists had believed that the human brain sort of hardened into a final form when one became an adult, leading to the belief that our "personalities" were more or less fully-cooked by that time. Modern brain science has learned that the brain continues to grow and change in a multitude of different ways throughout our lives, and that we can influence the ways that those changes occur. Because of *neuroplasticity* we have control to a certain degree over the types of people we are, the types of feelings we foster, and how those express in our lives. Following the logic of the violin player example above, then, there might likely be a change in the actual structure and/or operation of the brain by activities such as Loving Kindness meditations and recitations.

And, in fact, that *is* what the research shows. The fact that thoughts and feelings of different kinds cause different parts of our brains

---

116 <u>Destructive Emotions</u>, Daniel Goleman (2003) Bantam Books, Page 21.

to activate and deactivate is relevant to our Loving Kindness and Compassion training.

This was well illustrated by the true account of "Lama Oser", the pseudonymously named Tibetan monk who allowed himself to be scanned in a fMRI (functional Magnetic Resonance Imaging, which shows brain structure and activity in the form of a video rather than the snapshots of the standard MRI) machine, as part of research program related to the Mind and Life symposiums held by the Dalai Lama and western psychologists, philosophers, scientists, and others. Oser, who had been a practicing Tibetan Buddhist for thirty years, agreed to practice different kinds of meditations while in the fMRI machine, while Richard Davidson (a symposium member) and his associates at the E. M. Keck Laboratory for Functional Brain Imaging and Behavior at the Madison campus of the University of Wisconsin measured Oser's brain and neurological responses during each type of meditation, and during the resting states Oser went into between each type of meditation.

Oser did six types of meditation while in the contraption – visualization, one-pointed concentration, generalized Compassion, meditations on devotion and on fearlessness, and "open-state" meditation where the mind has no mental activity other than a vast openness. Each would trigger changes in the brain activity. Of particular interest to us here were the shifts in brain activity that occurred when Oser went from resting state to meditation on Compassion.

Davidson and his team of neurologists were already aware that there is an axis of activity in the prefrontal cortex, stretching from the left middle frontal gyrus in the left prefrontal cortex to the right middle frontal gyrus in the other side. Davidson's lab (which is pre-eminent for this type of research) knew from previous studies that when people have high activity levels in the left prefrontal cortex and left middle frontal gyrus, they report simultaneous "good" feelings such as happiness, alertness, enthusiasm and joy. High levels of activity on the other side – the right prefrontal area – are, to the contrary, usually accompanied by simultaneous reports of darker, "bad" emotions, such as sadness, anxiety, fear, and depression.

When Oser did his Compassion meditation – which he did by meditating on the compassionate qualities of one of his Tibetan teachers – there was a dramatic increase in good "gama" electrical activity in the left middle frontal gyrus, an increase that was considered by Davidson to be unlikely to have occurred by chance.

> *"The implications of these findings for our emotional balance are profound: We each have a characteristic ratio of right-to-left activation in the prefrontal areas that offers a barometer of the moods we are likely to feel day to day. That ratio represents what amounts to an emotional set point, the mean around which our daily moods swing.*
>
> *Each of us has the capacity to shift our moods, at least a bit, and thus change this ratio. The further to the left the ratio tilts, the better our frame of mind tends to be, and experiences that lift our mood cause such a leftward tilt, at least temporarily...*
>
> *In short, Oser's brain shift during compassion seemed to reflect an **extremely** pleasant mood. The very act of concern for others' well-being, it seems, creates a greater state of well-being within oneself. The finding lends scientific support to an observation often made by the Dalai Lama: that the person doing a meditation on compassion for all beings is the immediate beneficiary (among other benefits of cultivating compassion, as described in classic Buddhist texts, are being loved by people and animals, having a serene mind, sleeping and waking peacefully, and having pleasant dreams)."* [117]

As we do our Loving Kindness and Compassion meditations, then, they actually make our lives better, shifting our prefrontal cortex axis to the left, and our emotional set point towards positive emotional presence in the world. Rather than being silly, goody-goody exercises on no import, they are strong tools for the structural and functional improvement of the way we feel, and of how we conduct ourselves in the world.

---

117 <u>Destructive Emotions</u>, Daniel Goleman (2003) Bantam Books, Page 12.

What's in It for Others?

Loving Kindness and Compassion Meditations are not just prescriptions to make you feel better about yourself and your own life. They also have real impacts on those around you, and on the conflicts you involve with.

You will recall that the Buddha exhorted his *bikkhus* to "pervade" four directions with Loving Kindness in the Simile of the Saw, and advised *bikkhu* and non-*bikkhu* alike to let their "love flow outward through the universe, in every direction" in the Discourse on Good Will.

While there are many reasons for these exhortations, two major ones are that pervading the space around you with love has a definite affect upon others, and also lets you be a "hologram" (a fragment that reflects all of a whole image) for the power of love in this world.

There is in Buddhism the myth borrowed from Hinduism of Indra's Net, the net that the Hindu god Indra (the Father of Everything) hung over his palace on Mount Meru, the "Mount Olympus" of Vedic cosmology and Vedic mythology. If the reader is surprised at the mention of a god, he or she needn't be. In Buddhist cosmology, there are six realms of existence with corresponding emotional states – demons (anger), hungry ghosts (greed), animals (ignorance), humans (desire), demigods (jealousy), and gods (pride). The Buddha held that humans are more fortunate than the inhabitants of any of the other realms, including the gods, since we have the Dharma and can learn from our suffering – a need demigods and gods (who are "above" us on the chart) don't have since they are immortal!

Indra's Net, which is discussed in the Avatamsaka Sutra[118], is described elsewhere in the following fashion:

> *"Far away in the heavenly abode of the great god Indra, there is a wonderful net which has been hung by some cunning artificer in such*

---

118   The "Flower Garland Suttra" which was first fully translated in Chinese around 420 AD, and which is pivotal to the Hua-Yen school of Chinese Buddhism, and to the Kegon school of Japanese Buddhism.

a manner that it stretches out infintely in all directions. In accordance with the extravagant tastes of deities, the artificer has hung a single glittering jewel in each "eye" of the net, and since the net itself is infinite in dimension, the jewels are infinite in number. There hang the jewels, glittering like stars in the first magnitude, a wonderful sight to behold. If we now arbitrarily select one of these jewels for inspection and look closely at it, we will discover that in its polished surface there are reflected all the other jewels in the net, infinite in number. Not only that, but each of the jewels reflected in this one jewel is also reflecting all the other jewels, so that there is an infinite reflecting process occurring. "[119]

The image of Indra's Net has multiple levels of meaning. First, it shows that each part of the universe is a reflection of each other – that everything is one, and not the "separate" selves or objects we believe everything to be (we'll discuss this more later when we look at Dependent Arising). This aspect of Indra's Net goes to our understanding – however, a different aspect of it motivates our actions and shows the ultimate importance of acting with Loving Kindness and Compassion.

For just as each jewel at each interstice in Indra's Net was a reflection of each other, and contained within itself a reflection of each of them, so is each other jewel a reflection of it. Therefore, I am a reflection of the world, which is also a reflection of me.

This is not an egotistical statement, but rather a statement of the interdependence and interpenetration of everything in our world. So the war in Darfur is a reflection of the dis-ease each of us carries within, and vice versa. If I think evil thoughts, or carry anger in my heart towards another, that will be reflected in other evil events elsewhere. Sort of a doomsday butterfly effect.

But there's a positive side to this as well, for we are each reflected for the love and Compassion we have and share as well. Not that

---

119 Hua-Yen Buddhism: The Jewel Net of Indra, Francis Harold Cook (1977), Penn State Press..

we live in a perfect world – clearly we don't, as exhibited in the news and media every day. But the bad things that happen need to be counterweighted by the good, and we can each be part of that counter-weighting process. The goodness I generate when I practice Loving Kindness, or when I meditate on Compassion, will itself be reflected in all the other gems on Indra's Net, and will increase the density and proportion of goodness in the world.

One might ask what the use of this is, since there is so much cruelty and misunderstanding in the world today, seemingly on the increase. No one ever said that peace and harmony would be the only game in town, or that creating a world built on kindness and respect would be easy. However, neither did the Buddha (or any other great spiritual leaders) say that you should only practice Loving Kindness and Compassion when they seem to be winning the day. The Buddha did not tell the *bikkhus* in the Simile of the Saw – "practice Loving Kindness for the bandits, unless they get too rough, in which case it's okay to despise them!" Buddhism sets the bar high for self-understanding and for Compassion, yet has always acknowledged the quixotic nature of the quest to save all sentient beings from suffering, as in the Four Noble Vows of the Zen Buddhists:

> *"Sentient beings are numberless. I vow to save them.*
> *Desires are endless. I vow to put an end to them.*
> *The dharmas are boundless. I vow to master them.*
> *The Buddha way is unattainable. I vow to attain it."* [120]

If your goal is to resolve and minimize conflict, we could add a fifth Noble Vow – "Conflicts are endless. I vow to put an end to them." From the point of view of the conflicts in your life, or in the lives of those you wish to help resolve their own conflicts, the development of Loving Kindness and Compassion are additionally beneficial because they tend to create positive responses from others, which can lead to a deeper or quicker resolution of the differences.

---

120 <u>Essential Buddhism</u>, Jack Maguire (2001), Pocket Books, Page 77.

Not everyone will respond to your Compassion or Loving Kindness, nor will they work in every situation, but the mere presence of either quality will tend to lessen conflict for you and for others. It will make those around you trust you more, and feel safer in expressing their fears and concerns, which is often the first step towards resolving their conflicts (whether with you or with others).

Here we can look at another Lama Oser story for an illustration. For the very same day as he did his stint in the fMRI machine, he also did a Loving Kindness exercise involving himself and two scientists. In the exercise, during which each person was physiologically monitored and videotaped, he and each of the two scientists would have a 15-minute conversation on a subject about which they were bound to disagree – whether one should give up science and become a monk (which is what Oser had done, but the scientists had not), and reincarnation (which is part of Oser's religious belief system, but not that of the empirical, rationalist scientists). The scientists were chosen because they each possessed a different kind of character. One was mellow and relaxed, while the other was argumentative and confrontational.

Oser's conversation with the mellow scientist was unremarkable, perhaps because they both approach situations from a gentle place. In fact, they enjoyed the conversation so much they were sorry to see it end.

The aggressive scientist was a different story, however, for his physiological readings showed a state of high emotional arousal at the beginning of their discussion. In other words, he was preparing to fight (albeit verbally) with Oser. However, each time he tried to act aggressive or belligerent with Oser, Oser would very calmly reason with him and smile at him, practicing his habitual Loving Kindness for the scientist. The result of this was that the scientist's emotional arousal lessened and he quieted down by the end of the 15-minute discussion. In fact, he was so impressed by Oser's demeanor and presence that he offered the following comment at the end of the session, "I couldn't be confrontational. I was always met with reason and smiles; it's overwhelming. I felt something – like a shadow or an aura – and I couldn't be aggressive."[121]

Not every situation will of course work so effectively, and in many situations your Loving Kindness may be met with aloofness or coldness. On the other hand, in many situations the mere fact of your practicing Loving Kindness for the others involved, and of having developed your skills and depth in Loving Kindness and Compassion, will change the dynamics of the situation, and will start the parties towards reconciliation.

Loving Kindness and Compassion in Your Own Conflicts

In talking about Mindfulness, we noted that training it helps the contours and nature of our conversations with and treatment of ourselves becomes transparent, and thus the hidden players in those conversations are, like the Wizard of Oz, revealed from behind their curtains of mystery.

One of those players in many people's conversations with themselves is the critic or the self-loather, whose job is basically to make you feel bad about yourself. If the critic is not seen for what he is, then he operates beneath the radar with impunity. Once you see him (or her), it's helpful to have tools to retrain the critic to be loving and kind to you, and to have Compassion for the difficulties and suffering you have experienced in your life. Not to help you turn your life into a self-idolatrous pity-parade, but to actually be loving and kind and understanding to yourself.

One of the benefits of starting and finishing Loving Kindness and Compassion meditations with yourself as the beneficiary is that you can start to accept yourself more lovingly, just as you are. Somewhat in the same fashion that Mindfulness is "choiceless" in its awareness, Loving Kindness and Compassion meditation is "judgeless" – it

---

121 <u>Destructive Emotions</u>, Daniel Goleman (2003) Bantam Books, Pages 17-18.

bestows itself without requiring that the recipient respond in kind or be of a certain nature.

And in keeping with the Indra's Net "hologram" model of our lives, it's by healing yourself that the world becomes a better place – not just for you, but for the myriad other reflective gems across that vast net. As Dr. M. Erceg states:

> *"The task now boils down to taking responsibility for how we treat ourselves. Nothing else matters for everything is a reflection of this. There is no point talking about the world since it is secondary. How we treat ourselves is reflected in the world. Wars are based on the inner war. When we are filled with turmoil within such as through repressing, refusing to accept certain emotions or aspects of ourselves creating a war within, we infiltrate our methodology unwittingly into new generations of young people to fight amongst themselves and with other nations. We're infectious. That is why the most significant, globally-impacting act we can make is to create a loving, supportive relationship within. That's all we can do. That's all that matters. What else is there to do? Everything we do will be tainted by the way we treat ourselves."*[122]

Which is related to the point made by Ayya Khema in the quote in the heading of this chapter – it is only through the acceptance and love of ourselves that we can begin to have love and Compassion for the sufferings and aspirations of others. What Mindfulness shows us about ourselves we can learn to accept as a natural expression of the pain we have carried about, or of the ways we have learned to deal with how others have treated us, and learn thereby to love and have Compassion – as opposed to rejection and judgment – for ourselves.

The voice of the critic or self-loather is usually the voice of you as a small child, which has been trapped inside since then because of fear, or misunderstanding, or the internalized judgments of others. Because it got built into your internal dialogue before you knew

122 The Book of Life Questions and Answers, Dr. M. Erceg, (2006) Authorhouse, Pages 45-6.

what was happening, and usually during times of duress where your awareness and presence were in a diminished state, it has been largely invisible to you, even though it's been running virtually 24-7 ever since.

Mindfulness and self-awareness will let you hear that voice more clearly, and also let you begin to see the patterned behaviors you express in response it. Loving Kindness and Compassion, in furtherance, will let you use that new awareness to start to heal the wounds that the small child has guarded so tightly for so long.

Once the contours of the voice (or voices) start to become clear to you, you can take that knowledge and use it to increase your love for and kindness to yourself, in many ways. First, the very fact of hearing clearly the voice or seeing the patterns will almost immediately make you kinder to yourself, because self-hatred thrives in the dark.

But you can also do exercises to increase your self-love. For instance, let's say that you've heard the critic tell you that you are a bad person, and see as a result that you act in certain ways that make you feel ashamed of yourself, such as over-indulgence in drugs or food, shooting yourself in the foot in work or personal situations that are important to you, or in any kind of self-damaging behavior. When the critic was in clandestine control of the situation, his/her voice would have been unapparent, and the attendant behavior would have been painful but obscure. But having now heard the voice and seen the behavior, you can do exercises to a) be loving and accepting of yourself *as you are*, and b) be compassionate to the wounded child that the critic represents. These can be done in a format similar to the Loving Kindness and Compassion exercises described earlier.

So, for example, you could do the white lotus/golden light exercise that Ayya Khema suggests, and visualize your inner child as being bathed in the light of true Loving Kindness – since you are both the lotus and the light and the inner child, you will be loving yourself for exactly what you are, not for what the critic has been suggesting you are. Then, you could do that very same exercise for the Critic as well, for he or she is also part of you and no less deserving of Loving Kindness than the bandits in the Simile of the

Saw. Afterwards, you could do the first guided meditation that Khema suggests, wherein after allowing the breath to settle, you open yourself to feeling Compassion (not pity) in your heart for the *dukkha* you've felt, and for the *dukkha* of your inner child and of the Critic both, whether past, present or future.

Silly exercises? Not at all – by doing them you will open your heart, shift your prefrontal brain axis to the left, and polish your gem on Indra's Net, redounding to the good of both yourself, all the other gems on the Net, and everyone around you.

Loving Kindness and Compassion in Your Conflicts with Others

When we shift from your internal conflicts to your conflicts with others, we add two levels of complexity that are not present when dealing with "simple" internal conflicts. First, you yourself need to be mindful of the feelings and thoughts you actually have about the conflict, and then ascertain how to infuse or pervade the situation with Loving Kindness and Compassion – all while remaining true to the real needs of the participants in the situation. Second, and more difficult, those qualities need to be transmitted to the other in such a way that those same qualities infuse the situation and, hopefully, develop in them as well.

As we have previously discussed in this book, and as alluded to in our example of the foreign policy discussion between the three friends, the fact that there is a "conflict" between you and a friend, co-worker, or whoever means that there is something other than a simple "rational" disagreement between you two – there is something else, some added quality that immediately reduces Loving Kindness and Compassion to nothing. Rather than those two qualities, you will likely be feeling some one or more of the feelings from a different kind of list, like isolated, un-present, angry, resentful, unappreciated, etc. In other words, you're under the sway of the Three Poisons.

Your first step then is to realize that that's what you're feeling. While it is theoretically possible to nip such feelings in the bud, they generate so quickly that the likelihood of catching them before they develop is extremely slight. In classical Buddhist psychological writings, the gap between Original Mind (that is, the pure experience of anything) and the clouding of that experience by misconception or distortion is measured in fractions of a second.

So the first necessity to infusing Loving Kindness and Compassion into a conflict is to realize where you are – in other words, you and the other participant must recognize that a conflict has arisen, and somehow recognize what feelings and sensations and Poisons have arisen with it. Until that happens, it will be difficult to start to transform the situation.

It may take awhile, however, to develop that realization because the kinds of feelings and sensations – and attendant ideations – generated by conflict tend to create "Refractory Periods" where they are not really quite amenable to change, since they are still so powerful that they prevent true Mindfulness from developing. So, just as in small retail business the first rule of thumb is "location, location, location", in most developing interpersonal conflicts the first rule will be "timing, timing, timing". Because in fact, you can't think – or develop Compassion – until you've calmed down a bit. All of our forbears instinctively knew this when they said to "take a deep breath" when you get mad.

A good expanded way to take a deep breath is "doing Turtle", which is a technique developed by Mark Greenberg as part of the PATHS (Promoting Alternative Thinking Strategies) program, a program which helps schoolchildren develop emotional intelligence and resolve conflict as part of school curriculae. For 3-7 year olds, one of the learning tools involves telling them the story of a little turtle who didn't like to go to school, and who got angry at being in school or when his schoolmates would tease him or take his pencil. Unable to figure out how to control his anger, he goes to visit a wise old turtle who tells him the secret of controlling his anger:

"The wise old turtle said to him, 'You already have the solution to the problem inside yourself. It's your shell. When you feel very upset or very angry and you can't control yourself, you can go inside your shell.'

'When you're inside your shell you can calm down. When I go inside my shell , 'the wise old turtle said, 'I do three things. I tell myself to stop; I take one long deep breath, or more if I need to; and then I tell myself what the problem is.' The wise old turtle and the little turtle practiced this idea. And the little turtle said he wanted to try this when he got back to class."[123]

Based upon this story, the PATHS curriculum teaches the student who is angry and entering into a conflict with other students to cross their arms over their chest (putting their hands on the opposite shoulders), take a deep breath, and become aware of their feelings before acting out on the anger or other conflict-based emotion.

I actually like doing Turtle myself, and have also recommended it to clients and mediation participants who were in the throes of stress or negative emotions generated by conflict situations. Whatever the reader thinks of the particular technique, the point is that in an interpersonal conflict, some form of "time-out" (a deep breath, a walk around the block, delaying the next confrontation/meeting until the next day, etc.) may be necessary for both participants before either of you can generate Loving Kindness or Compassion.

Once the thorny Refractory Period of emotional upset has become manageable for you, and if the conflict was generated in the context of an ongoing necessary relationship, you need to check in on the other person in the conflict to see if they've cooled down a bit. If so, great – if not, you can help them move out of refraction by: a) acknowledging your part in the creation of the conflict; b) explaining

---

123 <u>Destructive Emotions</u>, Daniel Goleman (2003) Bantam Books, Pages 266-267.

the kinds of feelings that arose for you in it; and c) suggesting a compassionate course for the immediate future.

For example, let's say that you've had an argument with your employee about the vacation time they are due. Perhaps there was some confusion about how to compute their hours – you thought they were on a weekly salary basis, while she thought it was being calculated hourly. As a result, she is claiming she is owed some days of vacation time just at a time of year you thought she would be there to help. As you discuss this with her, some of the "Poisons" get generated – i.e. greed, hatred, and ignorance.

For your part, you start getting a churny kind of feeling in your gut, and start having a totally unsettled, un-present feeling in general, which creates a feeling in you that you've been mistreated. Along with this go rather unkindly thoughts about the employee, which try to "justify" or fill-out the feelings. "I've been a good and generous boss to so-and-so, and have been clear and fair in describing our vacation time policies. How can she try to cheat me like this? Why I ought to fire her, or do some other petty, mean things to let her know how good she's had it!"

She's not feeling any better, either, for now she feels both threatened in her livelihood (greed/attachment and fear at Maslow's "safety level") and resentful of what she sees as your cold and callous behavior (anger and hatred). So she has also had a set of physical reactions to the conflict, and has created her own story to go with them. "I've been a loyal, talented and diligent worker for so-and-so, and have made his life easier and more successful by my efforts. He doesn't appreciate me! He doesn't deserve me! If he thinks I'm going to take this lying down he's got another thought coming – I'll show him! I'll report him to the Labor Relations Board for unfair labor practices!"

When this first comes up, best to do some form of turtle before trying to resolve the conflict. Take a coffee break, or go for a walk. If there's no real possibility of manufacturing some sort of time-out, just tell the other person something like "Mary, I'd like to reach a resolution with you as soon as possible, but I'm not quite ready to talk right now. I know we'll be able to solve the problem once we've calmed down a bit. But we're both a little upset, and need to cool off a little before we discuss the vacation days. Okay if we talk about it tomorrow at noon?"

You've done three things with this conversation. First, you've acknowledged that a conflict exists, without blaming anyone for its arising. Second, you've made it okay for everyone to be upset about it for a while, and set up an agreed-upon Refractory Period for the poisonous feelings to dissipate. Finally, you've planted the seed of a future resolution without specifying in any way what it will be, and at the same time created a co-ownership of that process.

Once one of you cools down (I'll assume it's you that cools down first, because of your now-habitual Mindfulness training), you can perhaps check in with the other to see where they're at in the conflict refractory cycle. If they've cooled down enough to be amenable to discussion, you can start working on healing the situation using the techniques discussed below.

If not, you can speed up their Refractory Period by letting them know you're aware of the dynamics of refraction, and that you look forward to a chance to get to a point where a more rational conversation can occur. And you can shift some of the responsibility for this to the still-refractory person. In other words, if Mary is still psycho when you meet at noon the next day, tell her "Mary, even though I'd like to come to that resolution as soon as possible, I sense we're not quite ready to talk yet. Could you let me know when you can meet in the next few days to sit down and talk? As long as we deal with it by the end of the week, any time that works for you is good for me." By having this conversation, Mary has been informed that your Refractory Period is over, that it's okay that hers isn't, and that she can take responsibility for monitoring the dissipation of her own refraction within certain necessary bounds.

While you wait for her Refractory Period to end, make sure you practice Loving Kindness and Compassion exercises directed towards the particular conflict. When we've had a spat with someone, and one or more of the Three Poisons is coursing through our consciousness, they are the last people on earth we feel like doing Loving Kindness or Compassion exercises for – which means they're the very best people we can choose to focus our good energies on. So, while I wait for my employee to cool down, however long that takes, I can perhaps recite the following to myself while I walk, meditate, or wash dishes:

> *"May I be loved.*
> *May I have peace and harmony both within and with others.*
> *May I have a life filled with wisdom and compassion.*
> *I am loved.*
>
> *May Mary be loved.*
> *May Mary have peace and harmony both within and with others.*
> *May Mary have a life filled with wisdom and compassion.*
> *Mary is loved."*

Or I can imagine a beautiful white lotus flower opening in my heart, from which emanates a golden stream of light filling me with warmth and light and a feeling of contentment, and surrounding me with a feeling of lovingness and well-being, and which golden light expands outwards to encompass Mary, before returning to myself alone, where the white lotus closes and envelops the golden light within. I end this meditation by reciting to myself "May Mary and I and all beings be happy".

Or I can open myself to feeling Compassion in my heart for my own *dukkha* or suffering, then extend this feeling of Compassion to Mary, to feelings of Compassion for the *dukkha* she will no doubt feel in her life, including her pain over the present conflict, ending by reciting to myself "May Mary and I have Compassion for each other".

Whatever the technique, the point is that I will have started the process of converting my own poisonous feelings into ones of kindness and Compassion by modifying the "standard" Loving Kindness and Compassion exercises to fit the immediate situation.

Eventually, Mary and I will have our discussion, and during these I will try to utilize three techniques. I will:

a) *acknowledge my own part in the creation of the conflict.* Many of us are used to trying to deny our responsibility for conflicts or other problems in life. It's never me that did it – it's the other, or the situation, or the economy, or whatever. By acknowledging my role in the generation of a conflict, I free myself from having to keep the other person locked into the position of the "wrong other", and free myself to be just a person as opposed to someone who is "right". More importantly, it frees the other person to stop protecting herself in the same way – i.e. by making me wrong so she can be right –and allows her to start to move out of the conflict towards transformation. An even more powerful form of acknowledgement – namely, apology – can be incredibly effective in transforming conflict, since it validates the other through taking full responsibility for one's actions, when used in the right situation;

b) *explain the kinds of feelings that arose for me in it.* Mary needs to know that this was not some thought-based rational process for me but, rather, an emotional rollercoaster ride from which I am only too happy to free myself. By showing her that emotions or "poisons" were involved, it makes it okay for her to have had feelings as well, and lets her understand that the process I've followed – of letting the feelings play themselves out so that I can get to a more grounded, compassionate space – is a natural progression which is available to her as well.

c) *suggest a compassionate course for the immediate future.* Having accepted responsibility for my part in the conflict, and shown the feelings that I dealt with, I can now suggest ways to resolve the conflict. These are offered as possibilities, not as fiats. They are offered as much to generate mutual respect and kindness as they are to generate a result.

By acknowledging my role in the development of the conflict, I've freed Mary to acknowledge her own, without fear of judgment. The same goes for the recitation of the feelings felt – Mary is now okay to feel and/or express her own. By offering a compassionate suggestion for resolution, she is freed to develop her own capacity for Compassion just as I will mine. And, to the extent that I pervade the communications with Loving Kindness and Compassion, these qualities will tend to call forth similar qualities from Mary.

This is not to say that acting out of Loving Kindness and Compassion will always elicit similar responses from others. One look at the state of the world shows that Loving Kindness and Compassion have not yet prevailed as the dominant motivators in social behavior. As pointed out in the seminal work on negotiation *Getting to Yes*, there is the "Hard" negotiator type, who sees every offer of friendship as an admission of weakness and opportunity for manipulation. But you can have kindness and Compassion without being manipulated, and despite the fact that others won't always respond in kind. The Buddha didn't say he agreed with the actions of the bandits in the Simile of the Saw, or suggest that his bikkhus say to the bandits "hey, why don't you try my saw, since it's a newer model with sharper teeth on the blade!" He just stated the simple fact that Loving Kindness and Compassion are the sublime emotions to feel towards others in this life.

Loving Kindness and Compassion in Working with "Other Peoples' Conflicts"

While it might seem more difficult to help develop Loving Kindness and Compassion in the conflicts of others than in one's own – because as a mediator you have to try to develop these qualities in others as well as yourself – on another level it's easier, because as the mediator you haven't gotten any of your own Three Poisons revved up in the dispute.

The down side of the equation is that you can be sure the other people in the room *do* have their Poisons activated – if they didn't, they wouldn't need your help! So you'll likely be dealing with people who a) have objectified the others so that they don't see them for who they really are, b) are in some sort of refractory state vis-à-vis the others, so they aren't really "present" and fully functional in the situation themselves, and c) believe that they see things "as they really are", and that the other must be somewhat crazy to see the situation as they do.

Obviously, as the mediator you have chosen to resolve the conflict. Ultimately, you will confront the question of what "resolving" a conflict means. On the simplest level, it means that the issues in contention are no longer in conflict. So, for example, if you and I are arguing over who owns the copse of elderberry trees on the line between our two properties, if we agree to split the copse in two and keep half of the trees each, the conflict is "resolved".

But suppose that after that "resolution", I am still angry with you and wish ill to you and your family. Or that you, whenever you get the chance, speak badly of me, and carry rancor in your heart towards me and mine. In such a case, has there truly been a "resolution"? If our two interstitial gems on Indra's Net hold onto and echo ill-will towards each other, will this not be reflected throughout the Net?

Real resolution is somehow beyond this simplistic idea of "fixing" a problem. In a real resolution, ill-will is replaced by Loving Kindness and Compassion, and there will be no residue of rancor left to hold onto. Every mediator knows the difference between resolving a conflict situation and truly reconciling the warring parties. While there is some satisfaction in accomplishing the former, there is truly a bit of ecstasy in the latter.

The extent to which you as mediator can infuse and pervade Loving Kindness and Compassion into a conflict, and design your intervention to foster these qualities in the other participants, is the extent to which you will succeed in truly reconciling the situation. The difference between the two types of result can be quite profound for both you and them, as illustrated by the following examples.

In the first – the "Drama Queen" - I mediated a dispute between two co-owners of a building where issues stemming from their respective habitation of the two units in the building (like the airplane pilot and his neighbor) had caused friction between them. One of them, in particular, had become very angry and negative towards the other – disparaging her as an "irresponsible" person who never did anything for the benefit of the property – while at the same time feeling unappreciated by her for the work he had done on the property, which he felt to be quite valuable. She had somewhat less emotional investment in the conflict, but thought he was being a "Drama Queen". She primarily was just frustrated that the actual co-habitation issues were disturbing her enjoyment of her home. Because of their budgetary restrictions, they told me the entire issue had to be resolved in one hour and a half mediation session.

Which we did – they agreed on specific resolutions to all the bullet-point items of their conflict, but only after she agreed to his condition that she acknowledge him openly for the work he had done on the property. On the surface, therefore, the mediation had been a "success", in that the participants signed an informal agreement resolving all issues and said that they felt the conflict was "resolved" when they left my office.

Part of me knew, however, that the conflict was not actually resolved, because neither one had really let go of the Poisons they had invested in the conflict. He still thought she was irresponsible (the Poison of anger or dislike/hatred) and that he was unappreciated (attachment and pride), while she still thought he was a Drama Queen (dislike/hatred). The mediation had been a success in their eyes because it resolved her immediate living issues, and temporarily assuaged his need for appreciation. To me, the success was incomplete because there had been no real transformation, for the Poisons of hatred and attachment had not turned into their opposites, Loving Kindness and Compassion. I was therefore not surprised when she called with another problem between the two of them a year later. When I asked her how their arrangement was working out, she said, "It's still the same. He complains all the time about how unappreciated he is – such a Drama Queen!"

The second example – the Screaming Family -- was much more satisfying. I got a call from an extended family (a widowed mother, her grown son plus his wife, and his grown sister) telling me that they wanted to come discuss a "real estate problem", which they did not want to specify until the meeting. So I was curious, and actually had the feeling that the problem was really about something other than "real estate."

They arrived at my office early in the morning, and were already seated in the conference room when I walked in. To say the atmosphere was tense is understated – there was a palpable feeling of an impending explosion when I entered.

And explode it did! The minute the mother started talking, the son started yelling back at her, and then the sister started yelling at him, at which point the wife started yelling at the sister. It was a perfect storm of human misunderstanding and conflict, each person acting with anger from his or her own state of delusion. And it was incredibly loud.

I don't usually yell in conversation, especially when my job is to help resolve a dispute. In this case I did, because if I hadn't I would never have been heard above the din. I looked at the sister and yelled at her "Heyyyyyy! What are you doing? You can't just come into my office and start yelling at each other like that. This is *my* office!"

The room went silent, because they had all been so involved in yelling at each other that they were shocked when someone from outside the family yelled at them more loudly than they were yelling at each other. In fact, it turned out they had been acting this way with each other for many years, since the father had died. I told them that, the "real estate problem" aside, there was something "broken" about the communication between them all that suggested a great deal of underlying pain, and that without looking at and resolving their respective pain there was no point talking about the real estate problem in any event.

What unfolded thereafter was nothing short of miraculous. Each person took the opportunity to express their point of view, but more importantly also expressed the pain they felt about the way they were treated – or perceived themselves as being treated – by the others. When each spoke, I made sure that no one else interrupted with a self-defensive response, and that they simply listened instead. This was the "mindful" part of the healing, where each person saw clearly how they actually felt about what may previously have been inchoate internal responses to events, and where each saw things more clearly in light of the others' different experiences of the same events they had gone through.

But a second part of the event also started to unfold – a loving, compassionate part. For as the family's narratives unfolded, the mother started crying about the sorrow she had felt seeing her son so angry, which she had previously covered with sniping, bitter comments to him. The son let go of his anger as he heard and felt his mother's love, and was able to see and say that that anger had been due to his frustrated attempts to express how deeply he wanted to make sure his mother was safe, and how unappreciated he felt for working so hard to keep her that way. The sister started crying as she expressed and then let go of the resentment towards her brother she had felt because of perceived favoritism by the mother in his favor, after which the son let go of his anger at her for again not appreciating the hard work he did to help support the mom. And, finally, the wife cried when she finally realized that the family she had married into was not, after all, completely insane.

This whole process lasted about an hour and a half, and the change was dramatic. The family that entered that conference room was not the one that left it a little while later. When they came in, they were tense – yet they left relaxed and smiling. When they came in, they were estranged from one another – when they left, they were a group bound by mutual love and care. They had allowed Mindfulness let them see their conflict and pain clearly, and then let Loving Kindness and Compassion heal them all.

Of course, one could point out that an important difference between the first conflict between the Drama Queen householders and the second among the Screaming Family members is that the second group was indeed a *family*, and had ties of blood and marriage holding them together. No matter what you do, and no matter how good or bad your relationship is, your mom is your mom, etc. So perhaps there is often a natural reservoir of bonding and affection which makes it easier to have transformative conflict resolutions between them. But, as the Buddha's "Discourse on Good Will" suggests, Loving Kindness and Compassion can be fostered and are possible in any situation, if we have but the intention to foster them, and the perseverance to allow them to flourish.

For the mediator, there are a few simple guidelines you can follow to help foster Loving Kindness and Compassion in the disputes you mediate:

a) *Be an exemplar of the traits you hope to foster.* The disputants in your mediations are more likely to act with Loving Kindness and Compassion if you set the example. People are sensitive to the influences around them, and will often model behavior that they see as admirable or which seems to give them a good chance of achieving their goal, which in a mediation is resolving the conflict. If you model Loving Kindness and Compassion and work diligently towards the resolution of the disputants' conflict, you will augment the likelihood of success because you will create a harmonic resonance for the development of those qualities in the parties to the dispute.

b) *Be aware of fluctuations in your own empathy, and recharge it when necessary.* Mediation is demanding and, just as it is possible to lose your Mindfulness during the process, it's also possible to have your Compassion "batteries" run low. If you find your frustration with the participants rising, or see that you're favoring one side because of some dislike that's arisen in you for the other, recharge the batteries. Take a walk or do some other form of "turtle", and take the time to do the white lotus or other Loving Kindness or Compassion exercise to regain the ability to keep you aware of the suffering of the participants, and to keep the alleviation of that suffering foremost among your goals for the process.

c) *Let the participants know that Loving Kindness and Compassion are useful tools for the resolution of their conflict, and will in fact be fostered by that process.* It's common to want to be efficient and business-like, in which case mentioning empathy and the like might not be "cool". It's even perhaps a bit nerdy to bring things like Loving Kindness and Compassion up during the middle of a conflict. While we might be afraid as mediators to mention things like Loving Kindness and Compassion, actually there couldn't be a better time to mention and introduce them than during the resolution process.

The participants will likely come into the mediation process in reactive phase – like the family I mentioned above, they will be living a situation that is stuck in anger and misconception. They are each in their own solipsistic little world, seeing themselves as good and wronged, and the other as bad and an evil-doer. Letting them know that part of the resolution process is to develop empathy and Compassion for each other can actually be a first step towards getting them unstuck from these self-involved worlds.

You can do this by telling them that you and the other participants will be encouraged to listen to their story and acknowledge their feelings, as will they to the others' stories and feelings. Let them know that by doing so, they will get closer to seeing the big picture of the dispute they're in, and to seeing how inter-dependent on each other they are, and how the conflict has been co-created by them without anyone in fact being "right" or "wrong".

d) *Build real "listening" into the process.* One of the first thing that happens in a conflict is that the other person becomes objectified. Instead of "my co-worker, Mary", in my mind I'm now dealing with "that bitch who's trying to get the better of me." One of the ways to re-subjectify the other in a conflict is to listen to what they have to say about it – not for them to tell you what a bastard you are, but for them to relate what they see as the parameters of the situation and the kinds of feelings and concerns they have about it. In this way, Mary will again be Mary in my eyes.

So establish a safe environment in the mediation for each of the participants to show the other who they really are, and how the conflict has affected their lives. This is not so that they can have a self-pity parade. Rather, it's to let the other participant see them as real people not so different from themselves, and to understand the emotional impact of the situation from a different perspective than their own.

It's important that the mediator make sure that this listening time is not used by the other participant as a springboard for his/her own self-justification. I usually suggest to the person whose turn it is to talk that they speak directly at me while the other participant listens – that way it's less likely to seem like a furtherance of confrontation (there are also, however, times where having them turn towards each other aids in the resolution). I also suggest that they try to frame the story in terms of their reactions and feelings, as opposed to statements of what the other person did wrong. And, I make sure the other person lets them finish their narrative without interrupting them, so that it doesn't become a further conflict or an opportunity for that other person to justify their behavior – I let them know that they can do all that stuff during their narrative.

e) *Utilize techniques that allow for the development of Loving Kindness and Compassion.* Because the participants will likely come to mediation in a refractory or reactive state, there will often be resistance on the part of one or more participants to allowing Loving Kindness and Compassion. People invest a great deal of themselves in their conflicts, and it may appear at first blush to be antithetical to them to develop any kind of positive feelings for those they view as their "antagonists" or as their "problems".

There are ways to help them cross this bridge. The listening you've built into the process is of course one of these, since it is through hearing another, and through telling them one's own truth, that the seeds of Compassion are sown through the development of Mindfulness.

But there are other techniques – beyond ones that create Mindfulness and a better "take" on what's actually occurring in the conflict - that help people thaw their resistance to feeling positively towards the other person. These other techniques all attempt in one fashion or another to allow one person to put himself, imaginatively at least, into the "skin" of the other. By doing so, and because of the universality of human responses to types of stimuli, that person can begin to identify with the Other – which is the beginning of Loving Kindness – and to feel the predicament of the Other, which is the basis for Compassion. In other words, where building listening into the mediation process primarily (though not exclusively) fosters inter-Mindfulness, the "reversal" imaginative techniques primarily serve to create Compassion.

These reversal techniques owe a great debt of gratitude to the role reversal therapeutic techniques used in Gestalt therapy, as championed by Fritz Perls. In classical role reversal, which can be used in either individual or group settings, the party or parties switch viewpoints so that each tries to argue for the other's viewpoint, while the other listens. But since the mediation setting is somewhat different than the therapeutic one (though sometimes it may not *feel* very different), the techniques are modified in both form and depth to suit the genre.

The simplest way is for the mediator to use questions that direct the participant towards an awareness of or sympathy towards the feelings or experience of the other. Questions like:

"What do you really know about the other person?"

"What would make you act the way they are acting? (and if they respond) Could that be true for them now?"

"Have you ever acted that way? Did you feel justified in that behavior?"

"Why do you think they are engaging in it?"

"Was there anyone in your family of origin who engaged in similar behavior? How did you respond? Did that work?

"Do you know anyone else who has acted that way?" How did you respond? Did that work?

"How could you find out what's underneath their behavior?"

Obviously, the context of the particular mediation will determine the content and timing of such questions. If the Three Poisons are still virulent in him/her, it would be too early to ask these types of questions since that might lead the person to mistrust you as a mediator. And they should be used judiciously and subtly to avoid being obvious as to your intent, or to appear as if you're cross-examining the participant.

A second route to follow would be an imaginative one, which again would have to be used carefully to avoid alienating the participant. In this technique, you invite the participant to imagine themselves inside the skin of the other person – looking and acting like them, to see what they feel like from the inside. This is closer to a classical Gestalt role-reversal.

A third route, which again is akin to the classical role-reversal, is the one we mentioned in Chapter 5, where you invite the person to either write or recite a three-part story, with the first part being their version of the conflict, the second being what they think the conflict is from the other person's perspective, and the third being what a shared reconciliatory version of the conflict would be.

All of these three techniques – the "reversal" questions, imaginative reversal, and three-part stories – are ways to help the mediation participants, who have started developing Mindfulness through reciting their own perspectives and listening to those of the others, to develop Loving Kindness and Compassion through putting them into the experience of the others, thus lessening attachment to their own perspective on the conflict.

By following these guidelines – being loving and compassionate yourself and maintaining those attributes throughout, letting the participants know (in whatever words you feel appropriate) that these attributes are acceptable and desirable goals of a mediation, ensuring that the parties get to listen to one another, and using "reversal" techniques – you can increase the likelihood of developing Loving Kindness and Compassion in the mediations you orchestrate. Will they always be successful? No, because nothing is always successful. There are situations where the participants have so engrained the dislike of the each other into themselves that it won't shake loose no matter how compassionate you as mediator are, and no matter how much you get them to listen to each other. There are also conflicts involving people with substance abuse problems or mental infirmities that make them unable to develop Compassion in any true sense. But that doesn't mean you should lose faith in the basic efficacy of Loving Kindness and Compassion in resolving conflict, or that you should ever stop trying to develop these aspects of those you work with.

The Buddha once met a horse trainer named Kesi, and asked him how he did his work. The trainer said it depended on the type of horse, of which there were four. The first kind of horse was the quick learner who was easy to work with – these just needed a little guidance and a bit of kindness to be properly trained. Then there were the slightly more difficult ones – these took more time and more work, and were kind of a pain in the neck, but ultimately made good horses if they were trained with a combination of firmness and gentleness. The third kind were still more difficult ones who had to be trained by an iron fist only, though they were ultimately trainable still. The fourth kind just wouldn't heed or learn anything, no matter how firm the hand that trained them.

The Buddha then asked Kesi what he did when he found a horse that he couldn't train. Kesi said that these horses the trainer had to kill, because they would spoil the whole herd if left with the other horses.

Kesi then asked the Buddha how he trained his bikkhus, and he said it was just the same- the good bikkhus he trained gently, the more difficult ones with a mixture of firmness and gentleness, and the very difficult bikkhus with a firm hand only. When Kesi asked the Buddha what he did with a bikkhu he couldn't train, Buddha said "I do as you do. I kill him".

The trainer was stunned – "What? You kill him? I thought you were against killing?" To which the Buddha replied that he didn't really kill them, he just couldn't train them so they were made to leave the sangha.

It's a little like that with mediations. There are the good ones like the Screaming Family where the participants naturally develop Compassion as they resolve their conflict. Then there are the middle level ones like the "Drama Queen" pair, who can develop Compassion but are slow to do so, and with whom you have to invest a lot more work to have Compassion and Loving Kindness really take root. But there are the situations like the Hateful Neighbor who told his co-owner that he still hated him after working for three days to resolve their issues – in these situations, you as mediator must simply let go of your own expectations for the mediation at hand (while asking yourself what you might have better done to "reach" the participants, thereby focusing on your skills and learning rather than on what was "wrong" with them), and move on with enthusiasm to your next mediating opportunity.

7. THE RECONCILIATION OF CONFLICT – TRANSFORMING THE THREE POISONS INTO THE FOUR SUBLIME STATES

"Indeed, meditation is not about sitting quietly in the shade of a tree and relaxing in a moment of respite from the daily grind; it is about familiarizing yourself with a new vision of things, a new way to manage your thoughts, or perceiving people and experiencing the world.

Buddhism teaches various ways of making this "familiarization" work. The three principal ways are antidotes, liberation, and utilization. The first consists of applying a specific antidote to each negative emotion. The second allows us to unravel, or "liberate", the emotion by looking straight at it and letting it dissolve as it arises. The third uses the raw power of emotion as a catalyst for inner change. The choice of one method over another will depend on the moment, the circumstances, and the capacity of the person using them. All share a common aspect and the same goal: to help us stop being victims of conflicting emotions". [124]

---

124 <u>Happiness</u>, Matthieu Ricard (2003), Little Brown and Company, page 123.

Anyone who works with conflict – such as mediators, ministers, or couples counselors – knows just how resistant to dispersion conflicts are. People are very attached to their conflicts, and their brains and psyches are programmed to foster this attachment and the resistance to change that goes along with it.

Earlier in this book we discussed the fact that there is a certain something that differentiates debate from conflict. Debate is primarily an activity of the logical part of the mind, whereas conflict dredges up deeper responses. Once those responses kick into play, resolving the conflict becomes a multi-leveled process that has to accomplish three goals: a) resolving the external situation that led to the conflict in the first place; b) identifying the attachment & negative feelings that prevent the situation from resolving naturally; and c) transforming those feelings into positive ones that allow the situation to transform and heal.

Put another way, it is the central thesis of this book that *the transformation of conflict consists ideally of mindfully transforming the Three Poisons of greed, hatred and delusion into the Four Sublime States of Loving Kindness, Compassion, Appreciative Joy, and Equanimity, thereby liberating the person or persons to let go of the conflict.*

This is not to suggest every conflict is immediately resolvable in practice (think "Middle East"), nor that every resolved conflict has all of these characteristics. But in its purest form and in theory, the process of fully resolving a conflict will generally follow this pattern, leaving nothing but the memory of a former conflict when it has been fully resolved.

What It Means to "Resolve" a Conflict

There are both "small" and "big" ideas as to what we mean when we say that a conflict is resolved. On the small side, it's resolved when the immediate situation giving rise to the conflict has been dealt with. Thus, in the "Drama Queen" conflict mentioned above (the term "Drama Queen" is the participant's term, which I use to identify rather than to judge), the conflict was "resolved" as a settlement when the two co-owners agreed on the disposition of the immediate problem at hand, and went on their way. And, indeed, the immediate problems of their shared ownership of their home had been settled for the time being.

Yet, a year later, she still carried her same negative feelings about her co-owner, he still felt unappreciated, and a new set of particular issues had arisen. Since the feelings and perceptions underlying the new set of conflict issues were the same as they had been in the previous conflict, it would appear that the conflict had not been resolved in the first place – it had merely been settled. Had I had the time to work with the situation further, I could have explored the meaning of the term "Drama Queen" for her, and helped her to become mindful of how her own history may have made it difficult for her to deal with her co-owner's behavior, which might in turn have allowed her to feel more kindness and Compassion towards herself and the co-owner.

Ken Cloke has a flow-chart for the stages in the resolution of conflict, from which we can glean what was missing from the Drama Queen resolution:

1) Impasse (open conflict in a "stuck" situation)

2) Stop fighting – (a de-escalation of the open conflict)

3) Settlement – (terms agreed upon to end the open conflict)

4) Resolution – (the underlying emotional reasons for the conflict have been addressed and resolved)

5) Forgiveness – (of all persons involved, leading to closure of the conflict)

6) Reconciliation – (the disappearance of all residues of negative feelings)

7) Prevention – (the transformation of experience into learning, strengthening communications and relationships, and designing systems to prevent repetition).[125]

---

125 Kenneth Cloke, Heart of Dispute Resolution (2006), Janis Publications

In "Drama Queen", the first three stages of Cloke's resolution process were completed – the immediate hostilities had ended, and the present manifestation of the conflict had been settled by the parties. But the deeper, more lasting resolution, whereby the resentments they felt towards each other would have been converted into something more positive, had not. As such, the conflict had been settled but not reconciled, which is why it flared again.

In the Buddhist framework we've looked at in this book, the parties in Drama Queen had let go of their attachment to their positions on the immediate issues which fueled the conflict, but had not let go of the underlying negative emotions they felt towards each other – the Three Poisons as reflected in that conflict – and therefore never converted them into ones of Loving Kindness and Compassion. Because the Poisons had not been converted into Sublime States, the parties were ready to get into conflict again once a new set of external situations arose between the parties.

As a mediator of the Drama Queen situation, I met my immediate goal. The parties had reached a temporary truce and could get back to their "normal" lives. Because of the time and money constraints facing me in that situation (as in so many other conflict resolution situations), that result was "good enough" to meet the needs of the day. As a practitioner interested in human transformation, on the other hand, the result was not satisfactory, because the parties were still burdened with the destructive emotions they felt towards each other. The Drama Queen still felt unappreciated and therefore resentful to his house-mate, and she still looked down on him for his dramatic ways.

In the Introduction, we said that a Buddhist rewrite of Kenneth Cloke's flow-chart would look something like this:

Eightfold Path To Resolve Conflict:

1) a **Situation** causes Conflict

2) which is the arousal of one or more of the **Three Poisons**

3) which persist through a **Refractory Period** leading to stasis

4) after which the parties can **Acknowledge** to themselves and each other – through the development of *personal and interpersonal* **Mindfulness** -the nature of the Three Poisons present in the situation, making possible

5) a **Settlement** of the (external) Situation, during which process

6) the parties can develop **Loving Kindness** and **Compassion** for themselves and the others, which allows for

7) **Appreciative Joy** in the benefits that each side has gained through the Situation, which allows each person to achieve

8) **Equanimity** and peace with themselves, the others, and the outcome of the process.

The Situation can be anything – who takes out the garbage, the River Rohini Incident, the Dirty Basin Incident, a divorce settlement or child custody disagreement, the situation in Darfur, or the Drama Queen conflict. In some sense it doesn't matter what the situation is, just *that* it is. And we have already looked at the Three Poisons -- – greed (*lobha kilesa*), hatred (*dvesha kilesa*), and delusion (*moha kilesa*) – and some variations on that basic list.

Number three on the Eightfold Path To Resolve Conflict talks about a Refractory Period, at the end of which stasis has resulted, which means the situation is calm enough to generate a resolution. We should look a bit more carefully at the idea of Refractory Periods, so we can learn how to work with the emotions they contain.

Refractory Periods

It's interesting to watch the Buddha's timing in dealing with the various conflicts he was involved in:

a) in the River Rohini incident, he strove to intercede as soon as he possibly could, because had he not there would have been bloodshed;

b) in the Dirty Basin Incident, he left the disputants to their own devices, and allowed time to help them move through their own poisonous periods;

c) with Suddhodana, he didn't directly try to resolve it at all, although he did resolve it by making sure his Dad became enlightened and was able to let go of all his attachments to the issues in the conflict before he died;

d) with Devadatta, he did not try to resolve them at all – at least, not directly with Devadatta – perhaps because he knew there was no use. While some of the stories of Devadatta's death have him being swallowed up by the earth on the way to seek forgiveness from the Buddha, in which event there would be no resolution at all of the conflict in this lifetime, in others the Buddha forgives him on his deathbed, thereby effecting a reconciliation and making sure that Devadatta was firmly back on the Way before he expired. The Buddha did intercede in the conflict through secondary routes, however. He had his disciples deal compassionately with the renegade newly-ordained monks, he himself dealt compassionately with his would-be assassins, and he protected the other citizens of Rajagaha from Nalagiri, who he dealt with lovingly in the moment that the danger presented.

Each conflict situation has its own inner timing and rhythm, which one has to first intuit, and then have the patience to allow unfold. Sometimes, one has to intercede immediately, as in the River Rohini situation, because the risk of delay is too great or because the Poisons at play are actually concentrating in strength during the delay.

In other situations, like the Dirty Basin Incident, the attachments of the participants are so strong, and the consequences of the inherent risks so seemingly palatable, that one can allow time itself to heal the conflict. But it's slower that way, which is hard in our society in particular where we're always in a hurry, so one needs to be mindful of the urge to hurry and of the need to be patient.

There's also a significant difference in the rapidity with which different people go through their refractions. From the Buddha's life story, there is the example of Devadatta who never let go of his jealousy of the Buddha until his death-bed, if at all, whereas his would-be assassins and the Rohini River leaders were able to transform their Poisons on the spot. I also remember my Mom being mad at me for 30 years about a plastic mimosa plant I had thrown out by accident as a child – I finally told her in my forties that if she mentioned it again I would cease all communications with her (which made her stop mentioning it, though I don't know if she actually let go of the long-activated Poisons before her death a few years later)!

Richard Davidson at the E. M. Keck Laboratory for Functional Brain Imaging and Behavior at the Madison campus of the University of Wisconsin has studied the varieties of "recovery function" from destructive emotions, and has noted that some people have prolonged responses, while others return to an emotional baseline quickly. These variations depend upon a number of factors – the age of the person, the amount of activation of the amygdala, the amount of cortisol released by the adrenal glands, and the effect of this hormone on the hippocampus. To these must be added the psychological history of the person experiencing the emotion, because that will increase or decrease the likelihood and severity of the activation of the Poisons.[126]

Additionally, the likelihood of expressing certain destructive emotions in the first place can be a habitual tendency of a person towards such expression, which remains unconscious and dormant in the person until a triggering event unleashes it. The Pali term for

---

126 Destructive Emotions, Daniel Goleman (2003) Bantam Books, Pages 197-8.

these latent tendencies is *anusayas*, and it denotes the mental habits that have formed over time due to past experiences during a person's life. These propensities actually increase in strength with frequency, so that less and less of a stimulus will more easily generate more and more of a response – like an old muscle injury flaring up in response to a much smaller stress than caused the original injury in the first place.[127] The person who flies off the proverbial handle is an example of this – they end up in anger management class because they get madder and madder more and more often until their entire world is disrupted.

For all of these reasons, in dealing with conflict in your life, you will have to gauge and be sensitive to the vicissitudes of refraction, and learn to work with it. If you are in conflict yourself, and the Poisons involved are related to one of your *anusayas*, then you'll have to struggle for a little longer to get it resolved. If you're in conflict with your girlfriend or husband or partner, and you recognize that this same type of issue has come up with them before, and they react very strongly to it, then it's probably one of their *anusayas*, which means you need to have patience and Compassion to deal with it since you'll fully refract first. And every mediator is familiar with situations where a group in conflict is ready to resolve the conflict and needs to do so, except that one person in the conflict is stuck on an *anusaya* and virtually unwilling to even look at the possibility of letting it go. In that case, the mediator needs to structure the resolution around the recalcitrant party, leaving a compassionate invitation to him or her to resolve it when they feel capable of doing so.

Creating Mindfulness

If you want to create Mindfulness in your own life, you just need to resolve to do so and start practicing it – such as by using the Buddha's Mindfulness of breathing methodology outlined in Chapter 5. But how does one create Mindfulness when it's not just you, but you and someone else, or you as a mediator with a group of conflicted people?

---

127 <u>Destructive Emotions</u>, Daniel Goleman (2003) Bantam Books, Page 141.

When I first considered this question, the whole idea seemed a bit impossible – I mean, Mindfulness is historically considered an internal process, or at least that's how I saw it. But my friend Sasha said something to me one day that made me see things a bit differently. Sasha said that conflict resolution itself seems to be exactly the same as Mindfulness meditation, only on the outside rather than in.

In Mindfulness meditation, one has something one tries to focus on --such as the breath, a mantra, or a visual object -- and then witnesses what the mind generates around that attempt. All sorts of things come up unbidden – plans for the future, frustrations about the past, things you love, things you don't – and always you just get back to the job at hand of focusing on the breath after noting these things that have arisen.

And it's like that in all dispute resolution situations as well. Your focus is to resolve the conflict (which we've defined as converting the Three Poisons into the Four Sublime States), but other stuff just keeps coming up. If it's an internal conflict, you'd like to get right to the issue but need to swim through a sea of seemingly irrelevant other personal thoughts and feelings to do so. Similarly, if it's you and your partner, you're trying to resolve the issue of why the partner keeps getting mad about one of your personal habits, and instead the discussion keeps regressing into why he or she doesn't care about you, or why you said something earlier that's completely unrelated to the issue at hand. If you're mediating a conflict, you're trying to keep the group focused on the issue that ostensibly generated the conflict, and they keep getting mad at each other for seemingly completely unrelated past offenses.

When we talked about Mindfulness in Chapter 5, we noted that through it, one learns to accept whatever arises without attachment, watching it arise and dissolve, and seeing the underlying causes of what comes up. *This is exactly what happens in the resolution of conflict as well.*

Whether in a two-person inter-personal situation, or in the mediation context, though our goal is resolution and reconciliation, *all of the things that arise have meaning, and all must be allowed to arise and then dissipate in order to resolve the problem.* They are not, as many mediators assume early on, "beside the point" – quite often they *are* the point, which none of the participants in the conflict have been able to see or state clearly enough prior to this present moment. And so it's helpful to have some guidelines to foster and allow this "inter-Mindfulness" to develop and flourish. Some ground rules to allow this are as follows:

Fostering Inter-Mindfulness in Personal Relationships

First, you need to make it okay for the other person to open up to you. So make the possibility of a true communication real by stating that's what you're doing. In other words, say something like "We've got a problem with such and such, and I'd really like to resolve it so we can heal our relationship. So let's make a time and place to sit down and discuss it – I promise to be honest and to listen carefully to whatever you want to tell me." The emphases here are on the words *honest* and *listen*. If you're not going to be honest, there's no point having the communication. And as for listening, as Thich Nhat Hanh says, "the secret of creating peace is that when you listen to another person you have only one purpose: to offer him an opportunity to empty his heart." [128] This will mean allowing them to say things which may be painful or hurtful to you without interrupting them and trying to "defend" your position. Let their words arise and then dissolve, but listen with your heart.

Second, you need to make it okay for you to open up to the other person. For this you need two qualities: a) courage, and b) Compassion. You need courage because without it, you'll be too afraid to say the truth without trying to sugarcoat it into something you think the other person will be okay with, and thereby you'll become inauthentic which will generate even more Poisons in your life. And you need Compassion to understand how to say these courageous things without causing the other person not to hear them at all. In general, this means talking about your feelings as opposed to the other person's actions, and about what you need to satisfy your justifiable needs as opposed to what you need them to do.

---

128 Creating True Peace, Thich Nhat Hanh (2003), Free Press, Page 189.

Third, you need to allow for the unexpected, as opposed to what you're afraid will happen. The Buddha once told a story of a man who mistakenly believed his son had died when a house burned down. When the son later returned at night and knocked on the man's door, he was refused entry because the man refused to believe that his son wasn't already dead. As a result, the man never saw his son – who he loved more than anything in life – again. Our fears and expectations (to which we are attached by the Poisons of ignorance and greed or clinging, and by the very structure of the human brain) make us presume that there are only certain outcomes possible in many situations. And because of this, we are unable to allow the magic of what actually can happen to do so. So as an additional kind of courage to express, allow yourself to be a warrior of the unknown, and assume that the karma of the unexpected will work out as it should as long as you have a compassionate heart.

Fostering Inter-Mindfulness in Mediation Situations

First, you need to make it okay for all the participants to feel safe expressing their truth about the situation The participants in mediation usually come in with three characteristics: a) they feel somewhat powerless and self-absorbed; b) they are driven by or residing with one or more of the Three Poisons; and c) they are not seeing the true nature of the conflict situation.

The Budhha understood clearly the distortions of individual perspective when he told his disciples a parable wherein an Indian raja had each of six blind men touch an elephant, and then describe what he felt.

> "When the blind men had felt the elephant, the raja went to each of them and said to each, 'Well, blind man, have you seen the elephant? Tell me, what sort of thing is an elephant?'
>
> They assert the elephant is like a pot (head), winnowing basket (ear), ploughshare (tusk), plough (trunk), granary (body), pillar (foot), mortar (back), pestle (tail), or brush (tip of the tail).

The men come to blows, which delights the raja. The raja says:

> O how they cling and wrangle, some who claim
> For preacher and monk the honored name!
> For, quarreling, each to his view they cling.
> Such folk see only one side of a thing." [129]

So a significant part of the inter-Mindfulness of mediation is the approximation of actual truth by having all the blind men come together in one safe place to share their versions and hear those of the other participants. Through this process, they start letting go of their attachment to their Poisons by letting go of their attachment to their isolated perspective. This in turn allows them to come out of their self-absorption, and regain justifiable power by seeing the other participants as real.

Second, you need to allow each participant to speak his or her "truth" in such a way that the other participants can hear them. For this you need three qualities as a mediator: a) intuition, b) integrity; and c) Compassion. You need to be intuitive enough to understand how and when each party can speak in such a way that the others are ready and able to listen at all. You need the integrity to set good ground rules to make the others able to hear what is said. I usually make sure that the person speaking is speaking towards me rather than towards the other participants (so they can listen without feeling attacked in any way), and I try to have them speak in terms of their feelings and what they need rather than making negative comments about the listeners. And your Compassion, by which is meant your unending desire that the suffering of all the participants be reduced, will create an aura that allows the first two qualities to be effective.

Third, you need to get out of the way of your own expectations regarding the result, so that the unexpected can happen. Amazingly enough, I've never once been able to foresee exactly how any particular mediation

---

129 Udana 68-69, http://en.wikipedia.org/wiki/Blind_Men_and_an_Elephant#cite_note-Buddhist-1

would work out, though many times I've gotten attached to how I thought it should, as in the case of the Hateful Neighbors. So, in the service of inter-Mindfulness, see if you can remain present and compassionate, but allow the truth to emerge on its own without getting attached to what you think it should be. That way what arises will be true and clear and not be muddied by your expectations of the way it should look.

Transforming the Three Poisons

In the process of Mindfulness or inter-Mindfulness, the nature of the Three Poisons at work in the situation will likely be revealed. And it is the nature of Mindfulness that it not only reveals the Poisons, but also starts on its own to transform them into Loving Kindness and Compassion. Sometimes, however, the situation needs a little technical assistance to help this transformation succeed.

Earlier in the book we discussed the three techniques traditionally used by Buddhism to transform destructive emotions:

" The first consists of applying a specific antidote to each negative emotion. The second allows us to unravel, or "liberate", the emotion by looking straight at it and letting it dissolve as it arises. The third uses the raw power of emotion as a catalyst for inner change."[130]

The traditional usage of these techniques is by the practitioner internally, to help resolve the inner expression of destructive emotions. However, just as Mindfulness is mirrored and expanded by inter-Mindfulness, each of these techniques can be applied interpersonally.

Antidotes

The idea behind the use of an antidote or anti-venom is quite simple – the Buddhists believe you can't feel love and hate, or arrogance

---

130 Happiness, Matthieu Ricard (2003), Little Brown and Company, page 123

and modesty, or any two opposing feelings at one and the same time (which is not to say that you can't vacillate between the two).

Antidotes to a five-poison menu variation of the Three Poisons are:

Poison	Antidote/Anti-venom
1) greed, desire	a) *imaginative* -- contemplation of less attractive aspects of desired object
	b) *reality-based* - Mindfulness, balanced perception, generosity
2) hatred, anger	a) *imaginative* -- contemplation of positive aspects of reviled object
	b) *reality-based* - Mindfulness, patience, Loving Kindness
3) ignorance, delusion, distraction	meditation on Dependent Arising, meditation on Emptiness, Tranquility, Mindfulness
4) jealousy	Appreciative Joy
5) pride	Compassion, humility

Mindfulness is the key to all of the antidotes, because it is the factor that in each case either diminishes the relevant Poison, or helps create the Sublime State (such as Compassion, Appreciative Joy, etc.) that is the actual antidote needed to counteract that Poison. This reiterates the central importance of Mindfulness in the resolution of any conflict.

You will note that there are two levels of some of these – imaginative and reality-based[131] Actually, there are imaginative and

---

131 <u>Destructive Emotions</u>, Daniel Goleman (2003) Bantam Books, Page 96.

reality-based antidotes for all of them, only the imaginative ones are more readily adaptable to greed and hatred.

Let's assume that I really want something badly – to be with an absent sexual partner, or to buy a new car, for example -- I can meditate on or imagine the negative or less-desirable attributes of the desired person or object in such a way as to develop inner freedom from the desire for it. Even better, I can look at the negative qualities of the desire for the person or thing itself, and use that as the antidote. Similarly, even though I am angry at someone, if I imagine their better qualities for a while (or look at the negative qualities of the anger itself), it will have the effect of lessening my anger at them. As you might have suspected, these imaginative techniques are more readily suited to internal meditation than they are to mediated disputes.

However, they can be used in inter-personal situations as well. For example, let's say you're mediating a dispute where one of the participants is not seeing the bigger picture because of an almost obsessive need to control the situation. If the situation is a business and you believe the participant hasn't really thought through what the ramifications of getting the control they want will be in his or her life, have that person imagine out loud what those outcomes will be – e.g. less time with the family, less time for personal activities, less camaraderie with co-owners, etc. It's possible that (if the participant is neither a classical narcissist nor a psychopath) the Mindfulness of these countervailing factors will lessen the Poison of *trishna* for the participant, and thereby aid in the transformation.

Another example would be in a divorce mediation where one spouse has left the other for another person, and is subconsciously vilifying the abandoned spouse to cover up for the guilt they are feeling. If as a mediator you can get the abandoning spouse to admit to and be aware of the good qualities of the abandoned spouse, and thereby create some Mindfulness around the issue of guilt and projection, you can actually move both spouses towards a realization of the Compassion due to each other, and thereby facilitate transformation of the Poisons. This is a tough job, because the abandoning spouse will have a great deal invested in maintaining the Poison of hatred towards the other to avoid acknowledging what he/she has actually done, but it is possible and cathartic for both spouses when successful. If the direct antidote isn't working, you can accomplish a similar shift by getting the angry spouse to become mindful that they have trapped themselves into negativity to cover their own grief over the loss of the marriage, which again would tend to neutralize the Poisons of hatred and anger.

Substitution

Substitution is a corollary type of imaginative device that can be used to transform the Poisons, which acts much like an antidote but has as its subject something other than the person or object towards whom the Poison is directed as its object. The River Rohini incident is an excellent example of this technique. The kings of Sakya and Koliya were fixating venomous feelings on each other's sides because of greed for water, and the Buddha made them think instead of their love for the Khattiya warriors on their own side of the battle line. In this way, the positive feelings for the Khattiyas (who were oftentimes family members of that king) were substituted for the hatred of the other side, and the situation defused.

This technique is demonstrated in a less dramatic fashion by an example from family law mediation. When custody issues involve children, and the parents are venomous with each other, the mediator or other neutral will focus on the best interests of the children and thereby elicit the parents' love for the children to lessen the vitriol level and get them to agree to a reasonable custody-sharing arrangement. While I have heard people speak disparagingly of this kind of substitution as a "trick", it is actually a way to shift the focus of brain activity from one area to another, and thus shift the type of feelings from negative to positive as well. So the divorcing parents' activity comes from their love and Compassion for their children instead of their anger and hurt at each other. If that's a trick, it's a worthwhile one.

Priming

A corollary form of substitution (which substitutes the emotion rather than the object of the emotion) is *priming*, whereby with word choice (words like closeness, love, hug and support) or imagery conjured by discussion you can foster feelings of emotional security in the listener, which can have the tendency to shift their attention and focus away from their Poisons. It is a technique in which "the person is induced consciously or subliminally to access mental circuits associated with emotional security."[132] While one needs to be sparing in use of this technique (less the other person end up feeling like they're being groomed for a role in a Care Bears movie, and then become suspicious of you), studies have shown that these words tend to reduce standoffishness and judgmental feelings about other people (particularly if they are from a different ethnic or socio-economic group) and thus allow for a reduction in destructive emotions towards that/those other(s).

You may have noted in the antidote chart two of the antidotes to delusion or ignorance are "meditation upon Dependent Arising" and "meditation upon Emptiness". These are actually not just category-specific antidotes, but universal antidotes to destructive emotions in general.

Freeing Emotions Via a Universal Antidote

Ricard states that the second way Buddhists deal with destructive emotions is to unravel, or "liberate" the emotion by looking straight at it and letting it dissolve as it arises, as do all phenomena in this universe. He goes on to state that by doing this, one robs the emotion of all its power:

> "When we examine the emotions, we find they are dynamic flows without any inherent substance of their own – in Buddhist terms, "empty" of real existence. What would happen if, instead of counteracting a disturbing emotion with

---

132 Train Your Mind, Change Your Brain, Sharon Begley (2007), Ballantine Books, Pages 199-200.

its opposite – anger with patience, for instance – we were simply to contemplate the nature of the emotion itself?... The experience of anger is like having a high fever. It is a temporary condition, and you do not need to identify with it. The more you look at anger in this manner, the more it evaporates under your gaze, like white frost under the sun's rays"[133]

Internally, this sounds again like plain old Mindfulness practice. With regard to inter-personal conflict, it shows why it is so important to allow each party to the conflict some safe way to express their feelings in a real way in the process. Not just so the others may hear, but so the speaker can look at his/her own emotions and let them become "empty" as they do so.

The Dependent Arising of Conflict

A second specific antidote for ignorance which is also a Universal Antidote is "meditation on Dependent Arising". To understand and appreciate this Universal Antidote, which shifts how cause and effect are viewed -- and thereby how blame is allocated -- in conflict situations, we need to know what Dependent Arising means.

Dependent Arising (also called Dependent Origination, Dependent Co-Arising, Conditioned Co-Production, Conditioned Genesis, Interdependent Arising, Contingency, or any of a number of other translations of the Pali *paticca-samuppāda*) is the Buddha's teaching on the nature of cause and effect. Of course, the law of karma (or, in Pali, *kamma*) is also a law of cause and effect, but that has more to do with the nature of the effects caused by our unconscious and conscious volitions and behavior, whereas Dependent Arising is the teaching of the workings of the rising and falling away of the entire realm of human suffering.

---

133 <u>Happiness</u>, Matthieu Ricard (2003), Little Brown and Company, pages 126-7

Dependent Arising holds that nothing is caused by a simple single causative factor. So, despite the fact that in a conflict situation we tend to blame the other (or, if it's internal, to castigate a part of ourselves) for the conflict, in reality every situation arises because of everything else that has ever preceded it. In fact, both sides to a conflict arise dependently upon each other, for there is no conflict for the one without the presence of the other.

Two of the Buddha's top disciples, Sāriputta and Moggallana, converted to the Way after Sāriputta, who had been wandering in Rājagaha to seek a new spiritual teacher, heard the disciple Assaji (one of the original five disciples) express the following with regard to this first aspect of Dependent Arising:

> *This being, that becomes, from the arising of this, that arises; this not becoming, that does not become; from the ceasing of this, that ceases.*"[134]

This famous quotation holds that no causation is simple, and that each phenomenal event is part of a web of occurrence. And, in fact, the Buddha stated to his disciples that his Awakening under the Bodhi tree was an awakening to this truth of Dependent Arising:

> "What the Buddha awakened to (Bodhi means "to awaken") was the truth of dependent origination... This is the understanding that any phenomenon 'exists' only because of the 'existence' of other phenomena in an incredibly complex web of cause and effect covering time past, time present and time future. This concept of a web is symbolized by Indra's Net, a multidimensional spider's web on which lies an infinite amount of dew drops or jewels, and in these are reflected the reflections of all the other drops of dew ad infinitum.

---

134 A Survey of Buddhism, Sangharakshita (4th Ed. 1976), Shambhala Books, Page xxi. In Buddhist countries, the recitation of these words in Pali – "Imasmim sati, idam hoti, imass' uppādā, idam uppajjati; imasmim asati, idam na hoti; imassa nirodhā, idham nirujjhati." is believed to create merit for the speaker.

Stated in another way, everything depends on everything else. For example, a human being's existence in any given moment is dependent on the condition of everything else in the world (and indeed the universe) at that moment but, conversely, the condition of everything in the world in that moment depends in an equally significant way on the character and condition of that human being. Everything in the universe is interconnected through the web of cause and effect so that the whole and the parts are mutually interdependent. The character and condition of entities at any given time are intimately connected with the character and condition of all other entities that superficially may appear to be unconnected or unrelated.

Because all things are thus conditioned and transient (*anicca*), they have no real independent identity (*anatta*) so do not truly 'exist', though to ordinary minds this appears to be the case. All phenomena are therefore fundamentally insubstantial and 'empty' (*sunya*)."[135]

And so we revisit Indra's Net, only this time to see that every event/thing is a result of every other event/thing. Thus in a conflict resolution one of the purposes and results of Mindfulness or inter-Mindfulness, and one of the tools we use to deal with the Three Poisons, is to let go of our western idea of causation – "I'm feeling bad and it's your fault" – and see that the real truth of causation is more like "this situation and each of our behaviors in it is the product of everything that has ever gone before and led to this moment."

If we can see our conflicts in this clearer light, it frees us from having to blame ourselves or the other for being "wrong" or the "cause" of the problem, and thus allows us to shift from one causative system – that of Dependent Arising – into the volitional realm of karmic formation. In other words, the experience of the Dependent Arising of any conflict allows us to switch from being the victim

---

135 Pratītyasamutpāda, Wikipedia, http://en.wikipedia.org/wiki/Prat%C4%ABtyasamutp%C4%81da

of causation to being the planter of karmic seeds, a creator of a set of future possibilities. This perceptual shift allows us to let go of the Poisons that bind us to a distorted vision of the conflict, and to take personal responsibility for a role in both its creation and its transformation.

Using Emotion as a Catalyst for Transformation

Ricard's third technique for converting destructive emotion is "us(ing) the raw power of emotion as a catalyst for inner change". To do this, one needs to be aware that every negative emotion has certain positive aspects as well:

Poison	Positive Aspect
Anger	call to action, clarity of purpose, focus, effectiveness
Desire	bliss and appreciation
Pride	confidence
Jealousy	admiration, drive

In other words, each Poison contains within it other related qualities which are not in themselves poisonous and which can actually lead away from conflict instead of fostering it.

It is possible to – with Mindfulness and free expression – separate the aspects of emotions into constituent parts, and use the admirable parts as fuel for transformation. Ricard warns, however, of the difficulty of doing this:

"This kind of practice requires great command of the language of emotions. Allowing powerful emotions to express themselves without falling prey to them is playing with fire, or rather, trying to snatch a jewel from the snake's head. If we succeed, our understanding of the nature of the mind will grow accordingly; if we fail, we will find ourselves overwhelmed by the negative qualities of anger and its hold on us will be strengthened."[136]

---

136 Happiness, Matthieu Ricard (2003), Little Brown and Company, page
      129.

Ultimately, the choice on whether to chance this type of technique will depend on the context and how severe the repercussions of it backfiring are. If you're in a situation where antidotes are not working and no one is willing to look directly at the emotions to let them dissolve, then you might want to take a chance on working with emotions directly, and see where they lead. The Screaming Family was like that – no one in the room used any anti-venoms, and no one was willing to let their emotions dissolve into emptiness. Instead, each person expressed their emotions in such a way that the noble and loving parts of the emotion rang loud and true, while the negative aspects fell away like dross. So the mother's carping showed itself as appreciation and concern for her children, the son's and daughter's anger transformed into love and the desire that their protectiveness of their family be effective, and so on.

There was some risk in that scenario, which I as mediator took by yelling at them at the beginning of the session. It could have backfired, with the group accelerating their destructive emotionality and then leaving, worse than when they came in. On the other hand, my yelling was a veiled message to them, sort of like "hey, it's okay for you to yell and express your feelings – but what's that underneath them?" Perhaps if it had been a negotiation in the Middle East, and I knew that if one side walked out missiles would be raining on the others by sunset, the gamble would not have been worth it and I would have tried another tack. But that's one of the benefits of Mindfulness – hopefully, it gives us some insight into what's possible when, and the intuition as to how to make that possibility real.

The Anti-Refractory Period

The Refractory Period we discussed is the duration where the Poisons are so strong that transforming them is highly unlikely. There's another period of time – the *anti*-Refractory Period – which comes in to play after the "situation" has been resolved and the parties have quelled their Poisons and transformed them into Loving Kindness and Compassion. These are two of the Sublime States -- but you may recall that there are Four Sublime States (also called Supreme Abodes), not two. The anti-Refractory Period is the period during which the remaining two – Appreciative Joy and Tranquility – grow and express themselves. Like its opposite, this period can be short or long in duration.

Appreciative (or Sympathetic) Joy and Tranquility (Equanimity) are more subtle and delicate than their two companion states. And they are derivative, in that they grow out of the fertile soil created by Loving Kindness and Compassion. In fact, the ancient texts actually describe a cascading waterfall effect of the Four Sublime States, with Loving Kindness at the top of the waterfall:

> "Without Love, Compassion will turn to contempt, Sympathetic Joy to vicarious satisfaction, and Equanimity to heartless indifference. The texts invariably describe first the cultivation of Love, after which they repeat the same formula, with the variation of one term only, for the other three abodes."[137]

The directions that the Buddha thus gave his monks on the Four Sublime States were as follows (with identical portions of the second, third and fourth paragraph omitted:

> *"I. Here, monks, a disciple dwells pervading one direction with his heart filled with loving-kindness, likewise the second, the third, and the fourth direction; so above, below and around; he dwells pervading the entire world everywhere and equally with his heart filled with loving-kindness, abundant, grown great, measureless, free from enmity and free from distress.*
>
> *II. Here, monks, a disciple dwells pervading one direction with his heart filled with compassion… and free from distress.*

---

137 <u>A Survey of Buddhism</u>, Sangharakshita (4th Ed. 1976), Shambhala Books, Page 144.

III. Here, monks, a disciple dwells pervading one direction with his heart filled with sympathetic joy… and free from distress.

IV. Here, monks, a disciple dwells pervading one direction with his heart filled with equanimity… free from distress."[138]

It is common, therefore, that in the resolution of conflict Loving Kindness and Compassion will express during the actual resolution process. This makes sense since they are the eldest "children" of Mindfulness and the skillful means of the participant(s) and/ or the mediator, and in fact are necessary ingredients for any true "reconciliation" of the parties to occur.

But Appreciative Joy is a further step, for here one not only loves them, and feels their suffering, but is happy for any joy that has appeared in their life, or through the resolution of a conflict. And this can be hard. The old saw amongst mediators is that the mediation has been successful when each person can live with the misery it has garnered them. Under that adage, you haven't reconciled your Poisons, you've just learned to live with their residual bitter after-taste. But it doesn't have to be that way! For just as Mindfulness leads to Compassion, so does Compassion lead to Appreciative Joy.

Let's say a man leaves his wife and files for divorce, and out of guilt gives more than a fair share of the family's wealth to the spouse, and pays more than required amount of support to her as well. Eventually, when it comes time to finalize their settlement, his heart is rancorous because he misses the wealth he has given her, and feels she has "gotten the better of him", even though his actions created and structured much of the process. What constitutes a true resolution of the process?

He could ask that the agreement be revised so that it is fair to him as well. This is, of course, the ideal result, but there are circumstances that may militate against it, or he could finally become mindful of his real feelings only after the agreement is signed. So for purposes of this

---

138 Digha Nikaya 13, trans. Nyanaponika Thera, http://www.accesstoinsight. org/lib/authors/nyanaponika/wheel006.html

example, I'll presume that the agreement has been signed, and cannot be renegotiated.

He could enter the settlement agreement, and carry around resentment for his ex the rest of his life. Here's the old saw in action, which means he'll live with a shrunken heart (the "shrunken mind" of the Third Foundation of Mindfulness). So, while we can say that the divorce settled, the conflict didn't fully resolve.

He could enter the settlement agreement, learn to feel some love and Compassion for his ex, yet still carry around some resentment about the settlement for the rest of his life. This is of course better, but still he has a somewhat shrunken mind/heart, and is not at peace with the resolution.

He could enter the settlement agreement, feel love and Compassion for his ex, (and probably after a little while longer) let go of any attachment to the things he gave up in the settlement, and feel no resentment for his ex. This is a truer resolution, wherein the husband has achieved the sublime state of Appreciative Joy for his ex-wife.

To make a final, final reconciliation of not only the parties to each other but of each party to him- or herself, there is but one further stage – the achievement of Equanimity, which is a mind balanced by wisdom and insight into the nature of this human life of ours:

> "Looking into life we notice how it continually moves between contrasts: rise and fall, success and failure, loss and gain, honor and blame. We feel how our heart responds to all this with happiness and sorrow, delight and despair, disappointment and satisfaction, hope and fear. These waves of emotion carry us up and fling us down; and no sooner do we find rest, than we are in the power of a new wave again. How can we expect to get a footing on the crest of the waves? How can we erect the building of our lives in the midst of this ever restless ocean of existence, if not on the Island of Equanimity?"[139]

---

139 The Four Sublime States, Nyanaponika Thera, http://www.
       accesstoinsight.org/lib/authors/nyanaponika/wheel006.html

So a final, final resolution of the conflict for the husband is: *He enters the settlement agreement, feels love and Compassion for his ex, and (probably after a little while longer) lets go of any attachment to the things he gave up in the settlement, feels no resentment for his ex and is happy for what she gained through the settlement , and (probably after even a little while longer) recognizes the Dependent Arising of the factors in the situation and the fruition of the karmic seeds he planted therein, achieves Equanimity with the entire matter, and lives in peace with it.*

8. CONCLUSION:
CONFLICT AND THE WHEEL
OF BECOMING

Rebirth and Transcendence In Our Daily Conflicts

"Before my enlightenment, monks, when I was unenlightened and still a Bodhisattva, I thought: 'Into wretchedness, alas, has this world fallen, it is born, grows old, dies, passes away, and is reborn. But from this pain it knows no escape, from old age and death. When indeed from this pain shall an escape be known, from old age and death?'

"Then, monks, I thought, 'Now when what exists do old age and death exist, and what is the cause of old age and death? And as I duly reflected, there came the comprehension of full knowledge: it is when there is rebirth that there is old age and death. Old age and death have rebirth as cause.

"Then, monks, I thought, 'Now when what exists does rebirth exist, and what is the cause of rebirth? And as I duly reflected, there came the comprehension of full knowledge: it is when there is becoming (or desire to be) that there is rebirth, rebirth has desire as its cause.

"In the same way desire is said to be caused by grasping, grasping by craving, craving by feeling, feeling by contact or stimulation of any of the senses, contact by the six sense-organs, the six sense-organs by mind-and body (nāma-rūpa), mind and body by consciousness, consciousness by the aggregates, and the aggregates by ignorance.

"Thus, with ignorance as cause there are the aggregates, with aggregates as cause there is consciousness, with consciousness as cause there is mind-and-body, with mind-and-body as cause there are the six sense-organs, with the six sense-organs as cause there is contact, with contact as cause there is feeling, with feeling as cause there is craving, with craving as cause there is grasping, with grasping as cause there is desire, with desire as cause there is rebirth, with rebirth as cause there is old age and death. Even so is the origin of this whole mass of pain."[140]

---

140 <u>A Survey of Buddhism</u>, Sangharakshita (4th Ed. 1976), Shambhala Books, Page 78, quoting from Samyutta-Nikaya, II.10.

It is fairly common knowledge that the Buddha realized the Four Noble Truths, and formulated the Noble Eightfold Path, on the night of his Awakening. More specifically, he realized these on the Third Watch of that night. And within these Truths and Path are encapsulated a seemingly simple schema with which to approach the practice of Buddhism.

Yet during that Third Watch that night, the Buddha also realized the links between birth, death and rebirth, and the suffering that characterizes this "Wheel of Life" or "Dependent Arising". In fact, the Buddha told his disciples at various times that his Awakening *was* the full realization of Dependent Arising.

Dependent Arising includes the concept we have already discussed that each thing in the universe co-constitutes every other thing in the universe, but since that is a very nebulous concept the Buddha also devised a schema of twelve steps or *Nidānas* (which are the ones referred to in reverse order in the Buddha's quote at the beginning of this chapter) to show how the principle of Dependent Arising applies to the life of the individual, and how the karma generated by the individual affects him or her as they pass through this life. Actually, in the earliest Buddhist writings the twelve *Nidānas* were spread over three lives (with the first two steps from the previous life, the middle eight from the present life, and the final two being the next life) and were therefore entwined with the concept of reincarnation, but they are just as applicable to the single human life, or to any event or series of events (such as a conflict) that arises as well.

Because of its importance, the Buddha also drew a picture in the sand – the *bhavacakka* (in Pali) or "Wheel of Becoming" – to illustrate the workings of Dependent Arising for his monks, which they appreciated so much that eventually a painted version of it was placed in every Buddhist monastery in India. While these early prototypes were later largely destroyed by the Muslim invasions of India, stylized versions were copied and transported to Tibet, where they still exist, and also spread throughout the rest of Southern Asia.[141]   Below is a modern version of the Wheel of Becoming:

---

141 <u>When the Iron Eagle Flies</u> Ayya Khema (1991), Wisdom Publications, Pages 51-2.

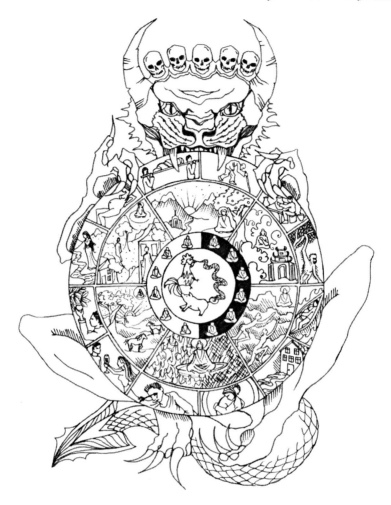

The iconography of the image is quite dense (having perhaps evolved beyond the sand-drawing stage), and local variations of the imagery change the specific items portrayed, but all exemplars have certain things in common. First, they all have an overarching tiger or monster hanging onto the rim of the system of concentric circles. The tiger/monster represents time and impermanence, and is therefore simultaneously beautiful and frightening to behold. Second all examples have a crown with five skulls on the head of the tiger/ monster – these represent the Five Aggregates, which give humans the illusion of a Self and of permanence, but which are all swallowed up by impermanence eventually.

All variations then have a system of concentric circles, the most central of which is one with three animals representing our old friends the Three Poisons:

At the bottom of the circle is the pig, which represents ignorance or delusion because it is always throwing dirt over its head and therefore can't see what's going on. The cock represents greed because he keeps a bevy of hens and likes to strut proudly about. The snake represents anger and hatred because it is itself filled with poison. The three animals are biting each other's tails, which suggests that they work as a tag-team, with delusion at the bottom because it is the springboard for the others and harder for us to become aware of in ourselves.

The next circle is of good and bad karma, with the white-backgounded half showing good karma flowing from following the Noble Path, and the black-backgounded half showing bad karma flowing from heedless behavior. Around that there is then a circle showing the six realms of human existence: hell, hungry ghosts (creatures with small mouths and big insatiable bellies), animals, humans, demi-gods and gods. These can all be taken as representations of different states of consciousness we each experience at different times in our lives.

The outermost circle, the Twelve Links of Causality or *Nidānas*, is the most important with respect to our look at the resolution of conflict, because conflict like suffering follows a similar path of cause and effect in its genesis. This circle represents the twelve causative steps in the arising of suffering and rebirth, as alluded to by the Buddha in the quote at the beginning of this chapter, with each picture representing one of the steps.

1. *Ignorance (avijja)*: the picture for this part of the circle is of either an old blind woman or man, wandering through a petrified forest. Ignorance – both in the sense of spiritual unawareness and of a mistaken view of reality in general - is not only one of the Three Poisons, but also the root cause of all suffering.

2. *Volitional Formations* (the Fourth Aggregate or *saṅkhāra)*: the image here is of a potter making pots, spinning his wheel which is thus set in a motion that continues after his action, and which also creates predispositions in his mind for future actions. Some of the pots are nicely crafted (creating good karma in the future) but some are broken (bad karmic results). This is the Aggregate we noted as a breeding ground for the Three Poisons and conflict. And, since it grows out of Ignorance, one of the Poisons is already at work in any event.

3. *Consciousness (viññana)*: a monkey holding a crystal goes from window to window of a house, or from tree to tree in a forest. The crystal is virtue, but is usually clouded. Consciousness, which is the Fifth Aggregate, organizes all the other Aggregates, but also like the monkey is drawn from window to window or from tree to tree by the contact of the senses with the world, and thus loses the focus it needs to keep the crystal clear. This step is also often called "rebirth consciousness" (in the earliest writings on the Wheel of Becoming, the ignorance and volitional formations of the previous life were reincarnated at the moment of birth into the consciousness of the present life) so it relates to Buddhist notions of reincarnation, but it

203

relates equally as well to each moment (or day, or phase, or situation) of our current life in which our consciousness is a rebirth of the karma already accumulated within this life.

4. *Body and Mind (nāma-rūpa)*: consciousness always knows that it has a body and a mind, which lead to the illusion of a fixed self. The image for this step is of a boat with two or more passengers. Some commentators say that the boat is the body or first aggregate, and the passengers are the remaining four aggregates, but since many versions of the image have a seated figure steering the boat with a prone figure lying down, a more lyric interpretation is that the seated boatman is the mind and passenger the body. In that latter imagery, the boatman may think he's in control of the trip, but really mind only thinks it can control the body (or itself, for that matter), and mind and body are "in this boat together" and thus perpetually tossed about by the currents.

5. *The Six Sense-Bases (or Sense-Organs, salayatana):* here there is a picture of a house with five windows and a door, which represent the five senses (sight, hearing, taste, touch and smell) plus the mind or consciousness as the sixth sense. The door, which is thinking and the mind, allows in anything unless it is either closed or guarded. In Buddhism, generally, one can attain only transitory happiness or satisfaction from any of these six Sense-Organs, and then must search out new satisfaction elsewhere.

6. *Contact (phassa)*: is shown by a man and woman kissing or embracing, which shows that where there are all or some of the six Sense-Bases functioning, there will be contact with sense-objects, and we will try to make them pleasurable, but as shown by the very next picture, that is not always possible.

7. *Feeling (vedana)*: shows a man with an arrow in his eye. Feeling will always arise out of contact of the Sense-Bases with the world, and we cannot make them all pleasant or even neutral. Because we would like to, however, we can be easily led to the next step.

8. *Craving (tanha)*: this step is alternately shown by a man gorging himself at banquet table, or excessively drinking at a bar, or shooting heroin. While all of these suggest the want of something, craving can also be the negative, that is, the desire not to have something or to avoid it. Indeed, the natural craving of the man in the previous step would be to remove the arrow from his eye. The word *tanha* is the Pali word for the Sanskrit *trishna* discussed elsewhere in this book – the grasping for what is not or for what you do not have.

9. *Clinging (upadana)*: once you are grasping for something, you cling to it as well, under the mistaken idea that you own it. The image for this step is either a monkey plucking fruit from branches, or a farmer picking fruit off a tree and putting it in a basket that is already overfull with produce. When we grasp for things, we cling to them even when we have enough, and even though we know on some level that since all is impermanent they can never be "ours". Devadatta wanted what the Buddha had, and clung to everything he felt brought him closer to that goal, which ultimately caused him to lose what he "had" in the first place.

10. *Becoming (bhava)*: is symbolized by a pregnant woman, about to give birth to a new reincarnation. That new "self" is not yet fully created, but all the constituent parts for it are ready – including the karmic ties to the past of craving and clinging, and the craving for a new life or reincarnation in which to cling to more things.

11. *Birth (jati)*: the new reincarnation is shown as a woman giving birth to a child, or a baby being carried or in a baby-carriage. Because of karmic links to the past, and causal links to the new life-cycle, this step must lead to the final step.

12. *Aging and Death (jaramarana)*: the final picture is either of a dying person, or a person leaving home with his possessions on his back, or an old man with a sack of bones on his back. In the reincarnation schema, the "self" is released to be reincarnated into a new form which will go through the same cycle from

ignorance through craving and clinging to becoming to yet another death.[142]

One of the interesting by-products of the Buddha having put the *Nidānas* into a circular format is that it reduces our tendency to see the progression as a linear, one-way progression. In the quote at the beginning of the Chapter from the *Samyutta-Nikaya*, the Buddha is referring to a 12-step progression that is continuously recommencing until nirvana is achieved, but the circular schema makes it clearer that: a) the process of reincarnation (of the individual, attachment, clinging, etc.) can start at any point in the circle; and b) that it can just as well end at any point that the cycle is transcended. In other words, the *bhavacakka* is like a roulette wheel of karma.

And, in fact, the classical commentators have noted as much. For example, in the *Visuddhimagga* (a 5th century Theravadan treatise on the Buddhist path by Buddhaghosa), he discusses four ways in which the *Nidānas* can lead to suffering and rebirth: a) the first method (bottom to top) begins with ignorance and ends with sickness, old age, and death; b) the second method (middle to top) begins with attachment and proceeds to birth; c) the third method (top to bottom) begins with birth and proceeds back to ignorance; and d) the fourth method (middle to source) begins with attachment and proceeds to ignorance. Wherever you start, the wheel keeps spinning until through Mindfulness you let it stop.[143]

You might be wondering at this point: "What the heck does this have to do with the resolution of conflict?" But this 12-step progression can be used to show how conflict develops through these same cycles – *and the introduction of actual Mindfulness at any stage starts the process of resolving the conflict.* So the use of the causal link-steps of Dependent Arising gives us yet another way to view the development

---

142 In writing this section, I referred to both <u>When the Iron Eagle Flies</u> Ayya Khema (1991), Wisdom Publications, Pages 51-63, and to BuddhaNet Basic Buddhism Guide's <u>Dependent Arising</u> at <u>www.buddhanet.net/e-learning/depend.htm</u>.

143 <u>The Twelve Nidānas</u>, Wikipedia, <u>http://en.wikipedia.org/wiki/Twelve_Nid%C4%81nas</u>

of the conflict through a Buddhist perspective. Let's see how the Twelve Nidānas relate to conflict using a real-world conflict.

The Aikido school where I study in San Francisco is in the Mission district, where there are a lot of car break-ins at night – in other words, when the owner returns to get his car in the morning there are lots of little pieces of glass on the ground, and any possessions that had been left in the car are gone.

One of our live-in students, named Constantine, had had his mini-truck broken into two or three times over the past few years, and as might be expected the whole thing makes him very angry whenever he thinks about it. So he was familiarly angry when he went out of the dojo one night to find his car window broken yet again. As he was leaning through the damaged window, he saw through the windshield a man across the street holding a tire iron in his hand standing next to the bed of a regular size pickup truck.

Constantine knew immediately what had happened – the man across the street had just used the tire iron to break his truck window and steal the stuff from the back seat. He noticed that the man was looking at him, and it was clear from the look on the man's face and his body language that he was looking and acting guilty – no doubt because he was afraid of being caught in his nefarious deeds! So Constantine decided to confront the man, and ran into the dojo to get a stick to counter the tire iron if the man tried to hit him with it.

The man across the street had a very different perception of the situation. He, like Constantine, had had his truck window broken in the neighborhood more than once over the past several months, and was sick and tired of being the victim of these senseless, expensive and irritating crimes. He was walking back to his truck this particular evening when he saw a man (Constantine) leaning into a car through a window he had apparently just broken. Finally, the man had his sights on the perpetrator of all the neighborhood auto break-ins! So the man reached into the bed of his own truck and retrieved a tire iron as "insurance" for the impending confrontation. Right about then the perpetrator looked out of the car directly at the man, who perceived immediately that the perpetrator (Constantine) was looking funny and acting guilty. When the perpetrator ducked into the martial arts school next door, the man started crossing the street towards the dojo to prevent the criminal from escaping when he re-emerged.

When Constantine came out, the man with the tire iron was standing there. Since each was the angered yet somewhat apprehensive defender of moral right, they exchanged angry accusations with each other for several minutes, until the true nature of the situation began to dawn on each of them. Finally, each saw that they had been angry about the historical break-in situation, that the current events had brought that existing anger flooding back into consciousness, that because of the anger each of them had skewed their perception of the current events to reinforce the emotional charge they had on the event, and they had each been "reborn" as the avenger of moral right in the situation.

If we run this situation through the 12 reincarnation steps of Dependent Arising, they look like this:

1. *Ignorance (avijja):* Constantine and the man were both ignorant of the actual genesis and nature of the other's actions and the situation that presented to them. Each failed to consider the possibility that there were innumerable other possible explanations for the behavior of the other. They have each become a blind man with an elephant, where "quarreling, each to his view they cling, such folk see only one side of a thing."

2. *Volitional Formations (saṅkhāra):* because of their shared, mutual ignorance of reality, each comes up with theories and explanations, based upon their temperaments as modified by the experiences they have already had in this life (or even a previous life), including previous car break-ins. These give rise to some or all of the Three Poisons of anger and hatred and resentment (towards the other for breaking into his car and stealing his stuff), fear for their safety (trishna), and delusion about the other person's actions and their own projected role

in the retribution for the wrongs. The specific mix of Poisons will depend on the individual's temperament once again.

3. *Consciousness (viññana)*: under the sway of the Three Poisons, each person involved starts to interpret sensory data to agree with the deluded assessment each has already made of the situation. Thus, each thing that the other person does is a further indication of their guilt of the imagined offense.

4. *Body and mind ((nāma-rūpa)*: Both Constantine and the man's body and mind begin to be taken over by the Poisons and therefore take on the physical and mental attributes of angry persons preparing for battle or confrontation, and are totally prepared to act in accordance with the dictates of that consciousness.

5. *The Six Sense-Bases (salayatana)*: Constantine's and the man's senses of sight, hearing, taste, smell and touch are now all geared to relate to and foster the anger, hatred and other destructive emotions built into the situation, thus aggravating the delusion of each party.

6. *Contact (phassa)*: the activities of each, plus all the other sensory input of the environment during these events are now impinging on the sense organs of Constantine and the man, many of which will be interpreted to foster the individual's perception of the situation, such as picking up tire irons, furtive expressions, running in to the dojo, etc.

7. *Feeling (vedana)*: Constantine and the man are now each experiencing unpleasant feelings – anger, resentment, fear, etc. – in general, based upon all the above.

8. *Craving (tanha or trishna)*: each party now craves release from the Poisons, and a desire for the other party to suffer retribution for their perceived transgressions.

9. *Clinging (upadana)*: in the throes of the Refractory Period, the transgressions of the other become obsessive thoughts and feelings of the other. Each party's behavior is viewed as

a threat by the other, who is seen as an enemy who must be dealt with.

10. *Becoming (bhava)*: each party's behavior will now be that of an enemy or a combatant, because of clinging to the feelings and perceptions that have arisen.

11. *Birth (jati)*: if Constantine and the man are allowed to have this "becoming" behavior to become set and distinct through time and/or happenstance, it will become an identity for Constantine and the man. Each will become the "neighborhood defender" and the other will become fully identified as the "criminal" or the "enemy". This will foster the illusion of the permanent self in this new, seemingly solidified realm of assumed roles.

12. *Aging and Death (jaramarana)*: this new identity will exist, flourish, and then dissolve based upon all the factors of Indra's Net that operate, which will include doubt (the first inkling either has that they may be deluded), insecurity (suppose his tire iron is tougher than my stick?), or changes in the real world such as the arrival of the police, etc. With the arrival of this new "self" also arise the seeds and intimation of its demise or non-existence, which will be followed by the next round of ignorance through death.

Again, the meaningful introduction of Mindfulness at any point in these links will stop this chain of conflict link-steps, and can return the parties to a non-conflicted state. If Constantine had been mindful in the beginning, he might have realized there were a lot of other possible reasons for the man's behavior, which the man could have realized as well about Constantine. When perceptions started to become slanted in favor of the Poisoned ignorance, Mindfulness could again have intervened.

As it turned out, Mindfulness entered the situation when Constantine came out of the dojo and he and the man met in the street. They were each probably in between the stages of "becoming" and "birth" when the truth of Mindfulness started to take over. In the process, they each saw their Ignorance, and how it had arisen. They ended up laughing at each other's and their own behavior in the incident, patted each other on the back, and went on their separate ways. In other words, Mindfulness had started to morph into Loving Kindness and Compassion.

While Constantine's drama may not be as serious or "important" as conflict in the Middle East or Darfur, it is part of Indra's Net and also part of the same Wheel of Becoming as are all other incarnations and reincarnations in human life. We all fumble along in a state of ignorance for most of our lives, and as a result end up in conflicts continually. Some of us more than others to be sure, but most of us sometimes surely.

Since that is the case, then as we stated in the introduction it's helpful to be somewhat familiar with the nature of conflict, and know how to resolve it when necessary. What we've looked at herein is that process in Buddhist terms, which provides a framework within which to organize our thoughts and actions to help us deal with conflict as it arises.

Concluding Recapitulation

From a Buddhist perspective, conflict – which can be either internal or external – has two significant features. First, a situation causes a perceived divergence of interest within an individual or between the opposing sides to a conflict. This provides the "attachment" which the Buddha stated underlay all conflict. Second, it becomes an actual conflict by the arising of one or more of the Three Poisons -- i) anger or hatred, ii) greed or grasping, and iii) ignorance or delusion. Ignorance is the most basic of the three, and helps engender the other two.

The severity of the conflict and the extent of the arousal depends normally upon the level of need at which the difference arises. The lower on Maslow's "Hierarchy of Needs" one gets, the stronger and more entrenched are the attachments to the needs – thus, the needs for food and shelter would ordinarily be stronger than the needs to feel good about how you're being treated or the need for a new car.

Once the frustration of a need occurs, the human brain is programmed to foster attachment and conflict rather than its resolution. While the hippocampus and the ventromedial cortex portion of the frontal lobe provide a memory of emotional contexts and some control, respectively, of our responses to situations, once the amygdala gets aroused it basically hijacks the brain so that we are responding in an emotional way, with even our very perceptions being controlled by the fear and emotional responses the amygdala is giving out.

And thus arise the Three Poisons. We looked at 5-, 6-, and 20-item variations of the Three Poisons list, but all are similarly based upon a "heightened" degree of ignorance (thus delusion), with heightened degrees of anger or dislike and either attracted or aversive desire growing out of that ignorance.

The dispute resolution process is the process of turning these Three Poisons into the Four Sublime Virtues (or Four Supreme Abodes). And there's a structured process that schematizes this transformative process, which we termed the "Eightfold Path To Resolve Conflict". On that Path, the first step is the arising of a Situation, which causes the second step – conflict - which is itself the arousal of one or more of the Three Poisons.

The third step on the Path is the Refractory Period, which is the period of time where the Poisons are so strong that it is exceedingly difficult (though not necessarily impossible, as shown by the River Rohini incident) to move towards resolution or transformation.

Different people have different Refractory Periods – some people return to baseline quickly, whereas others fume and have to hold on to their destructive emotions for longer before they can let them go. If you're one of the former, and in a dispute with one of the latter, you'll just have to bide your time until the other person catches up with you.

You can also try to build techniques that deal with the Refractory Period into the resolution process. For instance, you can do a "Turtle" of some sort – do an actual Turtle, or walk around the block, have a cup of tea -- to allow your negative feelings to quell. You can also structure delays into the process, such as meeting in a few days rather than trying to deal with the problem when feelings are running high. The ultimate skill with regard to Refractory Periods is to have the wisdom to recognize them and the patience when possible to allow them to play out before tackling resolution of the underlying dispute. Of course, in an emergency or perilous situation, you will have to structure the resolution despite the Refractory Period.

When the Refractory Period ends, it's time to enter the real transformative portion of the resolution process – the fostering of Mindfulness, and the development of Loving Kindness and Compassion. It is not possible to overstate the importance of this phase in the resolution process: as Thich Nhat Hanh says, the secret of ending violence and conflict is to show each side what the other is feeling long enough for the seeds of Compassion to be planted.

Mindfulness can be developed either internally, or between individuals as part of what we've called "inter-Mindfulness". To create the first, it's easiest to do just that – start practicing some form of Mindfulness meditation, such as Bhante Gunaratana's technique described in Chapter 5. That will let you start seeing just how your mind is working – what things it gets drawn away by, what angers seem to keep resurfacing, and what things or events make you feel which way.

If the conflict is between a couple or group, then techniques of inter-Mindfulness are called for. Generally, that means giving each person a safe opportunity to recount (whether verbally, in writing, or through pictures or other interpretive means) their perspective on the conflict -- not to show everyone it's right, but to allow each participant (including the speaker) to see which part of the elephant the "blind" speaker has been touching. As the other speakers recount their version(s) of the conflict, a shared vision of the conflict – the real elephant, so to speak – can arise in the room and allow the participants to see each other with renewed Compassion and understanding.

This process of getting people to perceive a more accurate sense of the truth isn't always quick or easy – quite often people resist the truth because they are quite strongly attached to their Poisons and to their desire for a certain result, or because they don't really want to acknowledge their own role in the creation of the problem. But don't lose faith in the power of Mindfulness to transform situations – remain courageous, persevering, and hopeful until it is no longer feasible to do so.

Mindfulness itself will tend to lead to Loving Kindness and Compassion, because through being mindful with yourself you can let go of the judgments with which you victimize yourself, and because in a group situation inter-Mindfulness will let all the participants realize that they each have similar needs, fears and aspirations. You can also foster Loving Kindness and Compassion towards yourself and others by doing exercises such as we discussed in Chapter 6 to increase the presence of these states in your life and those of the people around you. People often respond to Loving Kindness and Compassion in kind, because it resonates with similar energies in them.

Through the development of Mindfulness to fully comprehend the arising and letting go of the conflict, and Loving Kindness and Compassion to embrace oneself and the others involved, the conflict situation will itself be resolved. The full reconciliation of the conflict will involve a final two steps that occur during what we have called the anti-Refractory Period. These tend to occur naturally over time, often after the active resolution process has concluded.

First, the parties develop Appreciative Joy, which is the initial step beyond Compassion. Here, one learns to feel happiness for the benefits that have accrued to him/herself *and* to the other side in a conflict. This allows one to let go of the last vestiges of the conflict that one is holding onto inside – the last attachment to it – so that the mind is no longer clouded by residues of the Three Poisons.

And, finally, one reaches the state of Equanimity, where the mind has become at peace with the entire conflict situation. The surface of the pond is no longer rippled, and the water no longer muddy. Instead, the water is still, clear and pure, so that one can see the bottom clearly.

The Heaven and Hell of Conflict

As we said in the beginning of this book, we live in a world of conflict. Each of us – you, me, everyone we love – will have to deal with conflict continually throughout their lives. I hope this book has given each of you some tools to help transform your conflicts into opportunities for growth and prosperity in your life.

In many ways, conflict is what we make of it. When we call it "conflict" it sounds like kind of a bad thing – if we call it a "growth opportunity" it sounds just great! To some extent, then, conflict is a matter of perspective.

There is a Zen parable of a man who dies, and is happy to wake up in a shimmering world where he is guided by a celestial being to a glowing banquet hall where the tables are overflowing with edible delicacies. The only problem is that he and all the other guests have boards strapped to their arms so they can pick the food up with their forks, but can't get the forks to their mouths. Everyone is angry and dissatisfied, and grumbles and groans. The man thinks to himself: "This must be Hell! What is Heaven?"

Thereupon he is taken to another banquet hall by his celestial guide – once again, the tables are overflowing, and once again, he and all the other guests have their arms strapped so they cannot be bent at the elbows. But in this banquet hall the guests are all happily eating, having realized that they can easily feed each other by sticking their arms out straight to the right, so that the person next to them can eat.[144]

The resolution of conflict is a bit like the realization that one could feed one's neighbor in the parable, for two reasons. First, neither the hell nor heaven was really "perfect", since in each case the guests had their arms held straight. Neither is life perfect – in fact, conflicts arise because it *isn't* perfect. There's scarcity, competition, and the desire of each person to fulfill their perceived needs in a world populated by

---

144 <u>Essential Buddhism</u>, Jack Maguire (2001), Pocket Books, Page 137.

others with competing similar needs, to name just a few of the causes of discord. Second, and more importantly, the difference between hell and heaven wasn't a change in the actual physical situation but, rather, a fairly simple change in how the guests approached the situation. The change from hell to heaven required only that the guests first be mindful of the exact nature of the situation, then aware of their commonality in the situation, and finally compassionate with one another so that they could *all* enjoy the feast. This same shift from hell to heaven is essentially what we've referred to as the "Eightfold Path To Resolve Conflict" in this book – the shift from ignorant misery to Compassion and Equanimity that comes from seeing the true contours of a situation and realigning to it in such a way that allows all the parties involved to co-exist in peace with one another.

As I said, conflict is very much a matter of perspective. May the teachings of the Buddha help you learn to be happy and well-fed at all the banquet halls and conflicts in your life!

Appendix "A"

Meditation Techniques

A "SIMPLE" MINDFULNESS PRACTICE

- **Sit upright in a position that's comfortable for you** (in a chair, cross-legged, full lotus, whatever works for you).

- **Choose a quiet time and place if possible.** Early morning is good because the hustle and bustle of the day hasn't set in – early evening before dinner is also good. Try not to meditate right after eating.

- **Focus your attention on your breathing.** Once you've chosen your sitting position, the basics are simple – keep your eyes closed, and concentrate on the rim of your nostrils as the air enters and leaves the body through the nose. So, with your eyes closed, sitting upright, you simply focus your attention on the contact of the air with the inner rim of your nostrils as you breathe in and out. Try not to control the breathing – in other words, don't purposefully breathe deeply or try to equalize the inward and outward breaths.

- **Start with 15 minutes in the morning,** before you begin your day's activities. If you can, build up to thirty minutes twice a day, once early in the day, and once more before dinner or before going to sleep.

- **If any other thoughts or feelings start to arise**, just witness them, don't feel guilty, and return to your Mindfulness meditation as soon as you feel able.

A Loving Kindness Mantra to Recite:

May I be well, happy and peaceful. May no harm come to me. May no difficulties come to me. May no problems come to me. May I always meet with success. May I also have patience, courage, understanding, and determination to meet and overcome inevitable difficulties, problems and failures in life.

· the first round of this mantra is directed at the "me"

· then expand the feeling developed by the mantra in concentric circles out to those who you easily develop Loving Kindness and Compassion for (parents, then teachers, relatives, friends)

· then expand the feeling out to all those you would not ordinarily have those feelings for (strangers, enemies, persons for whom you feel aversion)

· and ultimately, expand the feeling out to all living beings (humans, animals, insects, etc…)

· before finally bringing the mantra back to the "me".

Recite the "Discourse on Good Will":

May all beings be filled with joy and peace
May all beings everywhere —
The great and the ordinary
The powerful and the oppressed
The mean and the generous
The healthy and the sick
The old and the young

May all beings everywhere —
Seen and unseen
Dwelling far off or nearby
Being, dying, or waiting to become —
May all be filled with lasting joy.

Let no one deceive another,
Let no one anywhere despise one another,
Let no one out of anger or resentment
Wish suffering on anyone at all.

Just as a mother protects her child from harm,
So within yourself let grow
A boundless love for all beings.
Let your love flow outward through the universe,
In every direction —
A limitless love, without enmity or hatred.

If you strive for this wholeheartedly
As long as you are awake — whether
Standing, sitting, walking or lying down —
Your life will be a blessing to the world.

Recite the "Discourse" in any position, anywhere, anytime. If you
want to do a formal recitation, recite it four times while standing,
once in each of the four directions of the compass.

The White Lotus Exercise

· Allow the breath to settle for a few moments.

· Imagine a beautiful white lotus flower opening in your heart, from the center of which "comes a golden stream of light which fills you from head to toe with warmth and light and a feeling of contentment, and surrounds you with a feeling of lovingness and well-being".

· This golden light is allowed to expand outward, touching first those close to you physically, then your loved ones and family, then everyone in your work and home worlds, then those with whom you have difficulties, finally returning the golden light to yourself alone, where the white lotus will close and envelop the white light within.

· End this mediation by reciting to yourself "May all beings be happy".

Tonglen (Taking and Giving) Meditation

· **the "boddhicitta" phase** (where you generate the wish to relieve suffering) – Visualize that your heart has an ocean of *bodhicitta* (the wish to move towards enlightenment for the benefit of all sentient beings) spreading out infinitely in every direction from it.

· **the "archetypal" phase** (in which you deal with universal suffering) –Visualize all the suffering of all the sentient creatures in the world as thick, dense, black, hot clouds or smoke that fills the air above the heart-ocean, darkening completely the light. Once this darkness has reached its zenith, you breath it in and let it saturate every pore of your body, and then change it into cool luminous light and exhale it out every part of your body and breath to thereby transform the universal suffering into happiness and tranquility. Do it for as many cycles as you feel appropriate.

· **the "personal" phase** (in which you work to relieve a specific, heartfelt instance of suffering) – Envision the suffering of the other participant(s) in your conflict situation, breath it in, and breath it back out as the cool white light of Loving Kindness and Compassion for him/her/them. Then allow yourself to feel your own pain and suffering about the situation – including any resentment or anger or other negative feelings – and likewise transform that with your breath.

· **the "universal" stage** (by which you extend the instant type of suffering to all persons who have suffered thusly) - Extend your Compassion from yourself and the other people in the conflict to all the millions of other people who are suffering or have suffered from this same type of suffering, and transform that suffering by exhaling the cool, white breath of relief, Loving Kindness and Compassion for them all.

APPENDIX B

CONFLICT RESOLUTION
CHEAT SHEETS

Mindfulness Techniques Cheat Sheet	
With Self	**Become aware of internal conversation with self** • Identify inner voices and identify what their natures are • Do Mindfulness Meditation (see Mindfulness of Breathing Meditation)

With Others	**Fostering Inter-Mindfulness**
	
	• Make it okay for other person to open up to you
	
	• Make it okay for you to open up to the other person
	
	• Allow for the unexpected as opposed to what you're afraid will happen
	
	Three Techniques for Creating Inter-Mindfulness
	
	1. Each person relates their perspective on the conflicts
	
	  • Speaker agrees to talk about his/her feelings (not what the other person did)
	
	  • And, what he or she would like to see occur (not what the other person needs to do)
	
	2. Each person in conflict will draw picture of how they see the conflict
	
	3. Each person writes a three part story
	
	  • Relate their version of the conflict
	
	  • Relate what they think the conflict is from the other person's perspective
	
	  • Share a reconciliatory version of the story

Mindfulness Techniques Cheat Sheet	
As a Mediator	**Fostering Inter-Mindfulness**
	1. Make it okay for all the participants to feel safe expressing their truth about the situation
	• The participants in mediation usually come in with three characteristics: a) they feel somewhat powerless and self-absorbed; b) they are driven by or residing with one or more of the Three Poisons; and c) they are not seeing the true nature of the conflict situation.
	• Allow them to come out of their self-absorption, and regain justifiable power by seeing the other participants as real.
	2. Allow each participant to speak his or her "truth" in such a way that the other participants can hear them.
	• For this you need three qualities as a mediator: a) intuition, b) integrity; and c) Compassion.
	3. Get out of the way of your own expectations regarding the result, so that the unexpected can happen.
	• Remain present and compassionate, but allow the truth to emerge on its own without getting attached to what you think it should be.
	4. Use Mindfulness to avoid becoming attached or reactively aversive to different participants in process.
	• These feelings will arise. Your job is to *not* get attached to them.

Loving Kindness and Compassion Cheat Sheet	
With Self	**Do Loving Kindness and Compassion Meditation** • White Lotus Meditation with your inner child and inner critic as the recipients of the golden light • Tonglen (Taking and Giving) Meditation, using the suffering of your inner child and inner critic as the subjects of the "personal" phase • Make up your own **Identify Voice of Inner Critic or Self Loather** • Do Loving Kindness meditations for that "person"

Loving Kindness and Compassion Cheat Sheet	

With Others	**Fostering Loving Kindness and Compassion**
	Be aware of Refractory Periods of self and other(s)
	
	• Do whatever form of turtle (some form of time out) that is necessary to get back to a workable state of balance for yourself
	
	• Acknowledge the other person's Refractory Period while suggesting a proposed time for discussion in the near future
	
	   ○ Plant the seed for future resolution without specifying what it will be
	
	   ○ Create a co-ownership of resolution process
	
	• Do Compassion and Loving Kindness meditations for yourself and the other(s)
	
	Creating Loving Kindness and Compassion in Resolution Process
	• Acknowledge a conflict exists without blaming other person(s)
	
	• Acknowledge your own part in the creation of the conflict
	
	• Create inter-Mindfulness
	
	   ○ Explain the kinds of feelings that arose for you
	
	   ○ Listen carefully as they explain the emotions that arose for them

Loving Kindness and Compassion Cheat Sheet	

As a Mediator	**Fostering Loving Kindness and Compassion as Mediator**
	
	• Be an exemplar of the traits you hope to foster
	
	• Be aware of fluctuations in your own empathy and recharge it when necessary
	
	• Let the participants know that Loving Kindness and Compassion are useful tools for the resolution of their conflict
	
	• Let participants know that Loving Kindness and Compassion will also be a *result* of the process
	
	• Build real "listening" into the process
	
	• Utilize techniques that allow for the development of Loving Kindness and Compassion
	
	  ○ Create inter-Mindfulness for the participants
	
	  ○ Make sure they hear each other express their feelings
	
	  ○ Use Reversal Techniques
	
	    1. Reversal Questions
	
	    2. Imaginative Reversal
	
	    3. Three Part Stories

Conflict Resolution Techniques Cheat Sheet	
Reversal Technique	**Reversal Questions** • "What do you really know about the other person?" • "What would make you act the way they are acting? (and if they respond) Could that be true for them now?" • "Have you ever acted that way? Did you feel justified in that behavior?" • "Why do you think they are engaging in it?" • "Was there anyone in your family of origin who engaged in similar behavior? How did you respond? Did that work?" • "Do you know anyone else who has acted that way?" How did you respond? Did that work? • "How could you find out what's underneath their behavior?" **Imaginative Reversal** Invite the participant to imagine themselves inside the skin of the other person – looking and acting like them, to see what they feel like from the inside. **Three Part Stories** Invite the person to either write or recite a three-part story, with the first part being their version of the conflict, the second being what they think the conflict is from the other person's perspective, and the third being what a shared reconciliatory version of the story would be.

Substitution	Substitution is an imaginative device that can be used to transform the Poisons, which acts much like an antidote but has as its subject something other than the person or object towards whom the Poison is directed as its object. So, for example, introduce thoughts of caring for people the conflicted person loves, to counteract the poisonous feelings they have about the other person(s) in the conflict.
Priming	Another form of substitution is priming, whereby with word choice (words like closeness, love, hug and support) or imagery conjured by discussion you can foster feelings of emotional security in the listener, which can have the tendency to shift their attention and focus away from their Poisons.
Using Silence –Freeing Emotions Via a Universal Antidote	Look straight at the destructive emotion and let it dissolve as it arises, as do all phenomena in this universe. _Silence_ is a very powerful tool which permits those involved to process their own emotions and which allow them to perceive the other side as similar to themselves.

Using Antidotes	<u>Poison</u>	<u>Antidote/Anti-venom</u>
	1) greed, desire	a) *imaginative* -- contemplation of less attractive aspects of desired object b) *reality-based* - Mindfulness, balanced perception, generosity
	2) hatred, anger	a) *imaginative* -- contemplation of positive aspects of reviled object b) *reality-based* - Mindfulness, patience, Loving Kindness
	3) ignorance, delusion, distraction	awareness of Dependent Arising, contemplation of Emptiness, Tranquility, Mindfulness
	4) jealousy	Appreciative Joy
	5) pride	Compassion, humility
True Causes of Conflict–Dependent Arising of Conflict	Dependent Arising holds that nothing is caused by a simple single causative factor. So, despite the fact that in a conflict situation we tend to blame the other (or, if it's internal, to castigate a part of ourselves) for the conflict, in reality every situation arises because of everything else that has ever preceded it. In fact, both sides to a conflict arise dependently upon each other, for there is no conflict for the one without the presence of the other. If you can get the participants in the conflict to understand this, they can let go of their attachment to their Poisons, and see themselves and the others as allies.	

Using Emotion as a Catalyst for Transformation	It is possible to – with Mindfulness and free expression – separate the aspects of emotions into constituent parts, and use the admirable parts as fuel for transformation, "us(ing) the raw power of emotion as a catalyst for inner change".

Poison	**Positive Aspect**
Anger	call to action, clarity of purpose, focus, effectiveness
Desire	bliss and appreciation
Pride	confidence
Jealousy	admiration, drive

GLOSSARY

Abhidhamma - The Abhidhamma is the last of the three *pitakas* ("baskets", so-called because the material was inscribed onto leaves that were carried about in baskets until being transcribed into permanent text) of the Pali Canon (the Theravādan scriptures), which contains a reworking of the material appearing in the Sutras according to schematic classifications, as well as a Buddhist analysis of the realm of consciousness.

Amygdala - An almond-shaped structure in the middle of the limbic system of the human brain that is particularly involved in the processing and expression of emotions, especially anger and fear.

Anatta - (Pāli) or **Anātman** (Sanskrit) refers to "non-self" or "corelessness", the idea that the individual has no fixed self or soul. The false belief in the fixed self is a primary cause of suffering.

Anicca – (Pāli) or **Anitya** (Sanskrit), impermanence; expresses the Buddhist notion that every conditioned existence, without exception, is inconstant and in flux from moment to moment, even the self we mistakenly believe we are/have.

Anusaya – (Pāli) proclivity, obsesssion; underlying tendency. (The etymology of this term means "lying down with", and the related verb *anuseti* means to be obsessed.) The mental habits that have formed over time due to past experiences during a person's life.

Appreciative Joy – **Mudita** (Pāli); take delight in one's own goodness and good fortune and that of others. One of the four "Sublime Abodes" in Buddhism (see also Sublime Abodes).

Arhant - a Buddhist who has "laid down the burden" and attained nirvana.

Atisha - (980-1054 CE) was a Buddhist teacher from the Bengali region of India. After a visitation by the Buddhist goddess Tara, he travelled to Tibet and became one of the major figures in the establishment of the Sarma lineages after the repression of Buddhism by King Langdarma (Glang Darma).

Attachment - Upādāna (Pāli); clinging; grasping; exaggeration of positive qualities, etc. Because attachment is ego-generated, it creates judgment and prevents transcendence.

Aversion – Dosa (Pāli); the avoidance of a thing situation or behavior because it has been associated with an unpleasant or painful stimulus; exaggeration of negative qualities. Aversion is the flip-side of attachment, or attachment in reverse.

Avidyā - (Sanskrit) or **Avijjā** (Pāli) means "ignorance" or "delusion", and is the primary cause of suffering in saṃsāra and one of the three kleśas. Ignorance is at the root of greed, anger, and craving, and is overcome by Mindfulness.

Bhavacakka - A circular symbolic representation of the twelve stages (called *Nidānas* in Sanskrit) of saṃsāra, also known as "Wheel of Becoming". It represents the causal chain from which arises the whole "mass of suffering".

Bikkhuni – female nun.

Bikkhu - a Buddhist monk. The word literally means "beggar."

Bodhi tree - The Sacred Fig (Ficus religiosa) tree under which Siddhartha Gautama attained Enlightenment.

Bodhicitta – literally translates as "enlightened (bodhi) mind (citta)". In Mahayana and Vajrajana Buddhism, it is a mind grounded in great Compassion and Loving Kindness that seeks to attain enlightenment for the benefit of all sentient beings.

Bodhisattva – One with the intention to become a Buddha in order to liberate all other sentient beings from suffering.

Brahmacarya – the spiritual life (literally means "under the tutelage of Brahma").

Buddha-Nature – the innate, unsullied Buddha-mind or Buddha-element possessed by all sentient creatures but which, prior to the attainment of complete Buddhahood, is muddied by the fetters of ignorance, attachment and other defilements.

Compassion – Karuṇā (Sanskrit; Pāli); awareness of and empathy for the suffering of oneself and others, and the desire to remove harm and suffering.

Craving – (Pāli: **Taṇhā**; Sanskrit: **Tṛṣṇā** or **Trishna**); the desire for anything one does not already possess (which can, however, also include the desire for the *continued* possession of something one does already possess). The three classical Buddhist variants are craving for sensual pleasures, craving for existence, and craving for non-existence, but these are subsets of the overarching craving. On the Bhavacakka, craving leads to clinging.

Dependent Arising – Dependent Origination – (Pāli: **Paticca Samuppāda**); the understanding that every phenomenon exists because of the existence of other phenomena in an infinitely complex web of cause and effect, symbolized by Indra's Net.

Dhammapada – is a collection of versified sayings ascribed to the Buddha himself, and is one of the best-known texts drawn from the Pali canon.

Dharma (Sanskrit) – **Dhamma** (Pali): *Dharma* is derived from the root *Dhr* – to hold – as in, to hold from suffering. The word has many meanings, but generally either refers to the workings of the universe (and of righteousness therein) itself, or, more narrowly, to the teachings of Buddha.

Dosa (Pāli) – see Aversion.

Dukkha – (Pāli): stress; suffering; pain; distress; discontent.

Eightfold Path, or the **Noble Eightfold Path**: the fourth of
the Four Noble Truths is that the way to the cessation of suffering
(dukkha) and the achievement of nirvana is to follow the eightfold
path of: 1) right understanding; 2) right thought; 3) right speech; 4)
right action; 5) right livelihood; 6) right effort; 7) right Mindfulness;
and 8) right meditation.

Emptiness – Sunyata (Sanskrit) or "Voidness": the nature of the
phenomenal world due the impermanent nature of form, which
means that all phenomena lack essential, enduring identity (see also
Anattā).

Equanimity - Upekkha (Sanskrit) (Pāli) **Upekkhā**: the state of
one who witnesses without becoming emotionally unbalanced,
which is a cultivated state rather than one of simple indifference or
lack of interest. Also sometimes referred to as "tranquility", although
tranquility is listed separate from Equanimity in the Seven Factors of
Enlightenment.

Five Aggregates – Skhanda (Pali); **Khanda** (Sanskrit): the
five elements that constitute an individual's mental and physical
existence. They are rupa (body), vedana (feeling), samjna (perception;
Pali sanna), samskara (mental formations; Pali sankhara), and vijnana
(consciousness; Pali vinnana). The five aggregates together comprise
the entity that we mistakenly call our "self".

Five Hindrances - (Pali: **Pañca Nīvaraṇāni**): the negative mental
states that prevent or impede success with meditation, and thus
lead one to stray from the Path: 1. Sensual desire (kāmacchanda); 2.
Anger or ill-will (byāpāda, vyāpāda); 3. Sloth, torpor or boredom
(thīna-middha); 4. Restlessness or worry (uddhacca-kukkucca); and
5. Doubt (vicikicchā).

Four Noble Truths – These were realized by Siddhartha on the
Third Watch of the night of his enlightenment. The truths are (1)
life is suffering; (2) desire, or craving, is its cause; (3) the cessation of
suffering is possible; and (4) the way to accomplish this is to follow
the Noble Eightfold Path.

Hippocampus – part of the limbic system, is a complex neural structure (shaped like a sea horse) consisting of grey matter and located on the floor of each lateral ventricle; intimately involved in motivation and emotion, and has a central role in the formation of memories.

Indra's Net – is a metaphor used to illustrate the concepts of interrelatedness and interpenetration in Buddhist philosophy. This idea is communicated by the net of the Vedic god Indra, which hangs over his palace on Mount Meru, at each vertex of which is a multifaceted jewel, and with each jewel being reflected in all of the other jewels.

Jataka – The Jātaka Tales (Sanskrit) is a folkloric compendium of tales concerning the many previous births and incarnations of the Buddha.

Karuṇā - (Sanskrit; Pāli) see Compassion.

Khanda – (Sanskrit) see Five Aggregates.

Khattiya – the warrior class in the classical Nepalese caste system.

Kilesa (Pali); **Kleśa** or **Klesha** (Sanskrit); **Nyon-Mong** (Tibetan): the "defilements", "destructive emotions", "mental afflictions", or "poisons" which prevent us from experiencing reality as it is. The most basic assemblage of these is the "Three Poisons" - greed (lobha kilesa), hatred (dvesha kilesa), and delusion (moha kilesa).

Limbic System – the "mammalian" part of the brain involved in olfaction, emotion, motivation, behavior, and various other autonomic functions not present in the reptilian brain.

Loving Kindness; **Mettā** (Pāli:) or **Maitrī** (Sanskrit); a strong wish for the happiness of others; a non-possessive non-judgmental love for others; one of the Four Sublime Abodes in Buddhism.

Mahayana - (Sanskrit, **Mahāyāna** literally 'Great Vehicle') is one of three main existing branches of Buddhism, and a term for classification of Buddhist philosophies and practice predominant in China, Japan, and Korea.

Maitrī - see Loving Kindness.

Mammalian Brain – see Limbic System.

Mara - (Sanskrit) the King of the temptations in life, or the Great Ensnarer, who attempted unsuccessfully to sway the Buddha from his enlightenment under the Bodhi tree. More generally, refers to *temptation*.

Maya – (Sanskrit); illusion generally, and more specifically the illusion of the reality of sensory experience and of oneself or one's perceptions as real and/or permanent.

Mettā - see Loving Kindness.

Middle Way – the Buddha's path (as exemplified by the Noble Eightfold Path) which is in between the extremes of severe asceticism and sensual indulgence.

Mindfulness - (Pali: **Sati**; Sanskrit: **Smrti**) calm awareness of one's body, feelings, mind–states (content of consciousness), or consciousness itself, which in Theravadan Buddhism form the four foundations of the path to liberation and subsequent enlightenment.

Moha – (Pali) delusion, one of the Three Poisons.

Mount Meru - is a mythical, sacred mountain in Hindu, Buddhist cosmology, and Jain mythology, and is considered to be the center of all the physical, metaphysical and spiritual universes. It is the home of Indra, the Hindu creator of everything.

Mudita - (Pāli); see Appreciative Joy.

Neomammalian Brain – the third and newest part of the brain, concentrated in the pre-frontal lobes or neocortex, which gives humans the ability to plan, develop morality, rationalize and develop a sense of "I", the latter of which in Buddhism is a primary cause of delusion.

Neuroplasticity - refers to the ability of the human brain to structurally change throughout life in response to and as a result of experience.

Nibbana (Pali): see Nirvana.

Nidānas (Sanskrit) – the twelve stages which bind humans to the cycle of suffering and becoming. They are: 1. Ignorance (avijja); 2. Volitional Formations (the Fourth Aggregate or saṅkhāra); 3. Consciousness (the Fifth Aggregate or viññana); 4. Body and mind (nāma-rūpa); 5. The Six Sense-Bases (or Sense-Organs, salayatana); 6. Contact (phassa); 7. Feeling (vedana); 8. Craving (tanha); 9. Clinging (upadana); 10. Becoming (bhava); 11. Birth (jati): and 12. Aging and Death (jaramarana). See Bhavacakka.

Nikaya - (Sanskrit; Pāli). 1. The five collections of sutras in the Pāli Canon: (i) Dīgha Nikāya (Collection of Long Discourses); (ii) Majjhima Nikāya (Collection of Medium Discourses); (iii) Saṃyutta Nikāya (Collection of Connected Discourses); (iv) Aṅguttara Nikāya (Collection of Incremental Discourses); (v) Khuddaka Nikāya (Collection of Lesser Discourses).

Nirvana – (Pali: **Nibbana**) the unconditioned state of being free from suffering.

Noble Eightfold Path – see Eightfold Path.

Nyon-Mong - See Klesha.

Original Mind – the mind in its pure state, unclouded by the fetters of attachment, delusion, and/or hatred.

Pali Canon - the scriptures in the Theravada Buddhist tradition, which were preserved orally until they were committed to writing during the Fourth Buddhist Council in Sri Lanka in the 1st century BC, approximately three hundred years after the death of the Buddha. The Canon has three categories, called *pitaka* in Pali, which have been known as the *Tipitaka* (three baskets). The three pitakas are: 1. Vinaya Pitaka, rules for monks and nuns; 2. Sutta Pitaka, discourses of the Buddha, with some by his disciples; and 3. Abhidhamma Pitaka, dealing with philosophy and psychology.

Pañca Nīvaraṇāni (Pali) – see Five Hindrances.

Paranirvana - (Sanskrit: **Parinirvāṇa**; Pali: **Parinibbāṇa**); is the final nirvana, which occurs upon the death of the body of someone who has attained complete awakening (bodhi), such as the Buddha.

Paticca-Samapudda – (Pali; Sanskrit: **Pratītyasamutpāda** Tibetan: **Rten.Cing**); see Dependent Origination.

Priming – a technique whereby with word choice (words like closeness, love, hug and support) or imagery conjured by discussion one can foster feelings of emotional security in the listener, thus reducing the sway of the Three Poisons.

Refractory Period - A brief period of time following the stimulation of a nerve during which the nerve will not respond to a second stimulus. In the context of conflict resolution, it is the period of time after the arising of a conflict where the Three Poisons are virulent enough to make any movement towards resolution very difficult.

Reptilian Brain – the part of the brain, which is dominant in the brain of a reptile but also present in the human brain, which includes the brain stem and the cerebellum, and which controls instinctive survival behavior, the muscles, balance and autonomic functions.

Samadhi - (Pali and Sanskrit) is mental concentration or composing the mind.

Saṅkhāra or **Saṃskāra** (Pali) (Sanskrit; **Devanagari**) – means 'that which has been put together' in the passive sense of conditioned phenomena generally, or 'that which puts together' in the sense of the mental "dispositions" or 'volitional formations' that constitute the Fourth Aggregate or Saṅkhāra-Khandha. See Volitional Formations.

Sati (Pali) – see Mindfulness.

Seven Factors of Enlightenment - are: 1) Mindfulness; 2) investigation of reality; 3) energy; 4) rapture; 5) tranquility; 6) concentration; and 7) Equanimity.

Siddhartha – the Buddha's birth prename, which means "every wish fulfilled."

Siddhus - yogic renunciates.

Simile of the Saw – a simile about bandits by which the Buddha expounded on the unwavering nature of Loving Kindness to his monks.

Six Internal and External Sense-Bases, - are: 1) the eyes (which know visible form); 2) the ears (which know sound); 3) the nose (which knows smells); 4) the tongue (which knows flavors); 5) the body (which knows touch); and 6) the mind (which knows the "objects" which arise therein).

Six Main Mental Afflictions – are 1) Attachment or Craving; 2) Anger (which includes hostility and hatred); 3) Arrogance or Pridefulness; 4) Ignorance or Delusion; 5) Afflictive Doubt; and 6) Afflictive Views.

Skhanda - (Pali); see Five Aggregates.

Sublime Abodes or **Sublime States** – the four states or qualities of Loving Kindness, Compassion, Appreciative Joy, and Equanimity which lead to and/or characterize liberation.

Substitution – a technique whereby one introduces the thought of something or someone about which the conflicted person has feelings which are antidotal or opposite to the poisoned feelings he or she is experiencing in the conflict.

Sunyata (Sanskrit, Pali **Suññatā**) – see Emptiness.

Tathagata - means both "one who has thus gone" (Tathā-gata) and "one who has thus come" (Tathā-āgata), and is the name by which the Buddha often referred to himself.

Theravada - literally, "the Teaching of the Elders" is the oldest surviving branch of Buddhism, and the closest to the Buddhism that the Buddha himself taught. It is widespread in Sri Lanka, Cambodia, Laos, Burma, and Thailand.

Three Poisons – see Kilesa.

Tipitaka – see Pali Canon.

Tonglen – is the Tibetan name (which means "giving and taking" or "sending and taking") for a meditation technique developed by Atisha in the 10th century AD, that works with both universal suffering and individualized suffering.

Tranquility – see Equanimity.

Trishna - (or also **Tṛṣṇā** in Sanskrit; Pāli: **Taṇhā;**) – see Craving.

Triune Brain - The triune brain is a model proposed by Paul D. MacLean, in which the brain is broken down into three separate brains (the reptilian, limbic, and neomammalian) that each has its own characteristics and abilities.

Upādāna (Pāli) – see Attachment.

Upekkha - See Equanimity.

Ventromedial Cortex - a part of the prefrontal cortex in the mammalian brain, which helps in the processing of risk and fear, and in the resultant decision making

Volitional Formations – see Saṅkhāra.

Wheel of Becoming – see Bhavacakka.

BIBLIOGRAPHY

Aikido, Kisshomaru Uyeshiba (1978) Hozansha Publishing Co. Ltd

The American Heritage Dictionary of the English Language (4th Ed.), Houghton Mifflin, New York

Being Peace, Thich Nhat Hanh (1987) Parallax Press

The Book of Life Questions and Answers, Dr. M. Erceg, (2006) Authorhouse

The Book of the Discipline: Vinaya-Pitaka Cullavagga, trans. I. B. Horner (1966)

The Buddha and His Teachings, Narada Mahathera (1988), Vipassana Research Publications

Buddha's Nature: A Practical Guide to Discovering Your Place in the Cosmos, Wes Nisker (1998), Bantam Books

Creating True Peace, Thich Nhat Hanh (2003), Free Press

Dhammapada: Sayings of Buddha, (trans) Thomas Cleary (1995), Bantam Books

The Heart of Buddhist Meditation, Nyanaponika Thera (1954), Weiser Publications

Destructive Emotions, Daniel Goleman (2003) Bantam Books

Essential Buddhism, Jack Maguire (2001), Pocket Books

Getting to Yes, Fisher and Ury (2d Ed, 1991) Penguin Books

Happiness, Matthieu Ricard (2003), Little Brown and Company

The Hero With a Thousand Faces Joseph Campbell (1949), Princeton University Press_

Hua-Yen Buddhism: The Jewel Net of Indra, Francis Harold Cook (1977), Penn State Press_

Integral Psychology, Brant Cortright (2007) State Univ. of New York Press_

In the Buddha's Words, Bhikkhu Bodhi   (2005), Wisdom Publications_

Introduction to Zen Buddhism, Daisetz Teitaro Suzuki (1964) Grove Press

King James Bible, World Publishing Company_

Mindfulness: Foundational Training for Dispute Resolution, Leonard L. Riskin, Journal of Legal Education, Volume 54, Number 1 (March 2004)

Mindfulness in Plain English, Bhante Henepola Gunaratana, (2002) Wisdom Publications_

Motivation and Personality, Abraham F. Maslow   (1970, 2d Edition) Harper & Row,

Old Path White Clouds Thich Nhat Hanh (1991) Parallax Press_

Ordinary Magic, (ed. John Welwood) (1992), Shambhala Press,

An Outline of Psychoanalysis, Sigmund Freud (1940), trans. James Strachey, Norton,

Social Conflict: Escalation, Stalemate, and Settlement, Pruitt and Kim, 2004, McGraw Hill_

A Survey of Buddhism, Sangharakshita (4th Ed. 1976), Shambhala Books

Toward a Psychology of Awakening, John Welwood (2002), Shambhala Press

Train Your Mind, Change Your Brain, Sharon Begley (2007), Ballantine Books

When the Iron Eagle Flies Ayya Khema (1991), Wisdom Publications

INTERNET SOURCES

Abhaya Sutta, trans. Thanissaro Bhikkhu (1997), http://www.accesstoinsight.org/tipitaka/mn/mn.058.than.html

http://www.ahaf.org/alzdis/about/AnatomyBrain.htm

The Buddha-Carita, Asvaghosa (trans. Edward B. Cowell 1895), http://www.ancient-buddhist-texts.net/Texts-and-Translations/Buddhacarita/index.htm

http://www.cs.unm.edu/~richards/sangha/buddha_on_community.html

BuddhaNet Basic Buddhism Guide's Dependent Arising at www.buddhanet.net/e-learning/depend.htm

Buddhist Stories from the Dhammapada Commentary, The Wheel Publication No. 73 (Kandy: Buddhist Publication Society), http://nt.med.ncku.edu.tw/biochem/lsn/AccessToInsight/html/lib/authors/burlingame/wheel324.html

<u>Digha Nikaya 13</u>, trans. Nyanaponika Thera, <u>http://www.</u>
<u>accesstoinsight.org/lib/authors/nyanaponika/wheel006.html</u>

<u>Digha-Nikaya</u> 16, trans Vajira & Story, <u>http://www.accesstoinsight.</u>
<u>org/tipitaka/dn/dn.16.1-6.vaji.html</u>
<u>The Four Sublime States</u>, Nyanaponika Thera, <u>http://www.</u>
<u>accesstoinsight.org/lib/authors/nyanaponika/wheel006.html</u>

<u>The Illustrated History of Buddhism</u>, <u>http://www.samakkhi.ac.th/</u>
<u>ih_bd/42.htm</u>

<u>The Illustrated History of Buddhism</u>, <u>http://www.samakkhi.ac.th/</u>
<u>ih_bd/52.htm</u>

<u>Informal Dispute Resolution and the Formal Legal System in</u>
<u>Contemporary Northern Afghanistan</u>, (2006), Page 2, Draft Report
to the Rule of Law Program, The United States Institute of Peace,
<u>http://www.usip.org/ruleoflaw/projects/barfield_report.pdf</u>

<u>Khajjaniya Sutta</u>, from the Samyutta Nikaya, trans. by Thanissaro
Bhikkhu, <u>http://www.accesstoinsight.org/tipitaka/sn/sn22/</u>
<u>sn22.079.than.html</u>

<u>Kutadanta Sutta</u>, <u>http://tipitaka.wikia.com/wiki/Kutadanta_Sutta</u>

<u>http://www.lakehouse.lk/budusarana/2007/03/03/Budu18.pdf</u>,
esoteric web publication, <u>*Digha Nikaya*</u> 14, condensed translation by
Late Ven. Bhikkhu Nanamoli's "The Life of Buddha"

<u>The Life of the Buddha</u>, A. Ferdinand Herold [1922], <u>http://www.</u>
<u>sacred-texts.com/bud/lob/lob42.htm</u>

<u>Life of the Buddha : Middle Years Stories & Teachings</u>, <u>http://www.</u>
<u>wisdom-books.com/FocusDetail.asp?FocusRef=18</u>

http://www.logoi.com/pastimages/buddha.html

Mahavagga, First Khandaka 54(5), http://www.sacred-texts.com/
bud/sbe13/sbe1312.htm

Majjhima Nikaya III (128), http://zencomp.com/greatwisdom/
ebud/majjhima/128-upakkilesa-e.htm

An Outline of Psychoanalysis, Sigmund Freud (1940), trans. James
Strachey, Norton, http://webspace.ship.edu/cgboer/freudselection.
html

Pali Canon Studies, Ryuei Michael McCormick (2006), http://
nichirenscoffeehouse.net/Ryuei/Devadatta

http://www.palikanon.com/english/pali_names/d/devadatta.htm
Pratītyasamutpāda, Wikipedia, http://en.wikipedia.org/wiki/
Prat%C4%ABtyasamutp%C4%81da

Sutta Nipata, http://www.ishwar.com/buddhism/holy_sutta_
nipata/book03/book03_11.html

Sutra on the Eight Realizations of the Great Beings, (trans Thich
Nhat Hanh),
http://www.buddhanet.net/pdf_file/beingssutra.pdf

Udana 68-69, http://en.wikipedia.org/wiki/Blind_Men_and_an_
Elephant#cite_note-Buddhist-1

Wikipedia, http://en.wikipedia.org/wiki/Arhant
Wikipedia, http://en.wikipedia.org/wiki/Image:Devadatta
Wikipedia, http://en.wikipedia.org/wiki/Image:Devadatta
Wikipedia, http://en.wikipedia.org/wiki/Kilesa
Wikipedia, http://en.wikipedia.org/wiki/Maslow
Wikipedia, http://commons.wikimedia.org/wiki/Image:Buddha_
with_the_Elephant_Nalagiri
Wikipedia, http://en.wikipedia.org/wiki/Skandha

Wikipedia, http://en.wikipedia.org/wiki/
Sa%E1%B9%85kh%C4%81ra#cite_note-4
Wikipedia, http://en.wikipedia.org/wiki/Tathagata
Wikipedia, http://en.wikipedia.org/wiki/Twelve_Nid%C4%81nas
  Essential Buddhi

INDEX

About The Author

Ross McLauran Madden is an attorney and mediator in San Francisco, California. He has an LLM Master's Degree in Dispute Resolution from the Straus Institute at Pepperdine University, where he studied mediation with many of the foremost practitioners in the field. In addition to being a practicing Buddhist, he has studied Aikido since 1980, and has been an instructor of the martial art since 1988.

CPSIA information can be obtained at www.ICGtesting.com
260270BV00001B/105/P